Stones of Witness

CHURCH ARCHITECTURE
AND FUNCTION

A church looms over the industrial city: a photograph of Bolton by Humphrey Spender from his 'Worktown' series of 1937. (Courtesy of Bolton Museum & Art Gallery)

Stones of Witness

CHURCH ARCHITECTURE AND FUNCTION

COLIN CUNNINGHAM

SUTTON PUBLISHING

First published in the United Kingdom in 1999
Sutton Publishing Limited · Phoenix Mill
Thrupp · Stroud · Gloucestershire · GL5 2BU

British Library Cataloguing in Publication Data
A catalogue record for this book is available from the British Library.

ISBN 0-7509-1225-1

Typeset in 11/13.75 pt Garamond.
Typesetting and origination by
Sutton Publishing Limited.
Printed in Great Britain by
Redwood Books, Trowbridge, Wiltshire.

Contents

Preface

The original idea for this book arose out of my own attempt to come to grips with the massive church-building and restoration effort of the Gothic revival of the nineteenth century; to understand the passion that drove such a range of men of genius to search out examples of the medieval builders' art and to create a new imitation medievalism for their own industrial age. Though they adopted medieval forms for schools, hospitals and even factory chimneys, it was in church building that their revived Gothic reached its fullest glory. My ideas were tested in a series of lectures on the Gothic revival given for students in the Department of Architecture at Cambridge in 1994 and 1995. I am grateful to the two groups, particularly the Chinese students for whom the whole world of Christian building was remote and unintelligible. Their thought-provoking questions sent me back to reconsider traditional approaches to church architecture and archaeology. As a result it occurred to me that it was important to provide an introduction to Christian architecture. But this is not an introduction to all such. Instead it focuses on the parish church, the most widespread of the Church's structures, and its very foundation. It also looks at churches of all periods, since so many are structures built up over centuries.

An important inspiration has been my work for the Diocesan Advisory Committee of St Edmundsbury and Ipswich, and I am grateful to colleagues on that committee, past and present, who have taught me much. The tension between the needs of ancient fabrics and the desires (and restricted resources) of parishioners at a time when fashions in liturgy are moving away from the traditions of past generations has been particularly instructive. The resulting book is an attempt to provide a basis for understanding how our churches have come to be as they are: to explore the interface between bricks and mortar and faith and ritual.

My intention is not to provide a potted history of church architecture or a simplified history of the Anglican Church. Rather I have set out to demonstrate how the developing liturgy of the

Church and the life of its congregations has determined the way churches are built and altered. I have tried to present in a straightforward way the relationship between the buildings that accommodated and resulted from a developing faith. Faith has determined the way the buildings were designed, but those buildings in turn have affected the way practices of worship developed. Now we live with the built results of centuries of evolving practice, and it is inevitable that we are all affected, one way or another, by the churches we see. Whether we merely explore them as visitors or attend them as worshippers, the impact of their architecture, their disposition and decoration are a crucial part of the reason why some churches simply feel good and some delight the eye. Of course there is much that is personal in our reactions, but we all need to understand how the spaces we use have come to be as they are.

The history of church-building is too often written as the onward march of succeeding styles, as though there were an inevitable progress from Saxon to Norman, through Early English to Decorated, and so on. The history of the Church as an organisation tends to be written as the politicking and theology of bishops and archbishops, the interaction of kings and abbots, parliamentarians and cathedral clergy. What is often forgotten is that even these powerful clerics had themselves begun as parish priests. Indeed in the centuries of pluralism before the Reformation many combined control of several lucrative parish stipends with more prestigious duties. Whether they were merely ambitious or outstandingly devout, it is at least likely that they made some impact on the parishes they worked in, and that impact will have reflected their theological position and liturgical interests. It is the interplay between theology and building, between liturgy and architecture, that gives rise to this book. It is based on the hypothesis that no one wastes money or effort on church building without having some purpose in mind – and those purposes, rooted in developing patterns of worship, are revealed in the architecture and fittings of our parish churches.

The ecclesiastical heritage is enormous: some forty cathedrals and literally hundreds of medieval monastic houses, priories and nunneries. The cathedrals still dominate the towns in which they stand and draw crowds of tourists as well as worshippers. The monastic houses are mostly in ruins now, and many are managed by English Heritage (or CADW in Wales). But the architectural heritage of the Church of England is really centred on that nationwide type, the parish church. It, together with its associated buildings, forms the focus of this book. This is not, however, simply a book about church architecture. It is an exploration of the uses of structures designed for Christian (and later Anglican) worship. It is an attempt to explain why churches have come to be the shape they are and why they are filled with the things they are. I hope that it will enable present-day worshippers to understand a little more about the nature and importance of the tradition of which they are a part. I hope, too, that it will allow students of architecture and uncommitted visitors to satisfy rather more effectively a natural curiosity about what is what in the churches that are such a major element in our architectural heritage. It is aimed at those who work with church buildings that were designed and built by generations long gone, and whose purposes it is difficult to recover. It is also for students of architectural history who have to cope with buildings whose complex functions they may not share. And above all it is for the many who simply enjoy exploring the heritage these buildings represent, and would like to know more about the way they have been designed and altered and why. I hope that it will go some way to overcoming the gap of incomprehension that all too often sits between the first inspection of the place and our attempts to draw from it satisfaction for our current needs.

I have attempted to illustrate my text not only with photographs of the architecture but also with images showing the various items in use, together with written comments and descriptions. I hope that people will then be able to unravel the way in which any church reflects the particular pattern of needs that has been recognised by its congregation over time. I have had much helpful advice from colleagues in the world of architectural history and in the various churches. The many scholars to whom I am indebted are acknowledged in the select bibliography. I have also benefited particularly from wise advice and helpful criticism from the Revd Anna Garvie, the Very Reverend Michael Mayne and the Revd Canon William Purcell and from colleagues in the Religious Studies department of the Open University. I am indebted to Andrew Anderson, Dr Nigel Bullock, Dr Paul Cattermole, Bob Maguire, Philip Orchard, Arthur Paxton, Chris Pickford and the staff of the Church of England Record Centre, Anne Riches, the Revd Dr Michael Sansom, Roy Tricker of the Churches Conservation Trust, Dr Chris Wakeling, to my colleagues on the Diocesan Advisory Committee of St Edmundsbury and Ipswich, and to the many parish priests and members of congregations who have welcomed me to their churches. I owe a special debt to my wife, Alisoun Cunningham, for her patience and for detailed criticism of the manuscript at various stages. Finally, publication has been made possible with a research grant from the Open University and the generous assistance of a Stroud Bursary from the Society of Architectural Historians of Great Britain.

Colin Cunningham
March 1999

The parish church at Sutton Valence, Kent, arranged for a live broadcast of The People's Service, a BBC Light Programme in about 1950. The choir has moved into the nave, and the vicar takes the service from a special microphone table. (Keystone Press Agency)

CHAPTER ONE

The Nature of a Church

Introduction

In almost every village the parish church is the most prominent, and often the oldest, structure. In our towns and cities, too, church buildings still make dominant features in the streetscape. Some twenty thousand parish churches are scattered across our island, with many more in the Anglican communion worldwide; some old, some new, large, small, rich, poor, they are all different, yet all linked by the common thread of their Anglican Christianity and a common liturgical function that has developed in many stages from the time of the Romans to the present day. Whether we use them for worship or merely visit as curious unbelievers, we are often left wondering about them, their shape, their contents and their history. Each is different, for each represents an accumulation of creative reactions to local events, to national and international pressures and to the long slow development of the liturgy that each was built to house. It is a process that in many cases stretches back over many generations; even when a church has been built from scratch in the last hundred years or so, the building is still the heir to that long tradition of development and worship.

Each parish church, therefore, stands as a mute witness to the hopes, fears, aspirations, wealth or poverty of its congregation. Yet each shares common features, for they all belong to the same tradition of faith. However much they have been altered and adapted to meet developments within the history of the Church, they remain structures designed to accommodate patterns of worship. So although there is great variety, it is always possible for a visitor to find elements of continuity with past traditions, or evidence of shared values and practices. Fascinating though it is to discover the rare or unique in some remote church, it is also important to distinguish what is shared from what is merely curious; and the building can offer an insight into its place in the history of its parish and of the Christian religion generally.

The spaces within a church are often discussed as though they were simply structures. But this is an oversimplification, for they were very seldom designed with their form as the only, or principal, determinant. They were for priest and people to use. We need to remember that each space has, or had, its function and it is the activity that justifies them. Thus it is important to try to rediscover the original functions, to see how present uses depend on past practice and how the spaces condition the activities within them and vice versa. I have not attempted to follow a chronological order in explaining the various features of a church. Instead I have tried to maintain the liturgical logic of their functions. The visitor to any church may be confronted with features and fittings from a number of different periods, representing a range of different attitudes to worship. Inevitably there is a degree of overlap, but my purpose will be achieved if the text and the images help the curious visitor, whether Christian or not, to understand why things are where they are and how they have contributed, or may still contribute, to the worshipping life of their congregation. There is a rich heritage of practices and furniture to which any congregation is heir, and a better knowledge of the whys and hows may help today's church users to get the best out of the amalgam of equipment, treasures even, that they possess.

Churches are particularly complex structures, having a range of both symbolic and practical functions which have developed over centuries. Not all are easily understood. The Anglican Church, as an organisation, has also accumulated a number of different functions: different patterns of worship, different rituals, different relationships with the local community and the hierarchy. These often overlap and always leave their mark on the structure. You cannot talk sensibly about buildings without considering how they were intended to be, or are, used. Buildings, even the sites of buildings, are not the result of chance, nor are they simply designs thought out in the abstract by architects. Rather they are a direct response to needs, in the case of churches the liturgical needs, of each congregation at a particular time. It seems to me axiomatic that buildings, alterations and additions (even on quite a minor scale) are unlikely to be made without their purpose being clear to the builders. If the works perform their function, then the building will reflect what that function was and how the different elements, changing patterns of use and of worship, have contributed to the architectural palimpsest that is the church building today. The general arrangement of a parish church, as most commonly seen today, needs to come first. We shall then explore the way builders have reacted to the different elements of the Christian liturgy over the centuries. The results, as Philip Larkin suggests, can be irresistibly curious.

Once I am sure there's nothing going on
I step inside, letting the door thud shut.
Another church: matting, seats and stone,
And little books; sprawlings of flowers, cut
For Sunday, brownish now; some brass and stuff
Up at the holy end; the small neat organ;
And a tense, musty, unignorable silence,
Brewed God knows how long. Hatless, I take off
My cycle-clips in awkward reverence.

(from *Church Going* by Philip Larkin)

The Function of Building

A church is, first and foremost, a place for worship, but we need to consider why congregations actually have buildings. The stories of the New Testament tell of great gatherings in the open air, and today there are plenty of open air services – the evangelical meetings of Billy Graham, papal masses at Wembley, street meetings of the Salvation Army or the daily acts of worship at Taizé in France, for instance. A church building is not the essential basic element in Christian worship, and there have been congregations that regularly worshipped in the open. For instance, after the Disruption – the great split in the Scottish Presbyterian Church in 1843 – many of the newly formed Free Church congregations were without buildings for decades, and were obliged to meet for worship in caves or in the open air. A congregation is necessary before a church – but that congregation will need somewhere to meet.

A church is not the first essential. In the absence of a church building this service is being held in the booking hall of Ribblehead railway station some time in the early 1950s. (*Manchester Evening News*)

The earliest congregations probably had just a sign, usually a cross, to mark their meeting area. Itinerant priests would hold services at the cross, which would usually be set up at a convenient place in the centre of a community or by the wayside. Such preaching crosses are often preserved, sometimes inside churches, as in Leeds parish church in Yorkshire. They often became a focus both for the acts of worship and for the community in general, and it is often impossible to distinguish between a cross set up for preaching and one that was erected as a focus for a market. Most likely these free-standing symbols had multiple functions in the eyes of those who built them but their form remains the Christian symbol.

The next essential for Christian worship was some sort of table or altar on which the bread and wine of the Eucharist could be offered, and these could take many forms. It can be argued, therefore, that the church building is only a secondary requirement, though it is the element that is most obvious today. This being so, then, of course, there are implications for the relative importance of the cross and altar. The building itself may be something of a paradox, for while it encloses the activity for which it was designed it is not itself essential for that activity. Betjeman described churches as being 'to atheists inadequately developed building sites; and often, alas, to Anglicans but visible symbols of disagreement with the incumbent',[1] which reflects the general vagueness as to their precise function and the extent to which their development has been driven by the ideas of clerics – often fiercely contested. They stand, however, both as functioning entities and as symbols; they are also the local focus of an organisation that reaches well beyond the locality, and are a part of a worldwide communion.

The Church as an Organisation

As a world religion Christianity is just reaching the end of its second millennium. It developed from the small band of followers of Jesus of Nazareth, himself an itinerant preacher, whose life is described in the four Gospels that form the first part of the New Testament. The books that form this section of the Bible, together with the Old Testament, are the core of Christian scripture. But the Old Testament also forms a part of the Jewish tradition, out of which Christianity grew. In today's multi-faith society we are readier to recognise that one religion is related to another, and that, for instance, Christ is also recognised as one of the prophets in Islam. However, that recognition is a modern preoccupation, and for most of the centuries of its development the Christian Church has been concerned with establishing and maintaining itself as unique and separate from all others. Until fairly recently the Anglican Church, along with other denominations, has been almost as keen to advertise its separation, as the established Church, from the many non-conforming denominations. It is usually fairly easy to distinguish older Anglican churches from later Roman Catholic ones, Nonconformist chapels or Quaker meeting houses. Indeed, it is often the age of the Anglican parish church that distinguishes it from its rivals, but the ecumenical movements of recent times have found less differentiated forms in modern architecture, where what is demonstrated is the Christian purpose of the building rather than any denominational allegiance.

It is often said that the worldwide Church has too frequently been involved in religious wars, such as the Crusades, or the brutality of the Civil Wars, which may have led to a certain triumphalism in church architecture. It is equally a fact that the riches of the earliest churches in Britain proved a tempting target for pagan raiders. Such upheavals led to a great deal of destruction or demolition, or to hasty replacement of the building or its contents. Yet there was some continuity, and in each parish individuals continued to worship, often changing their ways only slowly. Easy enough to recognise in recent centuries, this conservatism reaches back to the earliest years of Christianity, and architectural forms and features may turn out to have a remarkably long life.

It is also worth recognising that Christianity, in its missionary supplanting of older religions, was efficient in absorbing pagan festivals into its own patterns of belief. For instance, the timing of Christmas in midwinter, with Christ as the promise of a new life and a new order, neatly subsumed the ancient midwinter feasts. We also need to recognise that the early Church, though confined to the Mediterranean basin, developed simultaneously among a variety of different cultures. The Jewish centres of Palestine and especially Jerusalem were linked to the cities of the Graeco-Roman world, and Christianity developed in Ethiopia and Armenia at the same time that it spread to the western Mediterranean and the lands of the Celtic peoples. Yet for centuries Christians from one end of the Mediterranean to the other regarded themselves as part of a single unitary Church. There were disagreements, heresies and wide variations of practice but, equally, practices and specific forms of worship could pass from one end of Christendom to the other. From the fourth century Christianity was the official religion of the Roman empire, and Santa Sophia in Istanbul, probably its greatest church, was built as early as the sixth century, long before any surviving churches in this country.

At that time the Church recognised five principal bishoprics: Rome, Alexandria, Constantinople, Antioch and Jerusalem; the five bishops were given the title of patriarch. Increasingly, however, the pattern of worship in the eastern Mediterranean differed from the western, though the two churches did not formally divide until 1054 CE, a date that still pre-dates most of the surviving churches of

An ancient site for St Mary, Portchester, Hampshire, within the castle bailey whose walls are those of a third-century Roman Saxon Shore fort. The church, a former priory, dates from *c.* 1150. (Colin Cunningham)

this country. By that date the forms of worship and the structures which housed them had very largely been worked out, with the centrally focused domed church being the norm in the east and the longitudinal basilica or hall more common in the west. Most Anglican churches clearly derive from the western tradition, though it is possible to see that there were links and even now to find occasional echoes of eastern or early Christian practice in some churches.

After 1054 Christianity in the western Mediterranean developed under the leadership of the Patriarch of Rome, generally known as the Pope. His control of western Christianity lasted until the sixteenth century, by which time the vast majority of parishes in Britain had built, and often several times rebuilt, their churches. After half a millennium western Christianity was subdivided by the Reformation, in which Catholic priests such as Luther and Calvin, pressing an advanced theology and arguing for reform, were finally driven to break with the Church that had trained them. The position of the Church of England was not so far removed from the continuing Roman Catholic tradition, and traditional practices continued with little change in a number of parishes. In that sense Anglicanism can be seen as a compromise, and the fact that the new state Church simply took over the plant of the pre-Reformation Roman Church was a major determining factor in the development of its own practices.

What became known as the Roman Catholic Church itself underwent a considerable reform in response to the Protestant breakaway of the sixteenth century, but for the next three hundred years

Britain had little contact with the hierarchy in Rome and remained a part of the Roman Catholic mission field. Scotland, as is well known, followed more closely in the path laid out by Calvin, and its inheritance of pre-Reformation churches required a more radical reordering. But for the most part parish churches in England and Wales were only lightly overlaid with the requirements of the new liturgy, and worship passed into a new system of control and organisation while retaining much that had been designed for the uses of the previous centuries. Yet it was a new order. Under Archbishop Cranmer and King Henry VIII the new Church was established after 1534 with the monarch as its head, but retaining the hierarchy of bishops who had been the leaders of the Church since the start. However, this Church 'by law established' became henceforth the official religion of the kingdom. In an age of growing nationalism it developed into the Church of England, and of Wales and Ireland, though Ireland had a majority Roman Catholic population and most of the Welsh people followed one or other of the strands of Nonconformist worship. The Church of England today is merely the English, and oldest, part of a worldwide Anglican communion that came into being at the time of the Reformation.

When the English Church broke away from the Pope, of course, it inherited buildings that had been designed over the previous six centuries for Catholic usage, and many present-day parish churches date back to pre-Reformation times. Since then, however, they have been a part of an organisation led by the Archbishop of Canterbury, with a second Archbishop at the head of the Province of York. Henry VIII's actions made the monarch the Church's formal head, with the title Defender of the Faith; the legal requirement to display the royal arms in each church began at this time. More important, though less visible, results were the many and complex links between the Church and the State, which have had their own impact on church building. These political, legal and financial ties have only slowly been eroded (and are by no means all gone) as Britain developed into a largely secular and multi-cultural state, but they have left their mark on churches and their organisation. In Scotland the Episcopalian Church is similar, as is the Anglican Church in Wales, but those two bodies are disestablished[2] (that is, without the legal paraphernalia of the Church of England). Anglican churches in other parts of the world have been increasingly free to develop in different ways to meet their own local needs, usually as minorities.

In all cases, however, Anglicanism is a church of hierarchies. The most senior churchmen are the two archbishops who head the provinces of Canterbury and York. Next come the bishops who have charge of the forty or so dioceses of England (they are often assisted by suffragen bishops), and it is the bishop who gives the charge of each parish to the priest at his induction. For centuries the bishops made formal visitations to churches, striving to correct what they considered were lax practices and to see that buildings were well ordered. Provision may, therefore, need to be made for a bishop in any parish church. This usually takes the form of a special chair or throne reserved for his rank alone. Next in rank are the archdeacons who have administrative and disciplinary control over a number of parishes, usually about one-third of a diocese. They now have the duty of seeing that churches are properly ordered and maintained, and are responsible for ensuring that no alterations or additions are made without a Faculty (the legal permission issued by each diocese for such work). Their influence on the church building may therefore be considerable. More local contact comes from the rural deans, themselves always parish priests, who coordinate the efforts of a smaller group of parishes. The parish priest and the church (or churches) for which he, or now she, is responsible come at the end of a longish line, and in hierarchical terms it often seems that the laity, the actual worshippers, are even further down the ladder. Yet it is usually the actual worshippers and the parish priests who make alterations and additions to their own building. Until well after the Reformation responsibility for the chancel rested with the rector or patron, who might have been a distant abbot or corporate body. None the less ecclesiastical ambition might well lead an absent patron to embellish the chancel of any church for which he had a care. Maintenance of the body of the church was in the hands of the parishioners. What is actually achieved, therefore, in any church is usually in response to local needs, though to some extent regulated by the agreed standards of archdeaconry, diocese or province. A powerful archbishop or reforming diocesan may have a considerable effect on the church buildings of his area. Archbishop William Laud (1573–1645), as will be seen, made a deliberate attempt to impose liturgical uniformity on all. His methods were high-handed and he was finally put to death as the result of the hostility this aroused among the Puritan clergy. Samuel Wilberforce (1805–73), a man with influence at court, similarly did a great deal to encourage church building and rebuilding in his diocese of Oxford in the mid-nineteenth century. He was probably the first bishop to appoint a diocesan architect, in the person of the brilliant Gothic revivalist George Edmund Street.

Equally, on a smaller scale an energetic archdeacon can involve parishes in developments that sometimes seem to raise the spectre of inter-parochial competition. It is often a surprise to find quite similar facilities of more or less the same date in a series of churches that may be in the same archdeaconry or deanery. Rural deans may have similar opportunities, though the office had passed almost into oblivion until it was revived in 1836. Their present influence dates only from the turn of the twentieth century, and is linked to increasing ease of movement that brought parishes into closer contact with one another.

In earlier centuries parishes and their priests were a great deal more isolated, and it was easier for a recalcitrant or eccentric parson to act on his own initiative. That, too, could have a surprising impact on the church building, as, for instance, when the Revd Whitwell Elwin (1817–1900), who was also editor of *The Gentleman's Magazine*, decided to rebuild his little church at Booton in Norfolk with all the accoutrements of the grandest East Anglian 'wool' churches.

Finally there were the laity, who form the local body of the church; their influence on their parish church will be considerable. For centuries the lord of the manor, be he great aristocrat or modest gentleman, would almost certainly have been involved in paying the bulk of any building costs. His wealth and generosity, or lack of it, might be crucial. In towns the role of individual aristocrats was quickly subsumed by substantial traders, local corporations or guilds, who might adopt a particular church, or part of one, for their own worship. Such churches would closely reflect the prosperity of their congregations. Prominent and pious members might lead a drive for new work, which in turn would reflect both their piety and the extent of their power. General prosperity is regularly reflected in the splendour of churches. The medieval ports of Bristol and King's Lynn, for example, both boast outstanding churches, and the wealth deriving from the wool trade of the fifteenth century had such an impact on a number of churches in East Anglia that they are known as 'wool' churches to this day. Finally, and by no means least important, there was a long tradition, particularly in smaller churches, of local craftsmen producing individual items as a part of their witness. It is only the rapid progress of transport and the advent of professional architects and makers of 'church furnishings' in the last two centuries that has overshadowed their efforts.

An idiosyncratic Gothic revival style was adopted by the Revd Whitwell Elwyn for his church at Booton, Norfolk (1875–91). The small structure with three gables houses the parish bier. (Colin Cunningham)

Archdeacons, anonymous medieval craftsmen and wealthy or pious benefactors shared the belief that only the best is good enough for the House of God. Thus each parish church has, over the years, become a sort of collection or repository of the finest the local community could produce to reflect their aspirations or express their reaction to events. And because their aspirations and reactions were centred on a church building that was part of a national (and later international) community there is a continuous interaction between individual creativity and wider patterns of influence.

Working Parts

> It is related in annals of good credit that Lucius, king of the Britons, sent to Pope Eleutherius (AD 175–89) . . . [and] . . . there came, sent by Eleutherius, preachers to Britain, the effect of whose work will last for ever, though their names have perished through the long neglect of time. These men's work was the Old Church of St Mary in Glastonbury, as antiquity has not failed faithfully to hand down through past ages.[3]

The richly carved north doorway (*c.* 1325) of St Mary Redcliffe, Bristol, a grand church close to the port and built at the peak of the city's prosperity. (Colin Cunningham)

Patterns of worship developed slowly in the first centuries of Christianity, and there were a good many variations in practice to suit local needs or to accommodate different theological perceptions. Many of the common practices were agreed at ecumenical Councils that drew attendance from all the principal power centres of Christendom. Most took place in eastern Mediterranean cities, such as Constantinople (now Istanbul) or Nicaea (now Isnik) in Turkey; the Nicene Creed, though certainly not the product of the Council of Nicaea of 325 CE, probably spread from Jerusalem until it was in use in most churches. It is still the central element of the Eucharist today. What was important was that until 1054 there was only one Christian *oecumene* (literally the inhabited, and hence the civilised, world), though there was a range of different practices and a good deal of argument. Most surviving buildings for worship in Britain date from after that, and thus derive almost entirely from the western tradition. One result of this, and of the fact that the liturgy was conducted in Latin until the Reformation, is that many of the terms used to describe the different parts of a church derive from Latin or Greek. Many more are from Old English, since they were used to describe what was being built in the Middle Ages. (Where such words may be unfamiliar I have provided a modern meaning in brackets after the first mention of the term.)

As we have seen, an early requirement was for shelter for the altar and the priest, then shelter, even refuge, for the congregation. This produced what is known as the two-cell church where two spaces, one a sanctuary, or 'holy end', and one for the congregation, are separated by an archway. The structures that survive, such as that at Escombe in County Durham, are usually barn-like in appearance, massive and lit by small windows, with little surviving in the way of elaboration. They are probably the most basic form of church that can be found today. Over the centuries most churches have been enlarged and extended, so that the typical parish church of today may be a complicated sequence of different spaces. The original small apsidal sanctuary has generally been replaced by a large rectangular chancel containing both choir and sanctuary. The nave has often been extended to north and south with aisles. Transepts, a tower, spire, north and south porches, chapels to north and south of the chancel, a vestry, even an inner porch or narthex, and quite often a family chapel or mausoleum are all common features in the organic development of a church. The end result may be a rich and elaborate structure of great grandeur and beauty, but it must be remembered that all the elements had, and some still do have, their specific function, whether symbolic, practical or a mixture of both. What we see as we enter any church today is only the final coat, as it were, on a canvas that has been constantly repainted over many generations.

There has been constant, if slow, development, as well as some major upheavals, such as the almost total destruction of British churches by the Vikings or the radical reordering in the face of seventeenth-century Puritanism. The last seventy-odd years, too, have seen a revolution in liturgy as great in many ways as the Reformation. However, the majority of our churches today, apart from the few modern ones, are mostly the product of Victorian and Edwardian 'restorers', who are often accused of sweeping much away and restoring buildings out of existence. If they did so, it was because they were changing the way the buildings were used and perceived, and the process is continuing today, reflecting the needs and aspirations of the present generation of church users. The result is a huge diversity – of size and quality, of spaces, materials and facilities – but the churches still have one thing in common: they are all part of the 'plant' of the Anglican Church, and as such share certain basic functions.

However, the church, as a building type, has a much longer history than Anglicanism. Its growth from simple two-cell structure to wide-

aisled palatial temple was a slow process of responding partly to changes
in population, economic power and status, and partly to developments
in ritual. The oldest surviving structures are certainly not the first
churches built in this country. Spaces for worship were set apart in villas
by the first Christians at the time of Roman rule. It is now clear that
their successors continued to adhere to the faith and to build churches
in the centuries between the departure of the Romans and the arrival of
St Augustine, the Italian missionary monk who became the first
Archbishop of Canterbury, at the start of the seventh century. The
missionary effort that followed Augustine's arrival, as well as the work
of Columba and the monks of the Irish Church, undoubtedly led to the
construction of more churches, and it is likely that pre-medieval
structures underlie a good many of our current parish churches.

Fifteenth-century carved bench
end in St Andrew, Isleham,
Cambridgeshire. (Colin
Cunningham)

One cannot see much of this archaeological heritage, but the general
impression is that the seventh and eighth centuries saw the adoption of
the two-cell structure, usually with an apsidal sanctuary, as the norm
in church building. By the tenth century a few churches were being
built with towers, probably also as the result of Italian missionary
influence. These towers were usually placed just west of the sanctuary,
making three spaces, and though not standing very high were clearly a
dominant feature. They were also regularly used for defence as well as
to accommodate a raised belfry that would summon the faithful to
church or raise the alarm for the neighbourhood.

Most of the early churches of the seventh and eighth centuries in
Britain were of timber with walls of daub and roofs of thatch. These
were the commonest materials of the period, but they were horribly
susceptible to fire; during the period of Viking raids in the late eighth
and ninth centuries many churches were burnt to the ground. A
single church survives at Greenstead in Essex, its nave of split oak
logs built probably in the late ninth century, but that is all. The
fittings of the Anglo-Saxon churches, particularly the jewelled
chalices, crosses, candlesticks and altar hangings of fine workmanship,
made very portable loot, and the fact that major churches were such a
common target for Viking raiders is a reminder of the richness of the
liturgy in the Anglo-Saxon period. One has to look to the Byzantine
Church, with its rich treasures, for an indication of the splendour that
was echoed in the greater churches of Anglo-Saxon England.

The earliest remaining churches, and some four hundred survive in
whole or in part, can be divided into two groups: those built in the north
of England under the influence of St Columba and his Celtic
missionaries, and those built in the south, particularly around
Canterbury, under the influence of Augustine and his Roman
missionaries. The Celtic chapels are all of the two-cell type and without
aisles. Augustine's missionaries, coming from the more developed urban

centres of the Roman world, brought the tradition of *basilican* (royal hall) churches. Consisting of a central space divided by columns from side aisles, this type had been the common form for public halls throughout the Roman world. Originally used as halls of justice, they had *tribunals* (platforms) at either end for magistrates, but were widely used for other meetings. When Christians in the west first began to put up their own buildings they simply adopted the prevailing form of public hall, transforming one tribunal easily into the sanctuary, usually with a throne for the bishop in the place where a magistrate's seat had traditionally been set. The resulting buildings were wide, but Roman architects had already solved the problem of lighting the darker central nave by raising the roof and inserting clerestory windows in the wall above the level of the aisle roofs. This arrangement has been followed in almost all aisled churches. Churches of the Celtic tradition, in contrast, were usually small, and probably never intended for more than the priest and a few worshippers, with major festivals being celebrated in the open air.

The two traditions, Celtic and Roman, were divided over such matters as the date of Easter (something which still separates the Eastern from the Roman Church). It was agreed at the Synod of Whitby in 664 CE that the Roman tradition would be followed in Britain. Thereafter, with greater cooperation between the priests of both traditions, there was some sharing of architectural ideas. Roman-style basilicas were created in the north by piercing the walls, while two-cell churches became more common in smaller centres in the south. There was also increasing subdivision of church interiors to accommodate additional altars for additional priests as the late Saxon period recovered some of the wealth and richness of the

St John, Wantisden, Suffolk, a Norman two-cell church with chancel, tower and windows added in the late twelfth century, now isolated from its village. (Colin Cunningham)

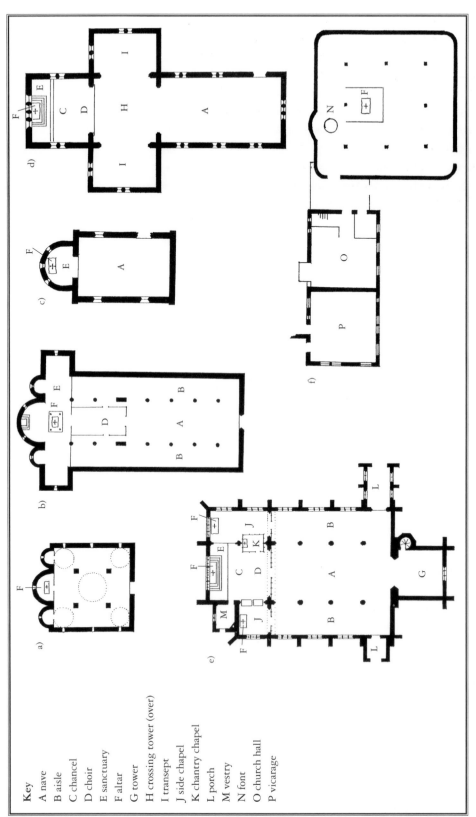

Key

A nave
B aisle
C chancel
D choir
E sanctuary
F altar
G tower
H crossing tower (over)
I transept
J side chapel
K chantry chapel
L porch
M vestry
N font
O church hall
P vicarage

Changes in the layout of churches are shown in this series of sketch plans (not to scale): a) Greek cross form of the Eastern Church with five domes, common by the ninth century; b) basilican plan of the early Western Church; c) two-cell church of the Saxon and Norman period; d) Latin cross form of the early Middle Ages; e) the fully developed late medieval church with aisles to nave and chancels, porches, tower and additional chapel; f) modern church with a unified space for worship, and church hall and vicarage to the side.

liturgy that had been pillaged by the Viking raiders. These extra altars were often housed in a *porticus* (side chapel), stretching out like one arm of a cross and entered only through a door from the main two-cell building.

A new symbolism was introduced in the cruciform church. There may be an echo of the symbolism of the great church structures of the east where the central dome is flanked by vaulted spaces in the shape of Greek cross (with equal arms). There the central dome represents the heavens and was usually filled with an image of Christ Pantocrator (Christ Ruler of all), surrounded by the heavenly host. In the west, however, the cruciform church retains elements of the basilica in its longer western arm or nave, giving the form of the Latin cross. The abbey church of Edward the Confessor at Westminster is thought to be the first such structure in this country, and the importance of that building meant that its form was enormously influential. The Christian symbolism of the plan was quickly recognised. Eventually this shape became the norm for larger churches, with a nave and chancel as before, flanked by two transepts, with a central tower over the crossing. The Normans, with their passion for rebuilding, soon ensured that most churches were reconstructed in fine masonry, and with richly carved ornament. The example of each new structure must have helped to spread the interest in new building, and the forms of each major church would have been studied and copied by nobles and clerics who were engaged in ensuring the presence of the church in every corner of the land.

There were other factors, too, that helped in the development of the parish church. The spread of monasticism was a major feature of the development of Christianity in the century and a half after the Norman conquest. Indeed Britain, in the period from the thirteenth century to the Reformation, was probably the most densely monasticised country in Europe. Many monastic churches came into the control of parishes at the time of the Reformation, and are an important sub-group of parish church buildings. The presence of large abbey churches and smaller priory buildings would have had widespread influence on parishes in the surrounding area, though the needs of a parish church were never the same as those of a monastery. However, the pre-Reformation service required more people to organise it, and there was a considerable range of staff available. Pre-Reformation clergy can be divided into those in major and those in minor orders. Only those in major orders – bishops, priests and deacons – were fully ordained, though they had previously to have received minor orders. Minor orders consisted of cantors, who led the singing, lectors, who read the scriptures, porters, who opened and guarded the church doors, exorcists, whose duty was to drive out evil spirits, and acolytes (literally followers), who assisted generally with carrying crosses, relics, incense and candles. Most of these would have been only part time, helping at services in much the same way as servers do today, but their inclusion in minor orders was a significant and permanent social distinction. Some churches were served by colleges of canons or by full-time priests living a monastic life; in addition, there might be a number of chantry priests and even the occasional itinerant preacher. Yet the main body of the building had to house only the local congregation, and not all parishes could rise to the full complement of staff, so for many years the two-cell structure, derived from the Celtic tradition, was sufficient for most parishes. In many small villages it is still all that is needed and all that there is today.

Aisles were among the commonest additions, and were often achieved by simply piercing the existing outer wall. This was none the less a considerable and expensive development for a parish church and it was seldom the case that two matching aisles were erected at the same time. In parish churches the aisles often had a double function, which alone could justify the expense. The processions of great festivals would certainly use the aisle, but at other times the space might be taken over by one or another of the guilds who controlled the trades of each town for their own activities. Some larger town churches, such as St Nicholas, Yarmouth, even had double aisles, creating a wide pillared hall of the whole body of the church. The eastern end of an aisle would often be fitted with an altar and could then be used as a separate chapel. In the later Middle Ages there was a proliferation of separate chapels, either in aisles or transepts or as aisles of the chancel. In some cases these were almost separate structures within the church, while a few were built to the east of the chancel. Each chapel had its individual function, and most were financed by individual donors.

This slow accretion of transepts, aisles and chapels was often completed with the addition of a western tower, and a porch to the south (and sometimes to the north as well). These last spaces further extended the activities for which the church provided a stage, and the resulting building was a complex series of interlinked spaces. The sense of movement through unenclosed areas, from aisle to nave, from nave to chancel, and so on, is the essence of the way churches were used. The subtle differentiation of spaces reflected important elements in the worship of which the original builders were acutely aware. Our problem is that in many cases practices have changed and the original function of some of the spaces is almost forgotten. Yet the complete parish church with all its parts has to be seen as a unified expression of the development of its parish. The fact that in almost all cases the church only grew to its final form over several centuries is also a reflection of the importance of continuity in a structure that developed to serve the spiritual needs of each generation. As a part of the continuum of worship each congregation is in effect only the trustee of what has been left in its care.

CHAPTER TWO

Sacred Space

Sacraments: the Christian Way

A church is not a building for worshipping in, it is a building for worshipping with.

(Edwin Lutyens)

The concept of a sacrament, an action that is somehow made holy, is difficult to comprehend but is none the less central to Christian belief and practice. Sacraments have had a major impact in shaping what is done in churches and thus in shaping the churches themselves. A sacrament is, after all, an 'outward and visible sign', as the prayer book puts it, of the gift of grace and the means by which it is received. The idea of the gift of grace is particularly related to certain key actions or celebrations, and the Church originally recognised seven such events: Baptism, Confirmation, Communion, Matrimony, Ordination, Penance and Extreme Unction. The first five of these continued to be recognised in the regular practices of the Church of England after the Reformation, while some churches still offer the sacraments of penance and extreme unction. These acts acknowledge the stages of the Christian life from birth to death, with the addition, in the act of ordination, of the special step of becoming a priest. They are, therefore, the determining ideas behind much of the liturgy that was developed over the centuries and they are the principal reasons why our churches have the form they do. The Bible offers little in the way of direct advice as to how to worship. So the liturgy and the spaces that house it have to be seen as the work of the people who made up the early church. Central to their worship in the first millennium were the seven sacraments which provided a means of marking the various stages of life from birth to death, including the possibility of admission to the priesthood. Since each sacrament was a means of expressing publicly the stages of an individual's relationship with God, careful provision was made for each from the very start.

A Mark of Difference: Baptism

Two of the sacraments – baptism and the Eucharist – have biblical authority,[1] and were regarded as special from early times, and it is the place of baptism that is the first to be encountered in most churches. Baptism involves marking or washing with water, a reminder of Christ's own baptism in the River Jordan. There needs to be a container for the water, and in a church this takes the form of a *font* (in Latin a fountain), which is the physical focus of the ceremony. The font is usually positioned near the entrance to the church and it usually consists of a low pillar on which is set a stone bowl. The bowl contains the water that the priest sprinkles on the forehead of each candidate for baptism before making the sign of the cross on their forehead. This was recognised as a mark of difference, signifying that each candidate had been accepted into the family of the Church. The place and the activity were both of great importance to every congregation. It was at baptism that the priest came into direct contact with each member of his flock, and so the font acquired a considerable pastoral importance. Without baptism there could be no congregation, and without a font there could be no baptism. The

The whole building is focused on the altar as the centre of the Eucharist. One step leads to the chancel and another to the sanctuary, and the altar is raised further for maximum visibility. (Church of England Record Office)

font, symbolising the beginning of each Christian journey, was therefore set up at the point of entry into the church building.

One early Christian manual[2] describes two methods of baptism: one of triple immersion and one by pouring water on the head of the candidate. Christ's own baptism is described as taking place in the River Jordan, and the earliest baptisms were in the form of total immersion. Baptism pools were constructed, often in special buildings; the earliest known baptistery dates from the mid-third century CE. However, most churches could not afford a separate structure, and for the most part baptisms were performed in the church itself from the tenth century on. Even so, the earliest were by immersion in sunken pools, a practice that some Anglicans and the Baptists continue to this day. Without a sunken pool, the practice of total immersion required a reservoir of considerable size, of a type found now only in the great churches of Italy. The cathedral in Siena, for instance, has a font some 15ft across, which incorporates separate dry compartments for the priests to whom the candidates were brought to be pushed beneath the water for their sins to be symbolically washed away. Presumably baptism by immersion was still practised in the western Church when this huge font was built in 1416. Yet in English churches much smaller fonts are all that survive, and the size of most early fonts would only allow infants to be baptised by immersion. Presumably by the time the west was securely Christianised there was less call for adult baptism and, significantly, the Sarum usage specifies immersion of infants only. The child was to be held with its head to the east and immersed three times, facing north, south and into the water, while the priest invoked God the Father, the Son and the Holy Ghost.[3] Thus all that was required was a bowl with the diameter of an infant's body; even the depth of water was immaterial, since the rite did not call for the child to be wholly submerged. Yet the symbolism of washing is important, and so the practice developed of using special water. This was blessed and poured into the font at Easter where it stayed until the next year. It seems likely that the practical difficulties of gathering large quantities of water, blessing it and keeping it clean and safe, not to mention the risks of plunging infants into water that might have been left in the font for six months or more, were factors in the change, by the end of the tenth century in most parish churches, from immersion baptism to baptism by simply sprinkling the water on the candidate.

The use of holy water had a curious side effect that has left its mark on many churches. The water once blessed was special and not lightly thrown away. Instead it was regularly left in the font, where the lead lining prevented it from soaking away into the porous stone. However, it became common for folk to draw off portions for

Baptism by affusion. The priest sprinkles water from the font using a scallop shell, the traditional badge of the pilgrim. A candle symbolises the injunction to 'shine as a light in the world'. (Church of England Record Office)

medicinal, or even for sinister, uses. By
the thirteenth century this scandalous
practice was so widespread that the order
went out for covers to be fitted to all
fonts. At first these were merely flat lids,
fastened with a strong hasp, the holes for
which are often all that remain today.
Later, conical covers were made, and by
the fifteenth century these were built, for
that is the right word, as enormous spires,
richly carved with miniature buttresses,
pinnacles, crockets and so on. Access to
the font basin was either by means of
doors in the lower section, which could be
securely locked, or by raising the whole
contraption with a variety of pulley
systems attached to the roof. Rich font
covers of this sort were a feature of many
East Anglian churches until the
Reformation, and there were even
attempts to continue the practice
thereafter, under Archbishop Laud. Rich
font covers were also a feature that the
most enthusiastic devotees of the Ritualist
revival in the nineteenth century tried to

The towering sixteenth-
century Laudian cover over the
font of St Clement, Terrington
St Clement, Norfolk.
(Colin Cunningham)

incorporate into their structures. Such covers could be decorated with
all sorts of details: biblical scenes, saints, or a whole menagerie of
creatures chosen for their symbolic appropriateness. The Pelican in
her piety was a favourite, since the bird was popularly supposed to
pierce her breast to feed her young, an act that symbolised the
sacrifice of Christ. Such stories seem fanciful to us but in an age when
every living thing was seen as a part of God's creation and a reflection
of his glory, the use of animals in the service of religious symbolism
was both natural and helpful.

For the process of baptism by affusion, however, all that was
actually needed was a bowl from which the priest could draw enough
water to pour on the candidate's head, marking each with the cross as
a symbol. So the earliest surviving fonts in this country are simple
round bowls, usually of stone and lined with lead. Because they were
so special they were carefully preserved, often surviving the
rebuilding of a church, so that the font may well be the oldest
element in a church building. The specialness of the activity meant
that the stone basin was carefully made, often richly carved with
patterns. By the eleventh century the patterns regularly included a

The font of 1499 in Holy Trinity, Blythburgh, Suffolk, stands on a high platform, with an additional step for the priest. (Crown Copyright RCHME)

symbolic element, typically a figure crushed beneath the base of the font signifying the devil driven out by this act of initiation. These Norman fonts are often square and more elaborate with pillars round the base, reflecting the increased status of their church. Later still, in the fifteenth century and especially in East Anglia, there was widespread replacement of fonts by fine new pieces. These are generally octagonal and often depict the seven sacraments with the eighth side reserved for an image of either the baptism of Christ or his crucifixion. Another interpretation of the octagonal font is that the sides are a reminder of the seven days in which God is described as creating the world, with the eighth referring to the Day of Resurrection, the day to which all Christians look forward. This symbolism was despised by many at the time of the Reformation, and the carved fonts suffered at the hands of the puritan iconoclasts. None the less the actual basins tended to survive, shorn or partially shorn of their carving, as baptism was accepted as important in the Protestant Church of England, and there needed to be some means of continuing the practice. A special Canon (or liturgical rule) was published in 1604 to justify the continued use of the sign of the cross in baptism, and to remove any scruples Protestants might have at this Popish practice. Another practice abandoned in the seventeenth century was the use of Holy Water on entering the church. Pre-Reformation worshippers used to dip their fingers in the consecrated water stored in the stoup and cross themselves as a reminder of their baptismal vows. Small built-in basins (stoups) survive in a number of churches.

The fact that baptism represents the start of the Christian journey explains why so many fonts are placed at the west end of their church.

Sometimes this area is made into a separate 'baptistery'. By the eighteenth century it had become common to construct a 'christening pew' around the font in which the child, the godparents and family would sit until the end of the second lesson of the morning service. The priest would then move to the west end of the church and conduct the baptism before the assembled congregation. The sense in which baptism was a public affirmation of faith was important, and the prayer book of 1662 actually admonishes 'that Baptism should not be administered but on Sundays, and other Holy Days, when the most number of People come together'.[4] Nowadays, while many churches prefer to incorporate baptism into their regular Sunday worship, it is also common to have a separate service involving just the child's family and close friends. The emphasis on public baptism, however, was another reason for so many late medieval fonts being placed on platforms, often with the priest having to climb up two or three steps, while the child was handed perilously up to him to be baptised in full view of all.

In some churches the actual baptising with water and signing with the cross is accompanied by the gift of a lighted candle, symbolic of the way Christians are urged to 'shine as light in the world'. This is a relatively recent practice which draws on the symbolism of light. But today most emphasis is on welcoming the baptised into the congregation, and baptisms are regularly part of the main family service. However, if the font is at the west end of the church this can be awkward as the family have to sit at the back, now that christening pews have been swept away. One solution, followed in a small number of modern churches, has been to set the font at the front of the congregation space. This reversal of the original order of progress has been made possible because from the Reformation until the nineteenth century there was a significant diminution in the size of fonts. Some eighteenth-century ones are no more than elegant bowls on slender stems. There are even a few made of Wedgwood pottery. These fonts are eminently movable and can be located wherever convenient, but in those churches where

The font designed by Robert Adam in about 1765 in St James's Church in the Earl of Coventry's park at Croome D'Abitot, Worcestershire. (Colin Cunningham)

the medieval stone font survives it does to a great extent control the way baptism can be administered.

Of course holding a baptism service at the west end of the church may be awkward today largely because of the fixed seating, almost certainly an addition of the seventeenth, eighteenth or nineteenth century. When the fonts were originally installed there would have been only a few benches set around the walls of the church, and the congregation would have been able to gather more freely. Yet it is interesting how far this first act of Christian worship has left its mark on the fabric and arrangement of the average parish church. It is perhaps even more important in our fluid society to feel, as you can at a baptism, that you are in contact with the many generations who have worshipped in much the same way before. This was recognised by the nineteenth-century restorers, one of whom wrote: 'The sanctity rightly and reasonably attached to the consecrated instrument of a Holy Sacrament caused the careful preservation of Fonts unchanged by centuries of rebuilding and alteration. Thus we cannot doubt that a considerable number of Fonts now exist in England wherein the Saxon infant received the waters of salvation from the hand of that ancient priest whose bones, for aught we know, may moulder under the pavement of a church reconstructed on its original foundations six centuries after his death.'[5]

A Gift of the Spirit: Confirmation

The next stage in the initiation of the worshipper has left much less trace, though it is hardly less important. Confirmation is the rite in which baptised members of a congregation affirm their faith and receive more fully the grace of the Holy Spirit. The concept is difficult, but it is most often described today as a sort of growing up in the faith, and each candidate is assumed to take up for himself or herself the vows made by the godparents at the baptism. Confirmation takes place in the presence of the bishop and involves a separate service at which the bishop lays his hands on each candidate in turn. It was not always so, and confirmation was originally linked closely with baptism. Some theologians still regard the two as inseparable.

The important factors in the early centuries were the laying on of hands and anointing with oil as well as washing with water. The first two acts were performed by the bishop, stressing the sense in which the individual congregation was part of a wider communion. However, as the number of Christians grew it became impossible for the bishop to be involved personally with all those seeking admission to the Church, and the responsibilities for the dual ritual were divided. The parish priest remained responsible for the immersion, the baptism, and the bishop for the anointing and laying on of hands.

This division was accommodated in different ways in the eastern and western Churches. In the Orthodox communion the bishop remained responsible for consecrating the oil, which was then transferred to the parish priest for actual anointing. This allowed the close connection of baptism and confirmation to be retained. In the western, Roman Catholic and subsequently Anglican, Church the bishop remained responsible for the act of confirmation, whether with consecrated oil or by simple laying on of hands. The involvement of the bishop rather than the parish priest immediately lifts this act of worship out of the ambience of the single parish church. Quite frequently today the confirmation service is held in the cathedral, the bishop's church. Alternatively, a bishop travels to one parish church, and the candidates come together from a number of parishes for the service. In such cases, though there may be an attempt to share out the privilege of an episcopal visit, it is usually the larger town churches that are used.

Confirmation is not a ritual that can be linked automatically with every church, although it is an essential part of every Christian's progress. This progress is, however, marked by the act of confirmation, the laying on of hands, which takes place in front of the congregation, usually at the chancel step. In this sense there is a real progression from baptism at the entrance of the church towards communion at the altar in the chancel. However, because the ritual involves the visit of a bishop rather than being a part of the regular activity in a church, all that is needed is somewhere for the bishop to sit. A few churches have a special seat or throne for the bishop's use, which is brought out for the occasion, but such a throne needs to be removed to allow for the regular

The moment of confirmation as the bishop lays hands on two candidates. They kneel at the chancel step, where the bishop's throne has been set for the occasion. (Church of England Record Office)

pattern of day-to-day use and movable furniture leaves little trace. However, the step that marks the division between nave and chancel, the site of the action in confirmation, is a crucial element in the symbolism of a church and an important feature in the architecture.

It might seem sad that confirmation, so important to the individual, should have such an ephemeral impact on the church, with no permanent reminder of the progression. But confirmation is merely another stage in the Christian journey, and it is linked with a third sacrament, the Eucharist, which does have a profound effect on the arrangement of churches.

Supreme Thanksgiving: the Eucharist

Jesus told his friends to do this, and they have done it always since. Was ever another command so obeyed? For century after century, spreading slowly to every continent and country among every race on earth, this action has been done, in every conceivable human circumstance, for every conceivable human need from infancy and before it to extreme old age and after it, from the pinnacles of earthly greatness to the refuge of fugitives in the caves and dens of the earth. Men have found no better thing than this to do for kings at their crowning and for criminals going to the scaffold; for armies in triumph or for a bride and bridegroom in a little country church; for the wisdom of a Parliament or for a sick old woman afraid to die.

(Dom. Gregory Dix)

The Eucharist, or Holy Communion, has been a central element in Christian ritual from the earliest times. It can be regarded both as a sharing of bread and wine and as a sacrifice. The sharing recalls the Last Supper in which Jesus shared bread and wine with his disciples before his crucifixion, telling them to 'Take, eat; this is my body' and 'drink ye all of [the wine] for this is my blood of the new testament'.[6] The sharing of Christ's body and blood, whether in actuality or through symbols, was a difficult concept and one that led to major theological differences, which in turn have affected the way churches are laid out for this ritual. The idea of the Eucharist as sacrifice, a remembrance of the sacrifice of Christ, also had implications for the way the ritual was conducted and so how the ritual space was ordered.

For the offering of a sacrifice an altar was the essential prerequisite, and can be regarded as more important than the church that shelters it. Stone altars have a long history in pagan religion and in Judaism even before Christianity, but it is assumed that the earliest Christians used some form of table for their celebration of the Eucharist (which usually took place in private houses). The use of stone altars may have come about through the practice of celebrating the Eucharist on the tombs of martyrs. Thus two forms of altars were justified, the table and the tomb, and these came to be associated with the two concepts of the Eucharist as the shared feast and the sacrifice. In fact the term altar really refers to the stone 'tomb' type, while the wooden altar tables that became widespread after the Reformation are more appropriately described as communion tables. The term Lord's Table is widely used among the Nonconformist Churches.

In Britain most early altars were probably of wood, like their churches; stone did not become common until the sixth century. However, the earliest surviving altars are later than that, and are all of stone. The altar was consecrated as a part of the dedication of the church and marked with the sign of the cross. Usually there are five small crosses inscribed in the surface, one at each corner and one in the centre. Because it was such a special element, the altar was often elaborately carved and decorated. It was also covered with cloths and furnished with a cross and candlesticks, making it the focus of the whole church. Originally, in larger churches, the cross and candlesticks were set on a separate table under a canopy, called the *ciborium magnum* (in Latin, the large bread-holder, ciborium also being the name of the vessel in which the bread or wafer for the Eucharist is held), leaving the communion table bare for use. This practice survives in the occasional use of a pillared canopy or *baldachino* over the altar, but such things, though common in Roman Catholic churches, are rare in Anglican churches today.

The altar was set in the holiest part of the church, the sanctuary, which formed the eastern end of the chancel. The manner of decorating altars, and the habits of use, developed fully in the early Middle Ages. Stone altars were often repositories for relics of martyrs and saints, as they are to this day in many Roman Catholic churches. The front was covered with an ornamented cloth and the whole was enriched with an ornamental shelf, called a *retable*, and a *reredos*, or background panel. These last were often extremely richly carved and incorporated images of Christ and the saints, and sometimes even the tree of Jesse, which depicted the ancestry of Jesus. The whole chancel area was generally decorated, and was more elaborate than the rest of the church; the sanctuary, if it was a separate space, was made richer still. The roof was usually enriched with carved and painted angels, stars and the name Jesus in painted letters. Often the eastern bay, over the sanctuary, was marked out with more carving, richer paint and gilding. In addition, as the centuries progressed there were larger and larger windows, filled with elaborate tracery and often with stained glass that would supplement the iconography of the reredos and fill the sanctuary with coloured light. There was no real limit, beyond available finance, to the adornment of this most sacred space in its special building. As the chancel was almost invariably set at the eastern end of the church, the light of the rising sun would flood in, providing a dramatic backlight for the altar. This in turn was a reminder of the centrality of Christ's rising from the tomb on the first Easter morning.

In many medieval churches the space within the chancel was considerable. Originally all that was needed was space for the altar and the priests but increasingly, as the ritual was elaborated, there was a need for more people – priests, deacons and acolytes and sometimes even choirs, following the practice of monastic houses and cathedrals, and the full complement of clerics in major and minor orders required a substantial space. Many medieval churches were, in fact, served by groups of monks, and functioned as outstations of monasteries as well as parish churches. Much effort was devoted to the building of chancels in the thirteenth, fourteenth and fifteenth centuries, and in these broad spaces there was ample room for all the clergy. One of the most impressive is at Walpole St Peter in Norfolk, where an eastward extension of the original church continued beyond the eastern wall of the churchyard, requiring the altar and sanctuary to be raised over the right of way running along the boundary. Thus the altar is not only at the end of a spacious chancel but is raised high up a flight of nine steps. Now that the screen there has been removed it makes a powerful focus for the whole church.

The sanctuary and chancel were often spacious, providing a splendid theatre for the celebration of the mass. The importance of the whole idea meant that in the medieval period careful thought was given to all the fittings that might be needed. Close attention was paid to each action and the beauty of the mass, and the quality and cleanliness of the items used was valued. Thus, in addition to the altar and movable furniture, there was often a shelf or niche, called the credence, on which the sacred elements for the mass (the bread, wine and water) were set out before consecration. More frequently this could be done on a movable table, which would not be likely to have survived the Reformation. There would also need to be facilities for washing the sacred vessels, and often a cupboard, or *aumbry*, for storage. These were often built into the wall and had a lamp to indicate the presence of the consecrated bread and wine reserved in them. The aumbry would have had a door, perhaps carved, and in the later Middle Ages would have had decorative iron hinges and locks. These, however, have seldom survived, and what is left is often no more than a rectangular hole in the wall. The washing basin, or *piscina*, is usually open and thus often quite richly carved. There is occasionally a second basin, or *lavabo*, for the priest to wash his hands.

Larger and more splendid were the seats for the clergy. Known by their Latin name *sedilia*, these were also built into the wall, often in the form of beautifully carved niches. Usually there are three, one each for the priest, deacon and sub-deacon who assisted with the liturgy, and the

At the central moment of the Eucharist the priest holds high first the bread and then the chalice. The action is focused by the cross and candlesticks on this altar. (Church of England Record Office)

three seats are often ranked, with the most important one tallest and nearest the altar. Other users of the chancel included members of the congregation who came on special feast days to participate in the communion. They stood or sat on benches. Very occasionally, if a church was regularly served by monks, the choir seating was arranged in the collegiate fashion, like the choir of a cathedral or monastery, with fixed seats facing inwards. These in turn may be richly carved, and some incorporate misericords, the tip-up seats that allowed the occupant to rest (but not actually to sit) during the long hours of the liturgy.

From the thirteenth century on it became common to set up other altars in a church, each of which would be used for masses on particular occasions. During the great festivals it was not uncommon for a number of priests to celebrate the mass at the same time, so that all the altars would be in use together and the building filled with chanting. These secondary altars might be in a separate chapel, perhaps dedicated to the Virgin Mary. In the twelfth and thirteenth centuries in particular there was a great emphasis on the humanity of the Virgin and her position as the mother of Christ in interceding for sinners. In some eyes this amounted to Mariolatry, but it resulted in the construction of a number of Lady Chapels dedicated to her. Other chapels or altars might be dedicated to saints; usually set at the eastern end of the nave or in a transept, these would have their own reredos, usually with small screens, or *parcloses*, beside them to mark out the specialness of that particular spot. There were also chantry chapels, often like miniature rooms within a church, built in memory of prominent or wealthy citizens, where a priest would be paid to celebrate masses for the salvation of the soul of the founder. However, at all times the main altar in the chancel was recognised as the high altar, as indeed it was by virtue of the raising of the chancel and sanctuary.

Until the Reformation the sacrifice of the mass was offered in a chancel separated from the congregation in the nave by a wooden screen called the Great Rood. There is a similarity here to the practice in orthodox churches of celebrating the mass behind the *iconostasis* (the wall or screen on which the sacred images are hung). The priest offers the sacrifice on behalf of the congregation rather than involving them in full, and the chancel space was thus reserved largely for the clergy. The rood screen had the effect of creating within the church a separate space whose rich decoration, half seen through the screen, served to heighten the special quality of the ritual.

In addition the chancel was almost always raised by one step above the level of the nave, and the sanctuary generally raised a further step, with sometimes more for the altar. The importance of this for visibility is obvious, but the value of steps for demarcating space was also well recognised, as was the added drama of moving from level to

The rich screen of *c.* 1450 in St John, Plymtree, Devon, crosses both nave and south aisle. It is now deprived of its sculptured rood. (Colin Cunningham)

level in processions. Such matters certainly concerned the men, usually clerics or nobles, who paid for the beautification of the medieval churches. Sometimes they seem to have considered the symbolic use of steps, and it was not uncommon to find an altar raised three steps above the nave in reference to the Trinity – the concept of God as Father, Son and Holy Spirit. In the nineteenth century this sort of symbolism was taken very seriously by the ritualists. At Studley Royal in Yorkshire the three steps leading up into the sanctuary are made of three different colours of stone: black for sin, red for redemption through the blood of Christ and white for purity.

In the Middle Ages, however, the rood screen itself was the most visible object as far as the congregation was concerned, acting as both a screen and a frame for the mass. It, too, was accordingly richly decorated, painted and carved. Many of those that survive are a testament to their makers' delight in rich ornament and a display of the best that the wood carver could produce. But there was more to them than merely a screen. The word *rood* in medieval times referred to the cross (or rod) on which Christ was crucified and thus the screen had a major symbolic as well as a practical function. The typical rood consisted of a screen with above it a beam and platform. On the beam was set a crucifix, usually with figures of St John the Evangelist and the Virgin Mary. The platform could be used on special occasions. Candles were often set there, and certain parts of major festival services, such as those at Easter, Corpus Christi and Christmas, might be sung by choristers or cantors stationed on the platform. Equally, the rood platform could be used for decoration. In some places, such as Stanton St John in Oxfordshire, the rood is decorated with a sheaf of corn at harvest time, which remains there for the whole year. There was further symbolism in the fact that a person could only reach the chancel by, literally, passing under Christ on the cross.

Nowadays all that remains of most rood screens is the vestige of an opening at the level of the beam or perhaps a blocked doorway at the foot of the rood stairs. The reason for their removal was that the remote and rich ceremonial of the mass hidden away in the chancel was increasingly unacceptable to the Protestant clergy and laity of the seventeenth century. The process of abolition was begun in 1538, when Henry VIII set about dissolving the monasteries, and there was a parallel movement to remove from parish churches shrines and images that were considered idolatrous. However, it was not until a hundred years later that the rise of Protestantism led to the almost complete disappearance of roods, the removal of statues of the Virgin and child from the church door, the levelling of chancels and the frequent vandalising of carved figures. Churches remained bare of such items until the Ritualist revival of the mid-nineteenth century led to their being reinstated in whole or in part.

The whole vocabulary of symbolic ornament was a part of the restorer's armament. The Middle Ages had regularly used pictorial images on the walls to reinforce the Christian message. There had been an almost standard arrangement with a Doom, or Last Judgement, painted over the chancel arch, the righteous rising to glory on the right, or south side, and the damned being flung into hell on the left, or north. In that position they literally framed the activity of the mass beyond the screen. Other paintings filled the walls; from the seventh century these had been common as the 'Bible of the illiterate' and well over two thousand churches in England retain some traces of their original paintings. Initially, they had shown the key scenes of Christ's life, from the Annunciation to the Ascension, but in the uncertain times of the Middle Ages there was a concentration on death and the horrors of hell or the expiation of sins. The images also reflected theological fashions, with Marian imagery being particularly common in the thirteenth and fourteenth centuries. Images of St Christopher were also popular because it was believed that by merely looking on his image death could be delayed. The

A fifteenth-century painting of
the Last Judgement over the
chancel arch in St Nicholas,
Stanningfield, Suffolk. (Crown
Copyright RCHME)

nineteenth century could not accept the rich mythology of the Middle
Ages, and so their decoration was confined to less specific images. The
monogram IHS was widely used[7], and in sanctuaries and on altars
representations of vines and ears of corn (symbols of the communion
feast), often with the letters Alpha and Omega (the first and last
letters of the Greek alphabet, referring to Christ's claim to be the
beginning and the end), were both common. A little less frequently
we find the crown of thorns, the whip and the hammer and nails that
are mentioned in the crucifixion story. In Lady Chapels Victorian
decoration was more frequently confined to patterns based on the
letter M, sometimes with a crown (for Mary as queen of heaven), and
sometimes without. Only in the most devotedly ritualist churches do
we find elaborate pictorial schemes of decoration, and even these tend
to illustrate biblical stories or major saints. But nineteenth-century
iconography was greatly enhanced by the developing art historical
scholarship of the period that searched out signs and symbols from the
many paintings of the Middle Ages and the Renaissance.[8]

   Of course, the destruction of carved and painted images did not
mean the abandonment of the liturgy, and many practices together with
their related items disappeared only slowly. The Eucharist continued to

The fifteenth-century roof of Holy Trinity, Blythburgh, Suffolk, decorated with the letters IHS and carved angels or Cherubim. (Crown Copyright RCHME)

be celebrated, though less frequently. By the end of the seventeenth century it was common practice to celebrate communion only three times a year, at Christmas, Easter and Whitsun; the chancel and all its surviving furnishings became almost redundant and in some churches it was even blocked off and used for other purposes. In most cases, where the chancel continued in use, attention was given to reordering on a simpler basis, more accessible to the populace at large. Commandment boards and boards with the Lord's Prayer began to replace carved reredoses and wall paintings, a practice that continued till the end of the nineteenth century and is now being revived, as fine boards left in store are rediscovered and restored. The walls themselves were often whitewashed and then decorated with appropriate scriptural texts. Occasionally one can find places where the sanctuary was redesigned with close attention to the actual ritual of the Lord's supper, as the Eucharist generally came to be called. Framlingham, in Suffolk, for instance, has a fine reredos made around 1700 in the form of a classical frame around a plain boarded backdrop painted with the letters IHS set in a circle of rays. This was carefully placed so that when the celebrant

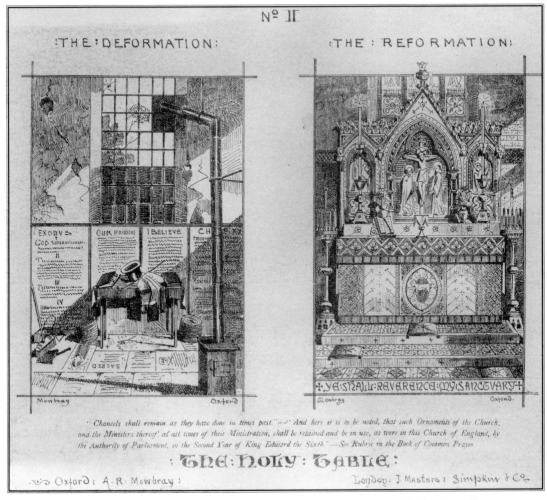

An 'unreformed' sanctuary
with Commandment boards,
stove, and Lord's Table used as
a coat rack, compared with one
'restored' to a nineteenth-
century ritualist ideal, from
Mowbray's *The Reformation and
the Deformation*, 1868.
(Courtesy of Pusey House,
Oxford)

raised the wafer at the central moment of the service, it was seen against
the centre of the circle. Such a concern for sight-lines would have been
unnecessary in the pre-Reformation period when the church building
was compartmentalised by the rood screen. Once the whole building
was thrown into one, it became more important to take thought for the
way that the congregation as a whole could see what was going on. The
same concern has led many churches in the last twenty or thirty years to
adopt the practice of using a nave altar, set at or just before the chancel
step, as a way of emphasising the corporate nature of the communion
service. This movement really only dates to the years since the Second
World War, when the parish communion service took the leading place
in the regular worship of congregations throughout the country.

Yet this concern for carefully conducted communion services was not
achieved at once. After the Reformation some churches ripped out their

St Peter, Bruisyard, Suffolk,
a reredos of *c.* 1870 with
Lord's Prayer, Creed and
Commandment boards.
(Colin Cunningham)

rood screens, but felt obliged to insert altar rails to maintain the special sanctity of that area. Others took a more determined line, rejecting what they regarded as popish ritual: they did away with altar rails and moved the altar bodily into the main part of the church, where it could actually be the centre of the Eucharistic supper. This practice is close to that followed by a number of Presbyterian churches, where the Lord's Table, in the form of a trestle table, is set up in the midst of the congregation only when needed for the communion service. The Puritan approach required a movable table, and there was a strong aversion to stone altars, many of which were broken up and replaced by sturdy wooden pieces. This objection to stone altars has lasted, and, although the ritualists of the nineteenth century often tried to insert stone altars, many Jacobean tables still survive as the current altar of the church. Indeed the insertion of a solid stone altar, admittedly a round one designed by Henry Moore, in the church of St Stephen Wallbrook in London proved controversial barely a generation ago.

Archbishop Laud (1573–1645), in his insistence on orderly services, demanded that altars be set back against the east wall of the

Jacobean altar rails in
St Andrew, Isleham,
Cambridgeshire. (Colin
Cunningham)

church, and from his time on, or rather from the Restoration of
Charles II in 1660, it has been customary to provide altar rails to
mark off the sanctuary space. The rails were at first required to be
sufficiently closely spaced to prevent dogs straying into the
sanctuary, but increasingly they were seen as mere ornamental
barriers, and are often lightweight and open. They became the focus
for decorative work, but never acquired the size or complexity of the
richest rood screens of which they are the effective successors;
moreover they mark off only the sanctuary and not the chancel.

Initially the Lord's Table needed only to be a small affair since it
was for occasional use. However, in the nineteenth century, when
there was a greater readiness to accept the concept of the sanctuary as
somewhere special and precious, the practice was adopted of first
putting candlesticks, then a cross and vases of flowers and finally a
crucifix on the altar. Larger altar tables were needed simply to
accommodate the other essential objects — a service book, a chalice
for the wine and paten for the bread or wafer, together with a flagon
for spare wine and jug for water — and nineteenth-century altars were

mostly much longer than their Jacobean predecessors. A number were actually built to incorporate the older table.

With the altar once again set against the east wall of the church, and communion seen as an occasional service in which only those who chose would participate, the practice returned of having the priest celebrate facing eastwards like the congregation. This had been the common form throughout the Middle Ages, and emphasised the way in which the priest was offering the sacrifice on behalf of his congregation. It was in fact a reversal of the practice in the early church, where the priest had faced west towards the congregation, emphasising their invitation to join in the common Eucharistic feast. This change had an impact on the size and arrangement of sanctuaries, since the westward position required space for the celebrant behind the altar. The eastward position made no such demand, and could be accommodated in a shallower sanctuary. That approach remained the norm until the twentieth century, when the emphasis began once more to be placed on the communion service as a shared feast. There was a short period when it was fashionable to celebrate from the north end of the altar in a typically English compromise, but the older westward position is now the one most regularly used, with the resulting need to bring altars forward once more.

The equipment on the altar is usually less visible to the casual visitor, though it is equally important in designing the space. Altar furnishings were very largely swept away at the Reformation, and more determinedly in the seventeenth century. They might have included reliquaries that were obnoxious, as well as richly decorated and jewelled chalices, which were attractive booty for the royal coffers. Much fine plate that survived the Reformation was looted or melted down in the civil wars. The few items of pre-Reformation plate that remain are now usually loaned to a museum or cathedral treasury, though parishes lucky enough to possess such treasures often like to use them for special occasions. It makes a particular and important point to the worshipper to realise that the cup from which the wine is offered has been used for that purpose in this place for hundreds of years. The link with all the past worshippers, who form a part of the whole communion of saints, is brought home in a particular way by the continued use of such things. For most of the eighteenth century, however, this was of little concern and attention in the church was directed elsewhere. It was not until the nineteenth century that much thought was given to the design and range of altar furnishings when the Cambridge Camden Society (the Ecclesiologists) in alliance with the theologians of the Oxford Movement set about bringing back the medieval concepts of the priest as minister and the church as sacred and symbolic.

The appearance of an altar fully decked for worship with crucifix, candles, flowers and a coloured altar cloth, and set with chalice, paten

An altar dressed for the Eucharist with two candles, service book, chalice and ciborium (container for the bread), seen during the prayer of consecration. (Church of England Record Office)

and service book is in marked contrast to what is seen when everything is cleared away. Sometimes even the coloured cloth that hangs in front of the altar is removed after the service, leaving only a plain one. This functions as a dust cloth, but is made of fair white linen, and is itself often protected by a dust cloth, often of blue. It requires a conscious effort of imagination to remember that the space was designed for the richer effect of divine service. Today most people would expect to see a cross, flower vases and perhaps a couple of candlesticks on an altar, but the range of items and the particular theological attitudes they represented were often the subject of fierce controversy.

An Honourable Estate: Matrimony

The 1662 prayer book describes the symbolic and sacred nature of marriage, another of the sacraments recognised by the Church, as 'an honourable estate instituted of God . . . signifying unto us the mystical union that is betwixt Christ and his Church'.[9] Those words are no longer regularly used, yet a wedding is one of the great festivals for any family, and for Christians an important element is the solemnisation of the marriage which brings the ceremony into the church. Since the Reformation, and because the Anglican Church has been the established Church of the country, the legal aspect of marriage has also been linked with the church. For many people weddings are some of the few occasions when they attend church. The rituals attached have a long history and reflect the social organisation of the congregation.

Marriage not only changes the social and familial status of the bride and groom, it also alters their legal standing. The ceremony links the sacred and the secular: the secular, legal elements as well as the sacred nature of the vows are both recognised in the way the service is organised, and in the way the church is arranged for the ceremony. Of course, weddings are not everyday occurrences, and churches are not built specifically to accommodate them. Yet the ceremony uses the various parts of the church in a way that reflects the hierarchies of space and also relates to the community, and churches are remarkably well adapted for the processional and ceremonial elements of the service. Originally this would have involved the village community as a whole and in many rural areas this is still very much the case. The 1662 prayer book actually instructs the couple to come with their 'friends and neighbours'. The aristocracy and gentry might arrange the religious ceremony in the private family chapel, but even so it was expected that the local community would have an opportunity to celebrate the wedding of the local lord or his children, and secular festivities, as extravagant and splendid as the family's purse would allow, would be arranged at the big house. The parish church, however, was the place where most members of any community were married, so there might be little difference from the normal Sunday congregation unless one party came from another village, except that there was probably a rather greater attendance.

By convention the bride, with her father (or whoever is to give her away), arrives last at the church, and there is inevitably a short pause at the entrance. This is a relic of a secular aspect that was more important in the days when matrimony involved property. In the church porch the marriage contracts were exchanged; these set out the dowry that the wife brought with her, and identified what was entailed on her or her children. The practice effectively died out towards the end of the nineteenth century after the Married Women's Property Act of 1870. Yet this was a secular commencement to the ceremony, which took place in an area halfway between the sacred space of the body of the church and the secular world outside.

The first ceremonial element is then the procession of the bride, her father and the bridesmaids up to the chancel step where the groom awaits her. This is an opportunity for the assembled congregation to see her finery, since the bride is very much on show; few people at this stage will see her face, because she processes from behind the congregation and is usually veiled. (At the point in the service when she is most nervous, this concealment may be some comfort.) The liturgy itself begins with the priest not at the altar, as would be the case at communion, but at the chancel step where bride and groom stand before him. This location acknowledges the fact that the marriage vows are taken in public in the presence of the congregation. It is here, too, that the ring, or more commonly nowadays rings, are given or exchanged as a sign to the world that the couple are married.

There follows a more solemn, though for the congregation apparently more boring, section in which the married couple, led by the priest, move to the altar and, kneeling there, receive their blessing. This most sacred element of the service is, like the pre-Reformation mass, removed from the congregation and celebrated at the heart of the sacred space. The 1662 prayer book continues: 'It is convenient, that the newly married Persons should receive the holy Communion at the time of their Marriage, or at the first opportunity after their Marriage.'[10] Many couples do indeed continue the service with a Eucharist, linking this sacrament with the one most central to the Christian faith. However, at most marriage services the blessing is followed by the signing of the Register, a legal document that reflects the Anglican Church's connection with the State and its laws. It often surprises people how awkwardly this is arranged, the couple and the four witnesses either sidling into the vestry or crowding round a small table squeezed in at the side of the chancel. The reason for this awkwardness is the mismatch between the space and its intended function. The chancel was never intended to be used for secular purposes, and its religious ones properly occupy its whole space. Originally the secular elements of the wedding were all taken in the church porch, but not all churches have porches, still less in town churches a surrounding churchyard that can be a pleasant place to linger or conduct such business. Thus in the last century or so the secular elements have been arranged in a part of the church not designed for the purpose. There is, it seems, one good reason for this. The marriage service is only a part of the whole celebration, and there is also the wedding feast. There is a certain awkwardness about interrupting this sequence too much with legal duties, so signing the register forms no major part of the ceremonial.

The final element of the church ceremony is almost totally theatrical, when the married couple, followed by their attendants and

The marriage vows are taken at the entry to the chancel. Bride and groom with their attendants face the priest in full view of the congregation. (Church of England Record Office)

parents, process out of the church. Their route starts at a point where they are raised some six inches above the nave, clear for all to see, and they move westwards facing, and so in full view of, the congregation who have come both to witness and to share the celebration. It is for this moment that the organist will probably reserve the most exhilarating music. A wedding service is certainly one of the occasions to which music makes a valuable contribution, and music has been a part of the tradition of worship in churches from very early times. Most often the music is played on the church organ, which by its nature is able to produce a considerable volume of sound and virtually to mimic an entire band. Although an organ is a relatively recent arrival in most parish churches, it seems entirely appropriate for this sort of ceremony. We also expect churches to be decked with flowers and often even more in the way of ribbons and so on. In fact this practice seems also to be a relatively recent one, dating back little further than the nineteenth century. It is, of course, natural that a celebration should lead to a desire to see the place set apart for it as finely decked out as possible. The present delight in numbers of flowers is probably partly a result of our distance, in this urban age, from nature – a sort of compensation. There is also an economic factor. In earlier times the average labourer, marrying in the local parish church, would certainly not be able to afford any large expense on flowers. As the urban middle classes became more prosperous in the nineteenth century, fine dress and fine decorations came into the reach of more of the populace, and became increasingly desirable.

After exchanging vows, the married couple move to the altar for the blessing. (Church of England Record Office)

The legal business of signing the register at a wedding in St Mary's, Ringmer, Sussex, takes place in a side aisle. (Church of England Record Office)

But the liturgy was the same whatever the social status of the couple, and the modest country couple in former times had the pleasure of leaving the church to linger in the churchyard. The green surrounding of the building had another of its regular uses here as a pleasant place of gathering, which undoubtedly explains the lasting popularity of some pretty country churches for weddings today. Outside the church the move from sacred to secular was completed, and the chief activities revolved around wishing the happy couple well as they left the church for the wedding feast, something that could easily (and often did) border on the bawdy. Tokens of good luck and symbols of fertility were often offered that can be traced to pagan rites, but the Christian Church has often found ways of absorbing earlier pagan rituals into its own liturgy. Yet the emphasis here is on the theatrical and public element of celebration. Frequently the church bells are rung as a way of announcing the completion of the great occasion to the world at large. Sometimes there are guards of honour lining the church path. Some people throw rice, though that can hardly be a native British practice. More traditional is confetti, which in fact is the Italian equivalent of the old English comfit or sweet. Originally comfits, or paper imitations of them (which were cheaper), were thrown. The Italian name suggests that the practice may be a continental import, possibly direct from Italy, where the tradition of public festivity is still strong. Nowadays confetti is always of paper and is frequently banned in the churchyard to prevent litter! What was always important, however, was that the organisation of the church and churchyard provided the necessary spaces for this linking of religious and secular elements.

Church organs, widely installed by the Victorian restorers, were capable of powerful sound, but required a trained keyboard player. (Church of England Record Office)

St Luke's, Cambridge, a church of 1874–5, with the full ritualist chancel decorated for a wedding in 1898. (Cambridgeshire Collection)

A Solemn Charge: Ordination, Induction and Installation

A parish church cannot function without its priest, and there is a link here with another of the seven sacraments, ordination. This is the act which confers on a priest the power to fulfil his or her office. Unless the priest is ordained he or she cannot administer the sacraments or take charge of a parish, so this element of Christian liturgy is intimately connected with the appointing of a priest to a parish and with the whole organisation of the Church. In that sense it is part of the way in which each parish church is linked to the wider body of the Church in diocese and province. The word 'ordination' is linked to order and the concept of rank, and the Church has always recognised a number of different ranks of clergy. Bishops and archbishops are at the top of the Anglican hierarchy, and by the later Middle Ages the western Church recognised three ranks – bishops, priests and deacons – as the major orders within the priesthood. There were also minor orders, and a parish church may have been served by all of them, which explains why so much space was given to chancels in the later Middle Ages. All that remains of this rich hierarchy in most parish churches today is the grading of the three seats of the sedilia.

Ordination, and the rituals involved, can be traced back to the Bible, when Jesus commissioned the twelve disciples; and just as Christian laymen consider themselves part of a long tradition of worshippers, the communion of saints, so it is important that the priesthood is seen as

At ordination the bishop, wearing his mitre, lays his hands on the candidate, while all the other clergy in attendance also reach out to him, stressing a continuity from Christ's charge to the disciples. (Church of England Record Office)

descended from those first missionaries. The actual act of ordination involved the laying on of hands, as described in the Bible,[11] and it has seemed important to many that this physical contact has continued through the centuries. Indeed it was regarded as vital at the time of the Reformation that there were bishops ordained before the break with Rome, who were therefore able to pass on the power of the spirit to newly ordained priests in the emerging Church of England. After the Reformation the priest also had to swear an oath of allegiance to the sovereign, since the Church was set up with the king as its head. Thus an Anglican priest has legal as well as spiritual status.

The attitude to ordination as conferring special spiritual power on the priest is not uncontroversial, but the very existence of an ordained ministry presupposes some sort of hierarchy. This is where the link between parish church and the wider Church comes in. In the Church of England ordination can only be performed by a bishop and so any ordained priest will have been presented to the bishop and ordained in the cathedral of the diocese. A bishop was not permitted to ordain a priest unless that priest had what was known as a *title*: a definite appointment with a guarantee of maintenance (unless, of course, the bishop was prepared to be personally responsible for maintaining the priest). This was sensible enough in a world where the business of a priest removed him from the normal practice of making a living. The community could not support an indefinite number of non-productive priests. Today the economic situation is very different and many priests are non-stipendiary, that is, they take responsibility for their own income and perform their duties as a priest in addition to that. However, for most of the history of the Church of England the normal support of a priest has been the parish, still known as a *living*.

The link with the parish church comes in the institution and induction of a priest as vicar. Here the wider ecclesiastical hierarchy comes to the parish, and the activities begin to leave their trace on the fabric. There are two elements to the establishment of a priest in charge of a parish, but even before that can begin he or she needs to be nominated by the patron of the living. Nowadays this is generally the result of a recommendation from the Parish Church Council after they have had the opportunity to meet the candidates, but for centuries priests were selected by the powers that be. In many cases this was the bishop, or some corporate body such as an Oxford or Cambridge College; very often the existence of such a patron will be commemorated in the church either in the form of a badge or coat of arms.

In the Church of England, particularly after the Reformation, there were a good many cases where the patron of a living was the local landlord or some other nobleman. The right to nominate a candidate for a church post, which gave its holder status in society and sometimes a very comfortable living, was highly valued, especially in the eighteenth and nineteenth centuries. It gave the patron the opportunity to promote friends and dependants, and often provided a useful career for a younger son. However, since it was a valuable privilege, it was carefully guarded and passed on in inheritance and through marriage. The right could even be bought and sold, with the result that a given nobleman might be the patron of a selection of different livings in different parts of the country, and the connection between patron and parish extremely remote. None the less patrons were expected to take an interest in 'their' churches. In the Middle Ages the custom developed that the patron, or the priest as rector, should be responsible for the upkeep of the chancel while the parishioners maintained the nave. Thus the existence of a powerful or wealthy patron often meant that the chancel at least was elaborately built and beautified.

In periods of controversy the system of patronage might also have an effect on the fabric of a church, since the patron would only be likely to nominate priests who were sympathetic to his or her views. This problem was particularly acute in the seventeenth century when Puritan patrons naturally appointed priests who were active in removing popish adornments and idolatries. Royalists preferred to see priests who moved only slowly in making changes. There was similar dissension in the nineteenth century between ritualists and traditionalists, or High and Low churchmen. A high church patron would be sure to select a priest prepared to transform his church by focusing on the Holy Communion and elaborating the furnishing of the chancel, while a low church patron would want to ensure that due attention was given to preaching the word. The presence or absence of a richly decorated chancel may be evidence of the attitude of a patron and his or her nominees.

Once nominated and installed in his parish, the priest had legal tenure and could only be removed with great difficulty. Thus opportunities to effect major change through patronage were limited; perhaps more important for the impact on the church, changes in the parish priest were not frequent. Secure in his living a man could, like the Vicar of Bray, ride out a good many changes in the world around. It was possible to stay in the same parish for fifty years or more – a practice that made good sense in an era when an individual might seldom venture as far as the next village and even more rarely to the nearest town. Most churches display a list of the priests who have served the church, and it is interesting to relate the dates of the incumbencies to the changes of the fabric. It is also possible to assess the status of the vicar at a particular period by studying the vicarage or rectory. Many eighteenth- and early nineteenth-century ones are very substantial.

The church itself, however, is the scene of the priest's installation, which involves two activities. The *institution* of the priest gives him

In an established church a parson has legal rights and takes a formal oath at the time of his induction into a living. (Church of England Record Office)

spiritual authority in a parish and involves the bishop handing the priest a commission to care for the parish. There is no requirement for this to be performed in the parish church. On the other hand the *induction* of the priest is what gives him the legal possession of the living. Clearly, since this is never a common occurrence, it leaves little mark on the fabric of the church, but it is certainly an occasion that the congregation will make every effort to attend, and other clergy from neighbouring parishes will come to show their support.

The ceremony draws attention to the important elements of the church building. The archdeacon, acting on the bishop's mandate, will bring the new incumbent to the principal door of the church, usually the west door, and lay his hand on the key, demonstrating his control over the building and his duty to it. The priest then has to ring the church bell, which announces to the parish at large that he is in possession of the living and responsible for holding services in church. A bell is a powerful symbol, and almost all parish churches have one as a means of calling the faithful to prayer. Bells were introduced in the sixth century CE and were in general use by the eighth. They were used to mark the hours of service, of which there were no fewer than nine covering both day and night. In monasteries these *canonical hours* are still kept, but in parishes it is only *mattins* (morning service) and *vespers* (evensong) that are regularly observed, with *compline* (late evening service) occasionally added. The 'hours', generally a shortened version of the monastic pattern, had been a regular part of worship until the seventeenth century, but by 1660 they had been reduced to a morning and evening service, sometimes with a communion service tacked on at the end. To announce these services the parish priest needed just a small bell in a bellcote for tolling, but larger churches soon acquired sets of bells, which were usually hung in a tower, so that the sound of the summons could be more powerful and heard more widely. Some churches had a second small bell, set in a bellcote over the chancel arch, that was used as a Sanctus bell and sounded at the key moments in the mass.

In addition to the 'hours' the church bells were regularly rung to announce the Angelus (a moment of prayer at morning, noon and evening) and the curfew (the time at which, by regulation, fires were to be covered or extinguished); they could also be used in times of trouble to warn of invasion. But the chief purpose beyond the call to prayer was for great celebrations, such as royal births or glorious victories and, of course, for weddings. Many churches have sets of five or more bells, and many bells date back to the Middle Ages. There was, however, an attempt to have bells silenced or removed at the Reformation. When they were restored in the Elizabethan period they were re-hung on wheels, which gave much more control. By the

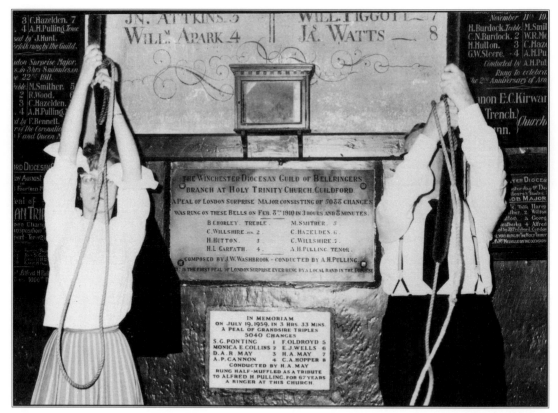

Bellringers at work in Holy Trinity, Guildford, surrounded by peal boards recording a century and more of successful change-ringing. (Church of England Record Office)

mid-seventeenth century the practice of change-ringing was introduced; this is almost unique to England, and gives the particular character to the sound of Anglican church bells. One of the originators of this system was Ralph Stedman, a member of the congregation of St Bene't in Cambridge, and his role is commemorated in a plaque in the ancient tower of that church. Bellringers have formed a close-knit fraternity, often visiting churches with particular sets of bells simply to ring a set of changes. Their achievements are frequently recorded on boards set up in the ringing chamber. For change-ringing a set of five, six, eight, ten or twelve bells is required, and they are rung in a developing sequence (1 2 3 4 5, 2 1 3 4 5, 2 3 1 4 5, 2 3 4 1 5, 2 3 4 5 1, and so on). This requires a substantial frame, which is usually set in a tower so that there is space for the ringers to stand beneath their bells. The upper chamber usually has large windows set with louvres to let the sound be carried far and wide. The music of bells is extended in a number of places by the use of handbells which give a more intimate sound.

The induction continues with the priest being taken to the various key elements of his church. The font and the pulpit are both visited and the priest is then conducted to his stall. Stalls are fixed seats for the clergy, and in the Middle Ages they were largely confined to cathedrals, monasteries and collegiate churches. In a parish church the priest's stall is most likely to be a nineteenth-century one, made in response to the movement for restoration which reintroduced surplices for clergy and choirs in parish churches on the model of cathedrals. A priest's stall was regularly made as a part of the set of choir stalls.

The final moment of the service of induction is, of course, the blessing given by the new incumbent from the high altar. The service establishes him as the incumbent of the living with all its responsibilities and rights, which included an income from the parish. This was provided by the parishioners through a system of taxes known as tithes, or more cynically among Nonconformists as 'steeple rent', levied on all who lived in the parish. One-tenth of all the produce of the parish was due, and a few tithe barns from the medieval period attest to the substantial income that this tax could produce. The whole sum did not always go to the incumbent and there developed a hierarchy between rectors who had the whole income and vicars who had only a lesser sum. Rectors drew their wealth from receipt of the greater tithes (one-tenth of all the major crops), though they might never see the parish. Vicars lived in the parish on the lesser tithes (one-tenth of minor produce such as lambs and chickens). Rectors, being wealthier, were responsible for the rectory and the chancel of the church, and for providing service books and vestments. Vicars were usually the nominees of some corporate body such as a monastery or a bishop, who was technically the rector. Tithes, however, were not finally abolished until about 1936 when they were replaced by stipends paid from centralised church income. By then their collection had become a source of considerable discontent, since they were levied even on members of other churches, and there were widespread protests. Priests' stipends are now controlled by the Church as a whole and there is less differentiation, though the varying economic power of earlier vicars often left its mark on their church.

In earliest times the pattern of population meant that the village needing only one incumbent was the norm, and the power and privileges of the individual vicar were restricted to his own parish. Before the Reformation it had become common for powerful and ambitious clerics to hold a number of different benefices with their rectorial stipends in what was known as plurality. This was one of the features that Henry VIII sought to change, though in practice many of the stipends that might have been released passed into the king's treasury rather than to the parishes. After the Reformation pluralism was much reduced and both rectors and vicars were encouraged to live permanently in their parishes. Prosperous parishes could provide a priest with a distinctly comfortable living and considerable status, where poorer hamlets might struggle to keep a priest and his family above starvation. In the eighteenth century the need, or often enough the desire, to increase their income once again led to many priests accepting several benefices, taking the tithes and appointing a vicar at a fraction of the tithe income to their secondary parishes. This practice was outlawed by the Pluralities Act of 1838, which also imposed stringent conditions about residence. The result was that there was a degree of competition for preferment and an ambitious priest needed to be sure that he was brought to the notice of a powerful or wealthy patron. Today, financial demands have once again led to the grouping of parishes, either under a single priest or in a team ministry.

One result of this system was that remote churches in small hamlets were unattractive as livings and the buildings were often simple to a degree. But the wealthiest parsons were often both generous and determined to ensure that their church was beautified in a way that would act as their memorial, and they mostly took their spiritual responsibilities as incumbents seriously. In the nineteenth century, however, especially in towns, wealthy or powerful vicars took the lead in carving new parishes out of their territory to cope with the increase of population and competition from other sects. The Revd John Sinclair, for instance, vicar of Kensington from 1842 to 1875, established no fewer than fourteen separate parishes in what had begun as his own single parish. The result was a diminution of his own income and privileges, but a definite increase in the service to Anglican worshippers. Another example was the Revd Brian King, the controversial vicar of St George in the East, Shadwell, who opened a mission for dockers in Wapping in the 1840s. He persuaded Charles Lowder to run the mission, which developed into the separate parish of St Peter, Wapping, with a large church (though not as large as Father Lowder had hoped). Eventually Lowder was rector over a separate parish with a church and attached priests' house and nunnery, and was supported by no fewer than seven curates.

Sure and Certain Hope: Penance, Extreme Unction and Burial

Penance and Extreme Unction (that is, confessing and receiving absolution for sins, and the anointing of the dying) are the last two sacraments that were recognised by the medieval church. Extreme unction, which involves anointing the penitent with consecrated oil, developed from the practice described in the Bible of anointing the sick. By extension, this was linked to terminal illness, the moment when confession of sins could be most complete, and when forgiveness would be most urgently wanted. These sacraments are not a common part of Anglican practice today, and in any case, since they were very much to do with the progress of an individual, they had little impact on the shape of churches themselves. Confession is, or used to be, a regular part of Roman Catholic practice and it is commonplace in Roman Catholic churches to find confessionals lining the walls of the nave or transept. All that is required is a place where the penitent can kneel in privacy and make his or her confession to a priest who does not have to, indeed should not, see the penitent. The result is something like a cupboard with a seat in it, flanked by a prayer desk on one or both sides. In many continental churches confessionals are often large and elegant pieces of furniture, and in a few churches they are even built into the wall like so many minute side chapels; some of the simplest (found in places such as rural Poland) consist of no more than a vertical board with a tiny shelf and a grille, which can be placed between whatever seat the priest occupies and the penitent. The impermanence and mobility of such items means that they were always unlikely to leave a permanent mark on the church building. When the practice of confession was largely abandoned in the Anglican Church in the seventeenth century, confessionals would have been easily removed and broken up. There is now no indication where they might have stood, and it is entirely probable that in small rural parishes the equipment was never elaborate.

Confession is rare in Anglican churches, and leaves little trace on the fabric. (Church of England Record Office)

Extreme unction was also abandoned after the Reformation but that sacrament, by its very nature, was not a part of the activities in a church building. Consecrated oil was simply taken to wherever the parishioner was dying, and the only element of the church that was needed for it was a space to store it. Almost invariably this would be in the aumbry, together with the equipment needed for the sacrament of the Eucharist. So, like penance, this sacrament has left no specific trace in most parish churches. However, both penance and extreme unction are linked, by implication or directly, to an activity and a set of rituals that do leave their mark: the burial of the dead.

Death is the end of the Christian life on earth, but since a belief in resurrection and life after death is central to Christianity, the business of dying has occupied the minds of many and engaged a great deal of expenditure. The link with penance is not least because of the fear of retribution for our sins, and the desire to leave a good name behind us. The results have ranged from the attitude of the Worcester monk, who wished to be buried where worshippers would walk over him daily as they entered the cathedral, with the one word *Miserrimus* ('the most wretched') over his body, to long laudatory inscriptions that leave the reader gasping in amazement at the hypocrisy of the deceased or the blindness of their admirers.

The fear of death and the energy exerted in achieving funerary fame have left indelible marks on every church in the land. The first public sign of a death, however, was the passing bell, rung by the sexton thrice for a man and three times two for a woman, followed by a stroke for every year of his or her age. In our noisy urban age it is difficult to recapture the impact of that bell ringing out suddenly across the fields, and to comprehend the shock when the tolling stopped at fifteen or twenty. Such a thought certainly underlines the importance of the bell in churches. Peals of bells have their place in the rites of death, too. It became traditional to ring a muffled or half-muffled peal at funerals, where the clapper of each bell has a leather pad tied over one side. There is a particularly haunting quality about the resultant sound, the clear notes of the first strike followed by the merest shadow from the muffled one, an interrupted sound that echoes the sense that the departed soul is now in another world. So here, too, the bells of a church have a particular role to play in reminding the world at large of the passing of another life.

Because of the belief in resurrection there was a sense in which the burial was an occasion for solemn rejoicing as well as for acknowledging loss. In medieval times even modest funerals were elaborate affairs, with processions through the village of priest, acolytes and mourners all carrying candles as well as the sexton ringing a handbell. Rites were also performed in the house of the dead before the corpse was brought to the church. These practices were largely swept away at the time of the Reformation, and few traces of them remain. The new rite of burial was restricted to the church and churchyard, and consisted of two elements: the funeral service and the committal in which the body was placed in its grave. Today, with professional funeral parlours and motorised cortèges, much of the original meaning of the special arrangements provided by each parish is lost, but the remaining traces remind us of the way each parish coped with this inevitable ceremony.

The priest meets the funeral cortège at the entrance not to the church but to the churchyard, where there is often a gate. Traditionally this should be a lych gate, whose name derives from the medieval word *lich*, or corpse. These 'corpse gates' are usually roofed structures, and some, like that at Monnington on Wye, are like small rooms with seats inside. There was good reason for this since the pause at the lych gate offered a welcome opportunity for the bearers to lay down a coffin that they might well have carried several miles to the church. Some churchyards are even equipped with 'coffin tables' – raised stone slabs on which the coffin could be laid for a few minutes. The pall-bearers would also welcome the roof over the lych gate, especially in the British climate and since more deaths tended to occur in winter. At the lych gate the coffin would be transferred to the parish bier, a special wheeled trolley

The lych gate of St George, Benenden, Kent, leads into a churchyard planted with the traditional yew trees. (Church of England Record Office)

that most parishes provided once the roads and pathways began to improve in the eighteenth century. Few of these are still in regular use though a number survive; they are usually kept in the church, or sometimes in a special building in or near the graveyard. Some churches even had a parish coffin, since, in the years before the eighteenth century, most people were buried in fabric shrouds only. The coffin was used during the burial service and the corpse then removed for placing in its grave. A fine parish coffin would add dignity to what might be a very modest affair, though the rich and powerful always provided their own coffins of either lead or elm wood.

The funeral cortège would pause again in the porch, that element of the church halfway between the sacred and the secular, before the coffin was taken into the church, feet first so that if the corpse were standing it would be facing east. (In medieval times priests were buried facing the other way, towards their flock.) It was then taken up to the chancel or the chancel step for the first part of the service, consisting of prayers and an affirmation of belief in the resurrection with, in most cases, a homily calling to mind the life of the deceased. Here, once again, the arrangement of the pews with a central gangway for processions is crucial. Most churches also have a space before the chancel step where the bier can stand if it is not taken into the chancel. This is another of the occasions where spaces that are

A funeral in West Wickham, Surrey. The coffin rests, feet forward, at the chancel step. There is a rich display of flowers in memory of the deceased. (Church of England Record Office)

empty for much of the year are important, and the use justifies what might seem to an outsider so much wasted space.

The final act of the burial service is the committal, for which the participants move to the graveside. The status of the vicar, at least in the eighteenth century, was acknowledged here, and at a few places such as Walpole St Peter in Norfolk there are preserved the special portable shelters, like sentry boxes, in which that dignified personage could read the committal sentences without being exposed to the weather. Today, this second element is regularly separated from the first part since many funerals involve a service in the parish church and a committal in the local crematorium which may be miles away. Every parishioner, however, formerly had the right to burial in his or her own parish churchyard. Burials were usually restricted to the southern side of the church, while the northern side might well be unconsecrated ground and so either free of burials or kept for those who had committed suicide or died unbaptised. Where the whole churchyard was consecrated, suicides had to be buried outside the churchyard and there are places, such as Hanbury in Worcestershire, where a single tomb just outside the churchyard bears witness to such a sad end.

In the eighteenth century a good deal of attention was paid to the niceties of social distinction and the funerals of the great and wealthy were often highly elaborate. This was the period when the practice of carrying painted hatchments in funeral processions became common, and this lasted until the beginning of the twentieth century. Each hatchment was a square panel with a black background decorated with the coat of arms of the deceased set on the diagonal. Since they were obviously only available to gentry who were entitled to arms these were a fine means of demonstrating the status of the departed. The hatchment was carried in the funeral procession, displayed in the church during the service and taken back to the house to hang over the door during the period of mourning. After that it was returned to the church for good, and many fine hatchments still hang in churches. Their presence is a reminder that a noble or gentry family is connected to the church; it is worth noting that there are plenty of examples of families with extensive interests or the patronage of several livings having several hatchments painted, one to be hung in each of the churches they were connected with.

After the burial it was common for the grave to be marked by a tombstone, and here it is possible to see all the social distinctions and changing fashions as well as the varying skills of local craftsmen. The range of funerary memorials is considerable, though now there is some degree of official control. After all, the churchyard is common to all, and each grave has only a share in the whole space – they do not even own the plot – so there are *Churchyard Rules* designed to ensure that individual memorials do not impinge on the character of the churchyard in such a way as to affect those grieving for others buried there. Generally speaking, gravestones are of three types: vertical slabs or memorials, table tombs and ledger stones set flat in the ground. At least until the nineteenth century they were of whatever local material was suitable, since stone was difficult to move around, and this lends each churchyard a degree of unity which enhances the sense of peace. There were fashions in what was regularly depicted on them. In the eighteenth century pairs of cherubs, as reminders of heavenly bliss, were popular, while at an earlier period skulls, crossed bones and sometimes the hourglass and scythe of Death were more common. All tombstones were carved with some identification that allowed the local mason to display his skill and taste in lettering. Some of the inscriptions are long, some in verse and in some the lettering is florid and decorative. Where the stone is soft and the surface decays, the record of so many earlier generations is rapidly wearing away and the remembrance of past generations is lost for ever.

Greater families might provide more substantial monuments, perhaps enclosing a small section of the graveyard with a kerb or iron fence, or their tombs might be set side by side repeating the same pattern. There are even occasions, as at Ketteringham in Norfolk, where the servants from the great house are buried in a row beneath identical

The Horton family tomb of
1866 at All Saints, Middleton
Cheyney, Northamptonshire.
(Colin Cunningham)

grave markers, dying, as it were, in livery in the way they lived. But the
gentry and nobility ensured that their family tombs were as grand as
could be afforded. In some cases they erected a mausoleum in which
successive generations could be entombed. Such things are not always
in graveyards; indeed they do not always contain burials, but are
principally for commemoration and may be set as prominent features in
a park. Yet there are a number of mausolea in graveyards or built
attached to churches. Sometimes they are in the form of a side chapel,
with burials in a crypt beneath, and the coffins, particularly of the
nineteenth century, are equipped with the whole paraphernalia of
funeral pomp with wreaths, studs in the shape of coronets, special
handles and coffin plates. Little of this, however, is usually visible.

From the nineteenth century, as transport improved, it became
possible to use a variety of different materials for grave markers.
Hard granite from Aberdeen gave better hope of permanence than
local sandstone, and white marble from Carrara could be carved into
the form of weeping angels, draped urns or broken columns. The
present century has seen highly polished marble that flashes in the
sunlight and grave plots enclosed with kerbs and filled with bright
green or coloured marble chips. Recent gravestones may even include
a photograph of the deceased on the same pattern as is common in
the Russian Orthodox Church. All of these continue the passion for
memorialising the dead, and it is this that has had the most varied
and persistent effect on the interiors of churches. The walls, and
often the side chapels, of churches are set with monuments whose
inscriptions reveal much of the detailed history of the local populace.

The nineteenth-century mausoleum of the Bruce family in the churchyard of St Mary, Maulden, Bedfordshire, contains monuments dating back to the seventeenth century. (Colin Cunningham)

Memorials inside churches may take the form of slabs, of either stone or marble, with or without attendant sculptures, or of brass tablets set on the walls. Initially only priests were actually buried in the church, but this privilege was later extended to noble families. Their grander tombs are often topped with figures of the dead, sometimes surrounded by figures representing their families. In some cases there is a family vault beneath the church, which is an extension of the practice in early medieval churches of providing a crypt, or underground chamber, beneath the chancel for the remains or relics of a saint. Such crypts were often provided with an altar, and regularly used for masses for the dead. However, they tended to be restricted to larger churches or abbeys where important relics were held. Their presence in a church may therefore indicate this earlier status.

Funerary monuments have provided subject matter for many books and there is no space here to say more than that they vary hugely in scale, opulence and subject matter. Large-scale memorials may fill whole walls of churches with a proliferation of pillars, cherubs and other statues in a variety of stone. At Framlingham in Suffolk the series of free-standing Howard tombs are almost of royal status, and match that family's political aspirations in the mid-sixteenth century. Other monuments speak more of individual lives and personal tragedies. Only the more prosperous could afford such things in any period, and the nobility regularly commemorated themselves with major monuments, often, as at Flitwick in Bedfordshire, setting aside a whole chapel for their dynastic collection. When the monuments of a noble family are not associated with a dynastic mausoleum or family vault, particularly before such things became common, their bodies were laid to rest under the floor of the church. This happened regularly in the Middle Ages, and gave rise to one of the most characteristic of medieval types, the memorial brass. These were in the form of brass 'portraits', often of great splendour, set in the top of the floor slab covering the tomb. In most cases these have been removed either to the church wall or to a museum, since they were vulnerable to wear or even theft. However, parish churches are rich with floor slabs in which shaped depressions indicate the former presence of a brass. The oldest medieval memorials feature figures of knights in armour, and in the later Middle Ages such figures were often made of expensive but easily carved alabaster. In the seventeenth century effigies were richly coloured and gilded, and the canopies that often surmount such monuments are gaudily painted, too. The eighteenth century turned to classical sources for much of its iconography and many fine sculptors peopled huge monuments with marble figures of the dead, their widows and

This sumptuous monument of 1587 in St Andrew Colyton commemorates Sir William Pole, with a splendour befitting his rank. (Crown Copyright RCHME)

attendant cherubs. The habit was extended to include some element of the story of their life, either in the accoutrements with which they are surrounded or in an illustrative plaque. There was a taste for broken columns, pyramids (which derive from pagan Egyptian funeral practice) and so on. The Gothic revival of the nineteenth century replaced these with canopied niches and coloured marble, angels and the like. In this century there has been a fashion, still prevalent, for finely cut lettering, usually on slate, which is left on its own to tell the story of the deceased.

The whole business of personal remembrance is acknowledged by the Church in a regular pattern of prayer known as the 'year's mind', the anniversary of each death. In some churches prayers are said for individual parishioners on the anniversary of their death, and this continues a medieval practice of holding special masses for the dead. Originally these were said every day for thirty days after the death and then there was an anniversary mass after a year. As we have seen, medieval funeral practices were largely swept aside after the

Reformation but there are a few details that have left their mark. Originally the corpse was brought to the church the day before the burial and left overnight in the church with a candle burning at each corner of the coffin. This exactly parallels the arrangements for lying in state. In a few inner urban churches, such as St Peter, Wapping, there are mortuary chapels where the coffin can lie securely before burial. The coffin usually rested in the home of the dead person but in the crowded slums of the nineteenth century such decency was often impossible. The privilege of lying overnight in the body of the church is still sometimes allowed to clergy. Clergy, too, could regularly be buried in a church, and in many cases their tombs are in the chancel in recognition of their status. Otherwise only the great and the good could be buried inside the church and their monuments often occupy extremely prominent positions.

The typically imposing eighteenth-century monument to Sir Lionel Tollemache (*d.* 1729), in St Mary, Helmingham, Suffolk. (Colin Cunningham)

One of the reasons for establishing family vaults or mausolea was quite simply that over the years burial space within the church filled up. The same happened, though rather later, in churchyards and quite a few rural churchyards are now full. The problem was particularly acute in town churches where there was little or no space to extend churchyards, and there are gruesome descriptions from the late eighteenth and early nineteenth centuries of churchyards where the graves have been filled with so many bodies that the top burials burst out of the ground in heavy rain. Quite apart from the rapacity of the body snatchers, who would steal corpses to sell to medical schools, this was a major health hazard, which led to the formation of many private cemetery companies in the nineteenth century. This removed from parish churches to a great extent the committal and the commemoration of the dead, and has left a legacy of richly varied memorials on the fringes of our cities. Many of the earliest cemeteries are themselves now full, and their place has been taken by crematoria. The practice of cremation only began in the Anglican church in the late nineteenth century and it took more than a generation for this change in practice to become acceptable to most Anglicans. Nowadays, particularly when the gardens of remembrance in crematoria are themselves becoming crowded, there is increasing pressure for the interment of cremated remains in parish churchyards. Typically these are marked by small slabs set in the ground. Their appearance in the churchyard marks yet another change. There is no longer a 6ft wide green space between rows of gravestones, but instead a largely paved area. Sometimes the difficulty of mowing between such close-set slabs results in the whole area being gravelled over, destroying the green tranquillity of a traditional country churchyard. In one case, Trimley St Mary in Suffolk, space is at such a premium that cremated remains are set between the older graves, inter-cropped like so much intensive agriculture.

This is not an entirely new problem and attempts have been made over the years to provide for the decent disposal of the dead and for a locus for grieving and remembrance. A few churches have ossuaries or charnel houses, where the bones of the dead are neatly stacked, often in piles 6ft high or more. This was a practice forced on many communities in the eastern Mediterranean where urban development was close-packed and where the soil was too shallow to allow endless burials. In some Byzantine towns corpses were routinely dug up after a fixed number of years in the ground and the remains removed to the local charnel chapel. However, the provision of ossuaries is rare in Britain. Crematoria have introduced *columbaria*, where ashes are stored in niches. This building type was common in the Roman empire, where cremation was the norm, but such things are extremely rare in Anglican churchyards. The most commonly accepted solution to the problem today is the provision of a Book of Remembrance or occasionally a wall of remembrance, where a number of people can be commemorated in a restricted space, while their actual remains are buried nearby. A few imaginative parishes are creating separate memorial gardens where the individual slabs can be laid together or set on walls, and the main space of the churchyard left green and open.

The matter of commemoration of the dead is one which touches everybody, and has exercised the minds and creative energies of generations. The church graveyard, as the gathering place of the dead of each community, is an important symbol of the way in which the present generation is a part of a continuity of faith. Day by day and week by week the graveyard is crossed, as it has been for centuries, by people walking to work or meeting and greeting neighbours after services. It reminds those who see the memorials that they, too, are part of the same long tradition, that they belong, as did their forefathers, to the wide communion of saints. Perhaps the extent to which our churches are affected by the rituals of burial and commemoration is an indication of how much they have meant to us over the generations.

CHAPTER THREE

Prayer, Praise and Preaching: the Order of Worship

Structures and Worship

The dead may have filled our churches and churchyards with their individual memorials, but the church is very much more than a place of remembrance. Corporate worship is an essential element in the Christian religion, and provides the *raison d'être* for the buildings. The importance of the congregation, the minister and the laity, rather than just the priest and his acolytes, were crucial to the Puritans of the Reformation. When they set about removing idolatrous images from the unreformed churches their concentration was on prayer and the preaching of the word of God, and it is easiest to look for its impact on church buildings by beginning from that period.

There was no change in the desire to encourage the faithful to attend worship and, although in some cases bells were removed from churches, they were soon restored. The tower and bells announced the services just as they had done before, indeed with the development of change-ringing in the late seventeenth century it could be argued that the bells made a greater contribution to churches after the Reformation than before. The sanctus or angelus bells were not wanted, however, and those small bells in their special bellcotes were generally left to rot. There was a ready acceptance of the tower and spire, medieval elements built principally for the glory of God and to demonstrate man's heavenward aspiration. These were felt to be important because they were a part of the public statement of the centrality of the established State Church. Spires were very much a creation of the medieval period, though they were later extensively copied by the Victorians in their attempt to revive the medieval sanctity of the Church. One might have assumed that in the seventeenth century they would be associated with the unreformed Church that the Puritans were keen to put behind them but this does not seem to have been the case. They tended to concentrate more on what went on inside the church, and the basic structure was in any case too costly to be destroyed altogether, so spires and their towers stayed. They did, after all confirm the church as the architectural centrepiece of its parish, and the spires advertised the fact far and wide.

It is difficult to find any practical justification for a spire beyond providing a roof for a tower, and even the most modest tower will require some form of roof. Most tower roofs are slightly peaked, and it is possible to regard a spire as no more than a hugely exaggerated conical roof. What made the spire significant was the very difficulty of its construction, thus providing an opportunity for the masons to demonstrate their virtuosity and the piety and prosperity of the congregation that could pay for such a thing. When life became more secure as the Middle Ages developed, the original function of the church as a place of refuge, with its tower as a look-out, settled into being a place of worship whose practical function could rightly be enhanced by splendid building. A tower and, if possible, a spire were simply additional benefits. In this, though, regional variations are important and the character of our churches changes dramatically from one area of Britain to another.

Much depended on what was available in the way of building materials as well as the economic or political status of the parish. Thus in East Anglia, where there is little good building stone, towers were of necessity built of the local flint cobbles. This material is extremely difficult to construct into sound corners, which take the force of the weather, so there developed the East Anglian round tower with no corners. In the far west, in Cornwall, where strong winds and storms are a regular part of the yearly cycle, it made sense to build churches in sheltered spots and to keep towers low. The same is true of many churches in Yorkshire and in the Welsh borders. There were other reasons why towers might be low and plain: Cornish stone is exceedingly hard and difficult to work, while Yorkshire grit-stone does not lend itself to fine carving, so churches and their towers in those areas tend to be relatively plain externally. On the other hand there are fine carving stones in Devon and Dorset and through the limestone belt of the Chilterns into Northamptonshire. It is no accident that where, for instance, it was economic to use the beautiful honey-coloured stone from Ham Hill in Dorset there are a number of richly carved churches. Towers, parapets and windows were the natural focus for such decoration.

Externally, as towers were built taller, and walls were pierced by increasingly large windows, it became essential to provide buttresses and pinnacles to transfer the thrust of roofs to the ground. Having developed their craft over centuries this was something that medieval masons understood very well and later medieval churches often have dramatic pinnacles as well as decorative parapets and deep buttresses. Of course, every detail could be involved in demonstrating the piety and the aspirations of the congregation. In that sense a spire is no more than a great pinnacle pointing heavenwards. It is perhaps the most dramatic external feature of a church but that did not mean that every church would want a spire. Like towers, they were restricted to areas where there was suitable building stone, and it is no accident that many of the best medieval spires are in counties such as Northamptonshire and Leicestershire, where the fine local limestone is ideal for building them. We need to remember that throughout the Middle Ages, when parish churches were developing, most of the populace moved only around a relatively small area, and the advertising value of the church and its tower and spire had a distinctly limited audience. Masons, however, did move from village to village and town to town, and it is usually possible to discover which churches were built by a particular team of masons. Yet there is no justification to look for widespread competition in the building of medieval parish churches. It was only in the great monasteries and cathedrals such as Norwich and Salisbury that the yearning to build as hugely as possible for the Glory of God and the importance of the diocese could be indulged. In the nineteenth century, when cities were larger and churches comparatively less noticeable, there were some deliberate attempts to build bigger and taller; it is no accident, for instance, that All Saints Margaret Street in London, the flagship of the new ritualist movement, built between 1848 and 1859, was designed as the first redbrick church in the capital and with the tallest spire in the city.

Of course that is not to say that the medieval masons and their patrons did not seek to display their very best efforts in their church. In

The 272 ft high tower of St Botolph in Boston, Lincolnshire, was both a demonstration of Christian aspiration and a useful navigation marker. (Colin Cunningham)

Late fifteenth-century carving
on the parapet of St Peter and
St Paul, Lavenham, Suffolk.
(Colin Cunningham)

general they reserved their most splendid carving for elements of the
building that were structurally essential. As glass became more
widespread, larger and larger openings were possible, and they
needed more elaborate frames for their glazing. Thus there developed
increasingly splendid and daring systems of tracery, stone lace that
held the delicate glass in place, but whose primary purpose was to
allow more light into the main spaces of the church. Where there
were difficulties in finding good building stone, such as in East
Anglia for instance, this attitude led to great ingenuity and
refinement. Fine stone could be imported for window tracery or for
those difficult corners, but it was expensive. Thus ashlar masonry, as
it was called, was frequently reserved for windows and corners only,
with the body of the wall filled with local rubble or flints. Even this,
however, could be turned to advantage, and once again East Anglia,
where there was great prosperity in the later Middle Ages, built a
series of large churches finely decorated with patterning of flint in
stone dressings. One of the grandest, Long Melford, even has a long
inscription round the top of the walls recording the generosity of the
citizens who gave the funds to pay for it.

   All this fine work was the culmination by the mid-sixteenth century of
almost half a millennium of building, rebuilding and extending, and it
was no part of the Reformation's agenda to sweep away all the pillars of
the establishment. Rather Henry VIII wished simply to bring the Church
under his control. It was the more determined Puritans of the mid-
seventeenth century who wanted nothing to do with the sinful idolatry of

Fifteenth-century flint
flushwork on the tower of
St John the Baptist,
Garboldisham, Norfolk.
(Colin Cunningham)

the established church; they turned their back on these splendid
buildings, preferring to erect their own meeting houses or chapels and
refusing to conform to the hierarchical pattern of the State Church. The
Church of England, however, inherited the plant of what had until 1534
been a unified church under the Bishop of Rome. Evidently there was no
immediate sweeping away of all that had gone before, and such changes
as were made were usually concerned with furnishings. We have already
noted that the attention previously paid to the mass was abandoned, and
that in some cases chancel spaces were blocked off for reuse. In many
parish churches there would have been relatively little apparent change in
the years immediately after the Reformation. However, the theological
differences that led Luther and Calvin also to break with Rome led to
developments that would have a profound effect on the pattern of use in
Anglican parish churches. Their followers stressed the importance of the
Gospel and of preaching so that the faithful should properly understand
the scripture on which their faith was based.

Preaching

It was some decades before the new theology of the Reformation had
much effect on the practice of worship in Britain. By the mid-
seventeenth century, however, the growing strength of the
Nonconformist Christians, and the determination of some of them to
destroy all altars, images and crucifixes, led to a revolution in church
practice that was a great deal more visible than the transfer of
political control effected when the Church of England was first
established. True, there had been a new order for services, and

Archbishop Cranmer had produced a simplified liturgy in English instead of Latin. But that first prayer book of 1544 did not satisfy all the reformers, and over the next half century there were increasing complaints that culminated in a petition from Puritan clergy in 1604 and led to further revisions, particularly in the catechism which provided the official instruction in the faith. The controversy did not end there, and religious divisions combined with political problems made the seventeenth century one of turmoil in which the established Church was sadly divided. It was not until after the Restoration that a new Book of Common Prayer was issued in 1662; this remained the sole official pattern for Anglican worship until the twentieth century. It is still regularly used by some parishes. (A new edition is shortly to be published by Everyman.)

Uniformity of worship in Britain had been achieved in 1544 with the First Prayer Book. Before that there had been a wide variety of practices, with different words and liturgy devised by various groups of cathedral clergy popular in different parts of the land. The Book of Common Prayer reflected the radical theological changes of the Reformation and established the new common liturgy. The preface pointed out that: 'whereas heretofore there hath been great diversity in saying and singing in Churches within this Realm; Some following Salisbury Use, Some Hereford Use, and some the Use of Bangor, some of York, some of Lincoln; now from henceforth all the whole Realm shall have but one use'.[1] This uniformity was partly intended to prevent the continuation of those varied practices that had involved attention to legends and ceremonials of doubtful authenticity. In particular the book, and the authority of the Crown that backed it, objected to the fact that in readings the Bible was not being properly followed. From earliest times the aim had been to have the whole of the scriptures read aloud each year, 'intending thereby that the Clergy, and especially such as were Ministers in the congregation, should . . . be stirred up to godliness'. In the pre-Reformation church, with the scriptures read in Latin, a full understanding was largely confined to the clergy, but departures from the original intention had involved more distressing variations than could be rectified by insisting on the use of the English language. As the preface noted: 'these many years passed, this godly and decent Order of the ancient Fathers hath been so altered, broken and neglected, by planting in uncertain Stories, and Legends, with multitude of Responds, Verses, vain Repetitions, Commemorations and Synodals' that the scriptures were never read in their entirety. Henceforth much greater attention was to be paid to the Word of the Lord.

It was important that the faithful should gather regularly for worship, but there was to be no more muttering of the mass. The 'multitude of dark and dumb ceremonies' were to be abandoned and the agreed order of worship was to centre on the reciting of the Psalms

The interior of the chapel of St Bartholomew the Great in London, a fragment of the ancient monastic buildings, shown in 1822 re-ordered for Puritan worship, with its two-decker pulpit against the liturgical south wall and box pews and galleries for the congregation. There is no sign of a Lord's Table. (Guildhall Library, Corporation of London)

right through once in every month and the reading of the whole of the scriptures once in every year. Thus a morning and an evening service were set out, to be read daily throughout the year, with a first reading from the Old Testament, and a second from the New Testament; tables were set out giving the appropriate passage for each day. It was a requirement for the priest to read the daily services, but the congregation as a whole would normally attend only on Sundays.

Although it had taken roughly a century of argument to reach the final form of the prayer book, its adoption forced a substantial change in the pattern of weekly worship. If the scriptures were to be read there was a need for both a reader and somewhere to read from. The priest would do the reading, of course, but now that the scriptures were read in English it was important that the congregation should understand them, and so there was also a need for exposition and teaching. These two requirements gave our parish churches their lecterns and pulpits. The act of reading brought some interesting recycling. In the pre-Reformation church it had been common to provide lecterns, or book-stands, beside the high altar to hold the service books for chanting the verses of the mass. Such things, of course, were superfluous under the new order but many parishes did not destroy their lectern, they merely relocated it in the nave, on the south side of the chancel arch, where it could be used just as effectively for reading the scriptures.

Not all parishes followed this course, and a great many lecterns were only provided much later, in the nineteenth or early twentieth century. Today, further changes in the liturgy are leading to their removal. Many

This fierce brass eagle is a fine example of one of the commonest types of Victorian lectern. The microphone is a later fitting. (Church of England Record Office)

medieval lecterns were in the shape of an eagle, which afforded a pattern for the large number of Victorian lecterns, often handsome objects of brass. Others were simple book-stands, sometimes double-sided or even four-sided with a revolving top. These last two were more useful for holding the various service books of the pre-Reformation liturgy, and are thus correspondingly rarer survivals. Most post-Reformation lecterns, in practice nineteenth- and twentieth-century ones, only needed to support one book, and so are single-sided. The most common materials are brass or wood, and obviously such items are movable. In the nineteenth century a few churches fitted fixed lecterns in stone, which may be handsome and elaborate pieces, though they are now often seen as a constraint because they cannot easily be moved.

In fact the commonest form of lectern in the years after the adoption of the new Book of Common Prayer was also built in, and it, too, has suffered from the difficulty of adaptation. Where there was a Protestant clergyman determined to lead his flock in the new ways, it seems that instead of recycling the old furniture congregations were asked to make new equipment. Where the lectern was concerned this took the form of a reading desk built as part of the pulpit. There were effectively two forms, the two-decker and the three-decker. In both types the priest read the service, and the scriptures, from the reading desk, and then ascended into the pulpit for the sermon in which he would expound on the scriptures. A three-decker had an additional seat at the bottom for the parish clerk whose job was to lead the responses and psalms. These structures, with their various sections at different levels, often with separate access, were a built embodiment of the hierarchies of the ritual.

The priest was more important than the parish clerk, and thus sat at a higher level. The sermon, taken from the highest level of the edifice, came to be the most important element.

There had, of course, been sermons and pulpits before the Reformation but they were not a major part, nor a requirement, of the liturgy. Preaching did not become widespread until the advent of the itinerant preachers, mostly Franciscan friars, in the mid-fourteenth century. They clearly required a raised platform to preach from, and a few medieval pulpits do survive in churches where they were fitted. It is, however, unlikely that all or even the majority of churches had pulpits, and certainly some pulpits were outside the church at convenient points on the wayside. In that sense they were like the earliest preaching crosses. The post-Reformation liturgy effectively made a pulpit an essential requirement.

The emphasis on preaching made new demands on the clergy, which not all priests were able to meet. Shows of any

The fifteenth-century pulpit in St Peter and St Paul, Salle, Norfolk, reorganised with a seventeenth-century sounding board, clerk's desk and reading desk for the parson. (Colin Cunningham)

kind were rare in small towns and villages, and the sermon was almost the only regular public performance available. Whether they were enjoyed or not, or whether the preachers were self-indulgent before a captive audience, we do not know. However, the survival in many churches of an hourglass or hourglass stand beside the pulpit suggests that sermons were long. A good preacher would certainly acquire a reputation, and skill in preaching became a route to preferment. Perhaps inevitably town churches or those attached to a nobleman's estate attracted the more influential preachers. Certainly the noble families and the increasingly prosperous and more educated traders in the towns were in a better position to judge the quality of a sermon, though the Church of England never adopted the Nonconformist practice of appointing ministers on the basis of a trial sermon.

There were, in the eighteenth and nineteenth centuries, a few places where the priest drew his congregation entirely by the fame of his preaching, and maintained himself from the pew rents. These proprietary chapels were unlike parish churches in that there was no responsibility for the care of souls in a defined area; indeed the incumbent of the relevant geographical parish had to give his consent, as well as the bishop allowing a licence, before a proprietary chapel could be opened. They were mostly in fashionable urban areas, but none now survives. The norm was the delivery of sermons by the parish priest from a pulpit in his local church. Of course, the more the priests were required to preach the more there was discussion, and the more attention some clergymen paid to scholarship. The status of the parson began to rise, and with it in many cases the elaboration and the height of his pulpit. Some eighteenth-century pulpits rise to a considerable height and dominate the whole church. In a few cases the pulpit was set in the centre of the church, in the same way as in many Nonconformist chapels. There was even a short-lived fashion for moving the pulpit to a point halfway down the church and rearranging the seating so that the priests could be better heard. In this the Church of England was adopting a practice already common among the Presbyterian Churches.

For the most part, however, the new arrangements simply reflected the different economic power and status of the individual parish. There might be just a simple wooden pulpit, or there might be a new, panelled three-decker of fine joinery with hourglass, book-rest, candles and deep cushions to the seats. In several of the churches in London, which were supported by the considerable wealth of the City merchants, the pulpits developed into timber extravaganzas, perched high on richly carved columns and with an elaborate canopy, or tester, overhead to help spread the sound of the preacher's voice to every corner of the hall.

New churches were increasingly designed as halls for preaching in. The preoccupation came to be the number of seats rather than the richness of the chancel. The destruction wrought by the fire of London in 1666 gave rise to a crop of new churches that were built to be the best that money could buy. Many were of fine white stone shipped in from the Isle of Portland well down the English Channel. They were usually built with no more than the shallowest eastward extension for the altar, raised one low step above the level of the nave and closed only by altar rails. The body of the church was the focus of attention, and the interiors were rich with fine woodwork, much of it carved by Grinling Gibbons, the walls panelled, the aisles fitted with galleries for extra seating and the nave fitted throughout with pews.

Seating was another consequence of the change in the liturgy. A medieval congregation would have done without pews, there being only a few movable benches for the older or infirm members of the congregation. If the service was lengthy it was possible to move about, even to take a break and sit outside. Once the service included an hour-long sermon it was clearly necessary to provide some form of seating, and church after church was fitted out with pews. Initially

This sumptuous reredos in Wren's St Mary Abchurch (1681–7) is the work of Grinling Gibbons. Its boards display the Lord's Prayer and Creed, with the Ten Commandments behind the altar. Above is a traditional pelican in her piety. (Crown Copyright RCHME)

A typical post-Reformation set-up in Old St Giles, Cambridge. A complete set of box pews and a gallery run across the transept arch and right up to the east wall. On the right the three-decker pulpit and even a set of pews are in the former sanctuary. (Cambridgeshire Collection)

these were not the uniform rows of fixed seating that we see in most churches today, and there may well have been some reuse of redundant woodwork from the chancel. At Earl Stonham in Suffolk some of the pews even appear to have been reconstructed from the redundant rood screen. The construction of pews at first proceeded piecemeal, with the wealthier families paying a carpenter to make enough seating for their personal needs; they would then own their pew. Movable benches could be set out for the lower orders. By the time the nave was filled with pews they might be 'of all dimensions and heights, being patched up according to the fancy of the owners' as Gilbert White wrote of his church at Selborne in Hampshire.

Noble families and great landlords constructed highly elaborate seating, often filling what had previously been a family chantry chapel. Such family pews could be equipped with doors to exclude draughts, stoves, cushions, even easy chairs, silk hangings and curtains for privacy. They were always prominent objects within the church designed to display the family's status, often liberally decorated with the armorial evidence of it. A few family pews were provided with a separate entrance, and one or two were built at first-floor level, a practice that was more common in Scotland and on the Continent. The Lutheran church at Swidnice in Poland (1656–8), with seating for five thousand has no fewer than four galleries and is extensively divided up into family pews or boxes, the more distinguished ones being fitted with marks of rank and even enclosed with glass windows. However, in Britain there was usually only one powerful family in a parish, and their pew would naturally be the grandest.

By the eighteenth century the disorderliness of random pewing was rapidly giving way to the provision of sets of pews, constructed of neatly panelled timber. The set might include two or three larger partitions for leading families, and in these square enclosures it was common to have seating all round, so that some of the occupants might actually be facing away from the preacher. All the pews were made with doors to keep out the draughts and this growing obsession with comfort meant that they were often surrounded with such tall panelling that it was impossible to see from outside whether a pew was occupied. Only the preacher high in his pulpit had a clear view of his congregation.

Although initially pew owners were expected to pay for and maintain their pews, the provision of uniform sets inevitably involved the church authorities, and by the mid-eighteenth century it was common for the occupants to pay a rent for their pew to the churchwardens. The greater the rent, the greater the church income and the greater the comfort that could be provided. In town churches the gallery seating was usually more modest than on the floor of the nave, and the benches there would be filled with the artisan class. But, of course, there were many who could not afford pew rent, and they were forced to sit on makeshift benches in the central gangway or at the back of the church. This practice lasted well into the nineteenth century, and the last pew rents were not abolished until the beginning of the twentieth. Often there is evidence of renting in sets of numbers painted on doors of the pews or on the bench ends.

The determination to be as comfortable as possible in church went along with the eighteenth century's increasing attention to the niceties of social status, and with that the status of the parson. The parson of an eighteenth-century parish was an important personality, and many, like Parson Woodforde,[2] acquired reputations for worldliness and good living. Others became increasingly dissatisfied with the way their church was bound to the hierarchies of society generally, and it was out of this dissatisfaction that Methodism was born. There was a general suspicion in the Church of England of the 'enthusiasm' which 'methodistical preachers' were supposed to display, and the established Church remained unmoved by these new reforms until the nineteenth century. There was, however, concern at the number of people drawn to Methodist and other Nonconformist sects, coupled with a growing realisation that the rapid growth of towns was leaving Anglican parishes with huge populations and only the old medieval church for them to worship in. There simply were not enough seats if they did want to attend. Accordingly the government set aside one million pounds for building churches in the new districts of towns. The project was administered by a board of commissioners, and the resulting structures are known as Commissioners' churches. They generally include some sort of tower, since the need to summon the faithful had not changed; and in towns there was an even greater need to announce the presence of a church by a prominent feature. Their layout was simply that of a large hall, usually with galleries, and a shallow chancel, since they were built specifically to accommodate the services of mattins and evensong with preaching and reading of the scriptures as the norm.

The preaching churches of the commissioners were succeeded from the 1840s by structures with a new emphasis on the Eucharist and an interest in pre-Reformation liturgies. Yet the preaching services of mattins and evensong remained the normal pattern throughout the nineteenth century. However, there was a good deal of tidying up and altering of older churches, much of it under the name of restoration. In many cases this was in the nature of tidying up and organising the interior arrangements, which frequently meant replacing the irregular box-pews with regular rows of benches. These could be supplied with doors as before, or given carved ends like the few surviving medieval benches, but they were uniformly lower than box-pews to prevent the inattention that was assumed to be the result of worshipping hidden away in private boxes. Now the whole congregation could see and be seen. Of course there were still hierarchies, and most of the great families retained their private pews. This was easier where they occupied a family chapel, as was often the case. There were also the poor who might still be relegated to benches. Sometimes there were even small fold-down seats for them attached to the outsides of the new pews. But the pews themselves could still be rented and the connection between a good seat in church and respectability was firmly maintained.

As the church of the establishment the Church of England has often been criticised as being middle-class, and there was some justification for this in the urban parishes of early nineteenth-century Britain. When new suburbs were laid out developers were anxious to get the best return on their outlay. It was more rewarding to lay out spacious suburbs that would attract comfortably established occupants who could pay good rents. These respectable suburbs often had a new church at their centre, which further enhanced the respectability, for these newly created

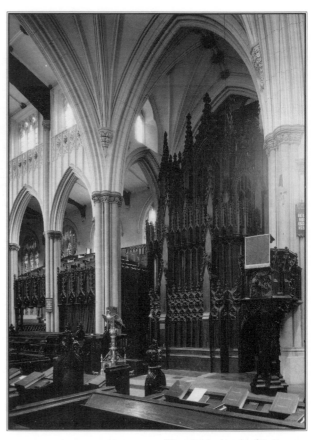

The parish church of St Peter, Leeds, rebuilt by R.D. Chantrell in 1838–41 for the dynamic Revd Walter Hook. This view shows the tall pulpit, the organ filling the south transept and the gallery on the south side of the chancel. (Crown Copyright RCHME)

parishes no longer contained the whole range of social classes as did village parishes. And the competitive respectability could be evident in church as well, where each individual was now firmly on view. One result was that pew rents remained popular and high. There were even complaints in *Punch* at the injustice of paying rent for half a pew only to find that your neighbour's wife and daughter in their crinolines were occupying far more than their half of the space!

Another result was more interesting and perhaps more Christian. Many priests and many congregations were dissatisfied with this conventional piety and set out to alter things. Not only were new churches deliberately built in the slums, but there was a distinct attempt to make the liturgy as rich as possible so that it should be more

Holy Trinity, Islington, built in 1826, is a typical Commissioners' church with box pews and galleries and a centrally placed three-decker pulpit. There are Commandment boards in the shallow sanctuary, and the loose benches in the nave are for poor parishioners. Lithograph, *c.* 1850. (Guildhall Library, Corporation of London)

attractive to those who lived of necessity in mean and cramped streets. A first step was taken by the Incorporated Church Building Society which was founded in 1818 to help finance new churches. It was a condition of their grants that the church should not contain any rentable pews. The followers of the Oxford Movement sensed that the church had moved away from its mission of service and, determined to ensure that worship was brought back to what they believed was its fundamental aim, followed the tenets of the Cambridge Camden Society in designing buildings that would most effectively foster this. Often they chose not to install pews at all, but to use chairs since these emphasised the equality of all before God.

Their attention to the chancel and sanctuary is a part of the story of the Eucharist, but they did not abandon preaching. A great many Victorian churches had new pulpits installed. Most often this was a part of a general refurbishment that involved the removal of box pews and their accompanying three-decker pulpit. If the liturgy was now to include the Eucharist on a regular basis as well as mattins and evensong, the priest needed to do more than sit in his desk and move into his pulpit. So increasingly the great preacher's structures were dismantled and stalls provided at the western end of the chancel, from which a priest could officiate efficiently at either the Eucharist or the preaching services.

Not surprisingly many poorer rural parishes needed to salvage some of the old materials, and a number of pulpits were reconstructed in the nineteenth century using finely carved panels from their Jacobean predecessors. But in the nineteenth century preaching was certainly not downgraded. The Oxford Movement was, famously, launched with a sermon that John Keble preached on the occasion of the Oxford Assizes in 1833 from the pulpit of St Mary's, the University Church, in Oxford. St Peter's Church in Leeds, under Walter Hook, vicar from 1837 to 1859, was an early example of major refurbishment. Hook had been determined to recapture the congregation from Methodism which, he complained, constituted the *de facto* religion of the town. Accordingly he rebuilt his church virtually from scratch, and arranged a sanctuary with more space than was usual for communicants. But he also provided a completely new set of pews in nave and aisles, and erected galleries with pews to match. In this great preaching building, with a seating capacity of over a thousand, he provided a new pulpit raised high up at gallery level and almost halfway down the church, like many Presbyterian churches. Leeds parish church was, in that sense, something of a compromise but, since development was slow and piecemeal, it is usually easier to find the results of refurbishment in compromises than in complete designs.

Where a church afforded a brand new pulpit in the Victorian period, it was usually of stone, often elaborately carved and set with polished coloured marble. The pulpit's richness is a measure of the importance that was still accorded to preaching the word, where the vicar might well be the most educated member of the flock. It was easy to make a pulpit fine with carving – the four evangelists are common and appropriate figures in niches on pulpits – and there was really very little limit to what could be done to make the whole thing splendid. All that was actually necessary was a raised platform, so that the preacher could be seen, and a rail or panels around it for his safety, but few Victorian pulpits are anything like as simple as that. In an age when appearance and a reputation for piety were still important, the gift of a fine pulpit to the local church was a popular and satisfyingly public means of commemoration. The problem was that the more elaborate the pulpit the larger it tended to be, and unless the church had been designed to accommodate it from the start, there was a risk that the pulpit would obscure important sight-lines. Where the church was built from scratch following the dictates of the Ecclesiological Society the sequence of spaces and placing of fitments would be considered in relation to the new patterns of worship involving both preaching and the Eucharist. However, in the majority of parishes that was not the case. In medieval structures the mass had been offered away from the congregation beyond the screen, and there might be only a narrow chancel arch. So the insertion of a large and elaborate pulpit might constitute something of a problem. As a result the altar might be

Preaching from a Victorian pulpit offset to the north of the nave so as not to obstruct the chancel. (Church of England Record Office)

invisible to a large section of the congregation or, alternatively, the pulpit might be so restricted as to make it – and by implication its function – unsatisfactorily insignificant. It has to be admitted that by the end of the eighteenth century the medieval churches of England were already causing problems for their congregations at a time when there was growing controversy about the varying importance of different aspects of their use. The nineteenth-century 'restorers' worked with a confidence that stamped its mark on the buildings they touched. Today we are perhaps more cautious, and many priests in any case now preach from the floor of their church without the need for a pulpit. However, there is no mistaking the attention lavished on this aspect of worship where pulpits, from whatever period, survive.

Praise

Perhaps because the traces they have left are more numerous it seems that the nineteenth and twentieth centuries have involved more changes than before. The changes were not as radical as those made in the century after the Reformation but it is certainly the case that fashions in worship and, as a result, fashions in church furnishing have swung to and fro steadily over the last two centuries. The only constant movement seems to have been a slow decline in the status of the vicar and a corresponding rise in the importance of the laity, and thus in congregational involvement in the acts of worship. But this was a gradual process, and many churches retained family pews and a hierarchy of rented ones until well into the twentieth century. The vicar's position, too, remained one of high status throughout the nineteenth century and for much of the twentieth.

One way in which the congregation became increasingly involved derives from changes at the Reformation. The new attention to preaching and reciting the psalms was linked to a completely new attitude to music as part of the service. From earliest times it had been common to sing hymns, non-biblical spiritual songs, as part of the service, and the first trained choirs began to operate from the sixth century. However, even by the end of the Middle Ages, trained choirs were only found in great churches such as cathedrals, abbeys and royal chapels. None the less the tradition of singing as a part of the mass had developed into a regular system of chanting. In the days before sound amplification this had the effect of throwing the voice further around the church, and by the end of the Middle Ages even quite small towns often had comparatively large churches.

This pre-Reformation music was performed by professionals – not in most cases musicians, but rather the clergy and the various lay clerks or acolytes who assisted in the mass. The congregation were little involved. After the Reformation the role was taken up by the parish clerk, the sole – and half-secular – survival of the numerous lay clerks and priests in minor orders. The parish clerk led the responses, and also read out each line of the psalms before the congregation repeated it. The resulting metrical psalms formed almost the only musical element of many seventeenth-century services, and a new version of them was published in 1692, not long after the official Book of Common Prayer that remained in widespread use until well into the nineteenth century. However, the emotional involvement of singing proved particularly fruitful in the eyes of enthusiastic priests, and especially among the Methodists, who developed this Puritan reciting into one of the best-known forms of Christian praise.

The Puritans had abhorred the chanting of the mass and everything that accompanied it. A great many medieval churches had been equipped with organs. This instrument has a long history and one is recorded in a church in England as early as the eighth century. Medieval organs were small affairs and many were designed to be carried in processions; they were more like accordions than the great instruments of the nineteenth century. The fixed organ of the tenth century in Westminster Abbey with its two manuals and four hundred pipes was regarded a something of a wonder! However, as the Middle Ages developed organs of some sort became a fairly regular feature of churches. Some were still the small portative type, while a few were set up in the rood loft; it would have been a common experience to have some musical accompaniment at least for major festivals. But in 1536 the newly reformed Church declared that organ playing was one of the

'Faults and Abuses of Religion', and many organs were destroyed at once. Those that were left were simply allowed to decay, and music was relegated to the unaccompanied voice of the priest or his clerk.

The development of congregational music, however, derives from the Nonconformist churches, and Isaac Watts (1674–1748), a Congregationalist, was probably the earliest post-Reformation hymn writer in this country. The Methodists also developed a strong tradition of congregational singing, and Charles Wesley (1708–88), brother of the Methodist leader John, provided a number of hymns which were soon regularly sung in Anglican churches. These inspirational poems were extremely popular and answered a very real need. There had been a set place for an anthem to be sung at morning and evening services from the moment the Book of Common Prayer was issued, but this was for 'quires and places where they sing' only. Hymns could be sung anywhere, and represented the first revival of popular religious singing on any scale since the sixth century. Hymns soon had their regular places in the morning and evening preaching services, one of which was often known as evensong.

It is, however, likely that the musical quality of most hymn singing was not high and there were many in the eighteenth century who poked fun at the performance of the average parish congregation. Horace Walpole even sniped at those churches, mostly Nonconformist, that did have trained choirs, likening Wesley's services in Bath to the opera, and commenting that they had a choir of boys who sang 'to Scotch airs'. In the Anglican Church trained choirs remained the preserve of cathedrals and major churches until well into the nineteenth century. Walter Hook in Leeds had introduced 'cathedral style' singing with a trained choir for daily morning and evening services, but was distinctly reluctant at first to make such a radical new departure.

The amateur singers of the average parish were not necessarily all unmusical – far from it, and by the time Hook was toying with his trained choir around 1840 there was already a well-established pattern of hymn singing accompanied by groups of local musicians. In the eighteenth century many of these church bands, together with groups of singers, were accommodated in a gallery at the west end of the church. There they were ideally placed to lead the congregation. The band varied in composition according to the local talent. Most contained fiddles, often a cello and a variety of woodwind. The inclusion of brass instruments was less common, and until the advent of the pneumatic valve in the mid-nineteenth century trumpets were less common among amateur players. Whatever its composition, the church band was a regular part of village life, parallel to the ringers, throughout the eighteenth and early nineteenth centuries, but they were increasingly superseded by the church organ until by the 1880s they were part of a rapidly vanishing rural culture.

An 'unreformed' choir with local musicians singing from a west gallery, the common early nineteenth-century practice, compared to the new fashion for surpliced choirs of men and boys in Mowbray's cartoon of 1868. (Courtesy of Pusey House, Oxford)

The reintroduction of the organ into churches actually began soon after the Restoration of 1660, when a number of town churches began to install them. There was a fine tradition of music in cathedrals and royal chapels in the later seventeenth century, a period when English composers were active and producing what is often regarded as the finest church music. This is particularly noticeable in London, where the influence of the court and the great churches of St Paul's and Westminster Abbey could be felt, and several of the fine churches built after the fire of London have substantial organs. Their cases continue the tradition of fine woodwork and are rich examples of baroque carving. Eighteenth-century organs, however, were almost all to be found in town churches where a congregation of prosperous and often well-educated traders would appreciate the more professional music of composers like Handel and Bach. The village band, involving as it did the varying local talent, proved a more lasting tradition in the countryside.

A surpliced choir in 'restored' Victorian choir stalls, with the organ in the commonest position on one side of the chancel. (Church of England Record Office)

By the mid-nineteenth century, however, there was a change in the attitude to choirs and hence to musicians. The Oxford Movement and their successors the Ritualists were passionately concerned to see that services were as well conducted and as beautiful as possible. These High Churchmen were the first priests to wear surplices and vestments. They were not the least daunted by resistance to changes they believed were bringing the Church back to its original purity, and they pressed ahead with other novelties such as choirs. A trained band of men and boys extended the cathedral-type service to each parish, and when the chancel was filled by a choir, it quite literally filled the gap left by the vanished clerks and acolytes of the pre-Reformation church. The choir, robed in white surplices emblematic of purity, would be seated in the chancel at the front of the congregation to lead the praise and help direct attention to the altar. Thousands of parish churches followed this arrangement, fitting out their under-used chancels with new stalls for the choir. These faced inwards as in the traditional monastic choirs, which made for antiphonal singing. The new fittings were inevitably in the Gothic style, copying the carved ends and other features of surviving medieval pews. In a few cases medieval pews were reconstructed, in another act of recycling, to make new choir stalls. The trend continued into the twentieth century.

With the advent of trained choirs there was an increasing interest in professional music. Increasingly hymn tunes were written down rather than simply memorised. In the nineteenth century there was a flood of hymn writing that ranged from translations of traditional early Christian hymns by John Mason Neale, through missionary invocations from people like Bishop Heber of Calcutta, to stirring songs such as 'Fight the Good Fight', originally written by Sabine Baring-Gould as a marching song for his Sunday School in Sheffield. These, along with many of the eighteenth-century favourites, afforded a considerable choice for congregations, and an opportunity for the collectors and composers of tunes. Many of the tunes in the *English Hymnal* were first recorded in written form by Cecil Sharpe in the last decades of the nineteenth century as he found them in use as traditional folk-songs. The tunes of every day had been absorbed into the music provided by the village bands and choirs for use on Sundays.

At first there was a variety of hymnals, often collected and published by the local vicar and each would include local favourites, well-known eighteenth-century tunes borrowed from the Nonconformists, plus a few by the vicar or very possibly his wife. Much of the verse was turgid and the sentiment trite, but the popularity lay in the familiarity of the tunes. On the other hand there were many churchgoers who wanted hymns that properly reflected the seriousness of their religion, and there was even one hymnal, from Yattendon in Berkshire,[3] that was specifically assembled to include only hymns of an acceptable literary standard. Two collections eventually became almost standard, *Hymns Ancient & Modern* and the *English Hymnal*, and their publication in 1861 and 1906 fixed Anglican hymn singing for two generations. Only relatively recently has it been common to hear hymns sung that were written with the dual intention of being relevant to the modern world both musically and in words.[4]

The progress from the first trained parish choirs to a common selection of hymns for all churches took almost a century, but it paralleled the increasing professionalisation of music in the world at large, with more and more printed music and a piano in almost every middle-class home. This had its effect on the church, too, in the increasing use of organs from the mid-nineteenth century on. These keyboard instruments required a different and more regular training than had been required for playing a flute or a fiddle in a village band, and since a trained choir automatically needed a trainer it could be assumed that he or she would be able to play a keyboard instrument. Thus the choirmaster, who might be the village schoolmistress or the vicar's wife, would also become the provider of music to a different standard from that of the traditional band.

The passing of the band was not always welcomed, as Thomas Hardy recalled in his novel *Under the Greenwood Tree;*[5] but the new professional music was considered to be an improvement and a sign of progress. An organ, after all, could mimic the sound of all the separate instruments of a band, as well as producing others. And the larger instruments, with two or more manuals, were capable of grand and powerful sound. Accordingly church after church acquired an organ, which sometimes physically replaced the old band in a west gallery, or more often was set in a side aisle or in a corner of the chancel where the organist could both play and conduct the choir.

Again there were awkward compromises, since many medieval churches had not been designed to accommodate large organs. Often they were set in front of windows (with disastrous consequences for their tuning), and the obscuring of windows often made churches darker than before. This was perhaps of less concern to the Victorians since from the mid-nineteenth century town churches at least had access to artificial gaslight. In any case they were busy filling the windows of their churches with stained glass which, while it enriched, also darkened the interiors. Rural churches, however, were less fortunate. A substantial organ was a common donation as a memorial to some wealthy local worthy or dearly loved vicar, but such a gift could not be relied on and many small parishes did the best they could with a harmonium, the poor relation of the organ, or simply continued with the increasingly old-fashioned local bands, some of which were still loyally performing well into the twentieth century. Their tradition is now being consciously revived with groups of local musicians and the importation of folk-songs into churches. This is a development that brings its own problems. Modern music requires all the electrical paraphernalia of amplification, and, now that western galleries have mostly been demolished, the group usually has to be accommodated somehow in the nave. A variety of ad hoc platforms provide visibility and a means of safely stowing electrical wiring, but such things are rarely considered in the context of the whole church like the organs they are supplanting.

Two other factors helped to foster the insertion of organs. First, the increased attention to the ordering of services and the spread of ritualism gave all churches a storage problem. Not only were there the chalice, paten and so on for the communion service, there were now cassocks, surplices and music books, all of which needed to be kept in the church. As a result a very common feature of nineteenth-century churches was a new or rebuilt vestry, designed for just this purpose. The vestry was most usually set to the north of the choir, from where the priests could easily enter the chancel to conduct the service. Quite often they were built in such a way that there was room for the new organ in a choir aisle that would be built up against the new vestry, making the insertion attractive as well as effective.

A substantial organ was often the crowning achievement of the Victorian 'restorers', and effected a dramatic change in the pattern of praise. However, there was also a desire on the part of many clergy to avoid what they saw as excesses of ritualism and its related restoration and rebuilding. Partly this was a matter of theology, with the Evangelical churchmen regarding too much colour and carving as dangerously Roman. Partly it was a matter of the conservative nature of a Church that was part of the establishment as well as dealing with concepts of eternity. A good many vicars felt and behaved like Richard Cobbold, the vicar of Wortham, who wrote in the 1860s:

> The church requires restoration and I am persuaded that this will one day be so, though I have been able to effect very little indeed in that way. When I came first to reside it was in a very neglected state – the parish coals being actually lying in a heap at the northern entrance! – and to this hour the stain is not out of the bricks! . . . My successor must not therefore marvel that I have not done more than make decent as far as I could the building of the Church. I am much more concerned in the instruction of souls in the Truth, and freely confess that I have more joy in the Holy Spirit in ministering to the living temple, than in adorning the human structure of the walls, windows or seats of a country Church. I would have every thing and every body decent and clean, but 'when least adorned – adorned the Most'.[6]

Richard Cobbold's account reminds us that the principal function of the church and its rituals was the instruction and salvation of individual souls. From the seventeenth century preaching and congregational praise had been at the heart of worship. Prayer was the other vital element to which we must now turn.

Prayer

> You are not here to verify,
> Instruct yourself, or inform curiosity
> Or carry report. You are here to kneel
> Where prayer has been valid.
>   (T.S. Eliot, *Little Gidding*)

Richard Cobbold's account reminds us that the function of the church and its rituals was the instruction and salvation of individual souls, and it was very much an element of Reformation thinking that the individual should be able to engage in direct communion with God. There had been widespread dissatisfaction with the remoteness of the Latin liturgy and of the mass offered beyond the rood screen. Instead the reformers were keen that every individual should study the Bible, and that the liturgy be taken in English. An emphasis on individual prayerfulness was a natural concomitant of this.

The body of the traditional church had been organised, and the common forms of service provided, for public worship, which has been at the heart of Christian witness from the start. Indeed it is officially a requirement that anyone claiming membership of the church should join in its public worship. However, there has always been a second axis of the Christian's relationship with God in the form of private prayer. It may at first seem difficult to see how this can be accommodated in a building which is by definition public and which developed as the focus of community life. Yet prayer, along with praise and preaching, is very much a part of the activity that goes on in a church. Although medieval church buildings were seldom specifically designed to allow for private prayer, the variety of places available for worship extended beyond the regular parish churches. This went a long way towards recognising the need of individuals for a place to pray and worship that was either in their own control or at least near to their home.

Of course, individual prayer formed a part of all corporate worship, but the act of praying really required no particular physical surroundings. A person might seek communion with God anywhere and at any time. The Puritan who sought his own salvation in his own tongue hardly needed regular forms of prayer beyond the 'Our Father' that he read in the Bible. Even the convention of kneeling to pray was seen as suspect by some. It followed that, beyond being the established spiritual focus of a village, the church building was not necessarily seen as a specific aid to prayer. Indeed the rich ornament, carving and colour and the separation of priest from people in the pre-Reformation church were felt to be an impediment to direct communion with God. All that the convinced Puritan needed was some place of relative peace, preferably with somewhere to sit. This approach has been most determinedly followed by the Society of Friends, or Quakers, for whom a plain white room and simple benches were all that was required for worship. A parallel cult of simplicity in the Church of England led, as we have seen, to much stripping of the altars and removal of features from churches throughout the kingdom. Yet it left little trace of one of its principal motivations in the individual's communion with the Deity.

The previous tradition had been of sacrificial prayers made on behalf of the people by the priests, and this approach has some justification in the notion of intercession. This was, and is, standard practice in both the Roman Catholic and the Orthodox Churches. The problem for the reformers was that the notion of intercession had been extended to the point where priest and people would regularly pray to the Virgin and the many saints to intercede on behalf of the souls of the righteous. Strictly speaking, the concept might be unobjectionable, but in practice it was difficult to distinguish between asking the Virgin to intercede and worshipping the Virgin, particularly since the medieval church had, over the years, expended a good deal of effort in adorning the places in each church where saints, martyrs and the Virgin Mary might be most conveniently addressed.

For the reformers of the new Church of England, the practice of intercession had to be distinguished from the practices that went with conventional intercessions. Petition had long been recognised, along with invocation and adoration, as one of the three strands of prayer, and intercession was one form of petition. This did not change with the Reformation, and remains at the heart of Anglican prayer. However, one visible aspect of intercession has recently begun to reappear. A number of churches in the last generation or so have revived the practice of providing a place where individuals may light candles or leave a note to accompany their individual acts of prayer and intercession. This is a borrowing back of a practice that is widespread in both the Orthodox and Roman Catholic Churches, where a lighted candle acts as a symbol and recalls both Christ as the Light of the World and the injunction at baptism that each Christian should 'shine as a light in the world'. The reappearance of this practice in the Anglican Church seems to be both the result of the absorption of the nineteenth-century reformers' interest in the traditions of the medieval church and a modern imperative, in our increasingly anonymous large towns, to leave some mark of an activity that is important to the individual. The candle stands and notice boards are almost the only physical evidence of a crucial act of faith. Such things are still uncommon, and seldom found in smaller churches, perhaps because it is easy to see the whole of a smaller village church as a haven of peace and quiet. Where they are provided they tend to be arranged in a side aisle or chapel in recognition of the need for a quiet place for prayer, and they are thus more often found in larger churches and especially in towns.

In medieval parish churches it was probably equally necessary to provide some sort of facilities for private prayer, since the whole congregational space of the church was largely open. Today it is possible simply to take a place in a pew and pray, and many visitors may be surprised to find a scattering of people at prayer in a busy church. However, the medieval practice of providing additional altars may have provided the answer. Each altar would be dedicated to one saint, and the most sumptuous would be in the Lady Chapel. The majority of these altars were built in the later fourteenth century, a time when the Virgin Mary was accorded almost cult-like status. Veneration of the Virgin centred on prayer since, as the Mother of God, she was believed to be in an ideal position to intercede for sinners. Yet since such prayers were often offered in corporate services it was in practice difficult to distinguish between asking for her prayers and simply worshipping her. This was one of the reasons that so many Lady Chapels were deliberately left unused at the time of the Reformation. Originally a Lady Chapel would have been used as the focus for special festivals involving veneration of the Virgin, such as the Annunciation (celebrated on 25 March), or the Assumption (celebrated on 15 August). Both of these were hugely important in the late Middle Ages, the first, Lady Day or Lammas ('Our Lady Mass'), especially so for its extension into secular life as the day on which yearly contracts were agreed.

The case was much the same with other subsidiary altars, though they did at least provide some means of breaking up the open space within the body of the church. Each altar would be enclosed on three sides by a *parclose*, or screen, made of metal or wood, sometimes even of stone. These structures were intended to delimit the individual sanctuary or holy space that surrounded each altar, but they also had the effect of creating subsidiary semi-private spaces where it was possible to venerate the particular saint or relic associated with the altar. Such areas might have been used for vigils in which an individual would pray for a period for a particular purpose, perhaps the recovery of a loved one or the return of an absent friend. However, the practice of public all-night vigils was subject to abuse in the Middle Ages, and so such events were usually restricted to day time. Besides, they were generally linked to major festivals and so should be considered as a matter of corporate worship rather than private prayer.

A side altar affords a quiet space for private prayer. This one is set with six candlesticks, and has a curtained aumbry for use in the Eucharist. (Church of England Record Office)

In the pre-Reformation period, it was more important that a priest was available to offer prayers and sacrifice for an individual, particularly for an individual's soul, rather than that an individual should have a space in church specially for his or her private devotions. Hence in many churches the additional altars were financed by wealthy individuals as *chantry* chapels where a priest would be paid to say masses for the soul of the departed donor. (The word chantry is derived from the French word 'to sing'.) Singing mass and devout praying were considered to be two of the most effective means of ensuring pardon for sins and redemption. This belief led to the widespread practice of building separate chantry chapels as additions to churches. In fact by 1547 when the chantry colleges were suppressed most large churches had at least one chantry chapel. They were often elaborate affairs. Some, as at Tewkesbury Abbey, were small structures within the body of the church, usually set between the piers of the choir arcade; others, as at Warwick, might be a completely separate chapel. In either case they would be staffed by priests funded by the donor, sometimes even during his own lifetime. The wealthiest founders (or perhaps those with the most guilty consciences) might even establish a chantry college with a group of secular priests. This was the ultimate achievement in the fourteenth and fifteenth centuries, and the foundation might also include almshouses or a hospital, but would be centred on the activity of prayer and intercession for the founder. Some parish churches originally operated as chantry colleges, and the survival of collegiate seating in places like the parish church of Ludlow point to this as the likely origin of such churches. However, the fact that chantry chapels were served by professionals effectively links them to intercessionary prayer (prayer offered on behalf of another) rather than private communion with God.

In fact private prayer was, as it still generally is, not so often a church activity. Most well-to-do medieval houses had some sort of oratory (a place for praying), usually with a small devotional picture and a prayer stool. Noble houses had their own chapel, which might be a complete church in miniature. These needed to be licensed by the bishop for religious use. A private chapel was unlikely to be built as a two-cell building, and still less with aisles; rather it was most often a single room in, or attached to, the house. There would usually be some space demarcated as a sanctuary, often with a raised step. Such chapels in the pre-Reformation period would almost certainly have been served by a priest as well as being used for daily household prayers. In the seventeenth and eighteenth centuries, where chapels continued in use in great houses, there was not always a separate chaplain, though the noble lord's taste might lead him to employ a professional musician and perhaps to add an organ or engage singers for his pleasure.

In many cases where a private chapel, or even a complete church, was in the possession of some important dignitary, or more especially the king, it would be exempted from normal Episcopal jurisdiction. Such places were known as peculiars, and the royal peculiars were carefully preserved after the Reformation, since the king was now Head of the Church rather than just the temporal lord of the land under the spiritual jurisdiction of the Pope. The few parish churches that were peculiars are rich structures, reflecting their connection with powerful dignitaries. It is, however, difficult to see a direct link between these semi-private chapels with their especial freedoms and particular forms of architecture.

Some peculiars were granted to chapels erected by members of religious bodies such as the Knights Templar, a worldwide organisation deriving their existence from the Crusades. Such organisations might have particular needs or requirements arising from their favourite festivals or practices, which they were free to pursue independent of the bishop's jurisdiction, and their structures may reflect the particular rituals of the organisation. The full title of the Templars was 'The Poor Knights of Christ and of the Temple of Solomon', and they took a special interest in the supposed form of that temple. Their headquarters were in the Temple Church in Fleet Street in London, a circular building that was supposedly based on the Church of the Holy Sepulchre in Jerusalem. They were also responsible for other circular churches, notably St Sepulchre in Cambridge. The order achieved enormous power and wealth before being suppressed in the fourteenth century, when its churches

Distributing the consecrated bread and wine and receiving the communion may be a rather cramped exercise in the sanctuary of a small medieval church that was originally designed for only one or two clergy. (Church of England Record Office)

became parish churches. Such examples, however, are not common. Each of the great military orders, notably the Templars and the Hospitallers (Knights of St John of Jerusalem), had only about fifty preceptories or commanderies in this country, and in most cases only a name, such as Temple Broughton, survives.

The medieval church really concentrated on spaces for corporate worship, leaving private prayer entirely as a matter for the individual in his or her home. Given the relatively sparse population of the country, inhabitants of remote hamlets must have been involved in considerable effort if they were to fulfil their obligations. The problem was recognised by the church, and a number of chapels of ease were built for the convenience of worship. These were subordinate to the parish church but were effectively the focus of the smaller, more remote communities. Thus they functioned in most ways just like a small parish church, and were used for all the normal services of corporate worship, though they were usually without rights of burial. Again, they are more public buildings than spaces for private prayer, and several have become parish churches in their own right.

Another common type of small chapel was for wayfarers. There are a number of bridge chapels or chapels near ferry crossings, which are a reminder of the difficulties of travel in the Middle Ages. Such chapels probably served a dual purpose, not only as a place to pray for a safe crossing or safe journey, but also as a place to rest and shelter while waiting for the ferry. The practice of providing numerous small chapels which were sufficient for a few people, rather than a full congregation, to pray in was widespread in the Celtic Church in the very early centuries. Such chapels were built for particular purposes, such as burial, or were served by hermits whose solitary way of life was a common feature of the Celtic Church.

Holy wells were particularly common sites for such chapels. Natural sources of water have always appeared miraculous, and it is a safe bet that almost all such wells were places of veneration in pre-Christian times. The Christian Church found no difficulty in accepting their sanctity, and the water was used for baptism or, more often, for healing. Once a well or spring had acquired the epithet holy it was almost always cared for by a professional religious, either a priest or a monk, and the erection of an attendant chapel soon followed. The sites were often credited with miraculous occurrences, and wonderful myths survive about the restoration of decapitated maidens, as at St Bueno's well in Flint. They also regularly became sites of pilgrimage. Many are still so to this day, and for believers their little chapels have a special sense of the numinous.

There were many other shrines in the Middle Ages, apart from international pilgrimage centres, where it was felt important to mark the place of some particular miracle or the dwelling of a particular saint. It was a common element in early Christian belief that the remains of a saint or an object they had possessed retained something of their real presence. The second Council of Nicaea in 787 CE had actually ordered that no church should be consecrated without relics. Contact with such items, particularly the bones of martyrs, could produce miracles. As a result the shrines where the relics were preserved were elaborately constructed and richly embellished. They frequently took the form of a table tomb with a canopy, a form that was particularly appropriate since most relics were the mortal remains of those who were recognised as saints. Shrines might also focus on other memorabilia, such as clothes, instruments of martyrdom, or miraculous statues, in much the same way that wells had proved a particular focus.

Medieval shrines at which a number of miracles were attested brought both fame and wealth to their churches, and naturally the most important were in major centres. The shrines of Edward the Confessor in Westminster Abbey, Thomas Becket at Canterbury and Cuthbert at Durham are three of the most famous medieval British shrines. The practice of granting or even selling indulgences to those who visited particular shrines to pray vastly increased the popularity of pilgrimage, and people might travel long distances either for penance or in hope of a cure; indeed, the practice of pilgrimage is by no means dead. But shrines were never confined to great cathedrals. Their renown had an immediate impact on the churches that housed them. Space had to be found for the shrine, and if it began to attract pilgrims, that space might need to be enlarged, or the shrine moved to a new area. There might be huge attendance at special festivals, which would require additional altars for celebrating the mass, as well as congregational space. In most cases pilgrims visiting the shrine would leave some offering, and there was a need for storage space for such treasures. Finally, of course, there was a need for security, usually provided by a watching chamber. This would normally take the form of an upper room with windows into the church, with a view of the shrine area, and such rooms can still be seen in a number of cathedrals (though they are extremely rare in parish churches). In addition to the shrine and the church there would also be a need for lodgings for pilgrims and often facilities were also provided for the sick. The whole business of pilgrimage could have a major impact on the local community and its economy as well as on the church that housed the shrine. The effect of even a minor shrine in a parish church might be considerable. At Madley in Herefordshire the presence of a wonder-working statue of the Virgin proved such an attraction that a new chancel, chapels, enlarged naves and even a crypt for the statue had to be added.

At the Reformation all shrines were destroyed, leaving only the enlarged shell of the church. It was not always easy to obliterate all signs of the veneration. At Dorchester in Oxford, for instance, the shrine of the local bishop St Birinus was broken up and the windows showing scenes of his life replaced with clear glass, but it was not so easy to remove the related carving on the tracery of the window. All these had been added when the choir was rebuilt and the church greatly enlarged in the fourteenth century at a time when the saint's relics were moved, presumably to create more space for pilgrims. However, it takes a leap of imagination to recover the bustle, the noise and the colour that attached to the medieval shrines and their use. For four hundred years Dorchester, and places like it, lived with overlarge churches and empty spaces that were of little use. Only antiquarians took any interest in curiosities such as shrines and their remains. Now archaeology has helped to establish the form of many of the lost shrines, and some are even being re-erected, at least in part. At Dorchester the nineteenth-century restorers collected and reset the surviving medieval glass. In the 1950s the fragments of the shrine itself were collected and set up as a reminder of the saintly bishop and of those who came to pray under the influence of his example.

This example of earlier generations of the faithful seems to be important to all Christians. Many churches proudly record their contact with leading preachers and priests, even when such people would have had little truck with the medieval business of relics. At North Leigh in Oxford, a small plaque on the pulpit records the first preaching of John Wesley, when he was a newly ordained clergyman of the Church of

The tiny, two-cell church of St John the Evangelist at Little Gidding, Huntingdonshire, an eighteenth-century structure on the site of Nicholas Ferrar's church. (Colin Cunningham)

England. Holy Trinity in Cambridge, on the other hand, preserves an umbrella used by Charles Simeon (1759–1836), a former vicar and leader of the Evangelical revival. It seems impossible for a religion that deals with concepts of eternity to escape from the past, and the Church of England, because of its direct link with the pre-Reformation church, is linked to a whole host of medieval and earlier Christians who together form the communion of saints. Their example survives in dedications and decoration here and there, as well as sometimes in the shrines to which long-past generations of believers went to pray. It was a phenomenon that T.S. Eliot recognised when he wrote his poem inspired by the church at Little Gidding, in Huntingdonshire, and the community that had lived and prayed there for generations.[7]

The Offices

Though the adornment of a church can be seen as the fruits of devotion, the activity of individual prayer has left little trace in the buildings apart from the side chapels set apart for it. However, the practice of intercession by professionals was a key element in pre-Reformation religion and has left a particular mark on a number of churches. Even after the Reformation there had been a few devout Christians who felt the need to withdraw from the world in order to be able to pray and worship more effectively. Perhaps the best example from this period is Nicholas Ferrar, who in 1626 established a small community at Little

Gidding near Huntingdon. It was to be run with strict rules within the doctrines of the established Church of England, and a principal activity was regular prayer. Their small church was a reconstruction of a dilapidated earlier one, with the seats arranged facing each other as in the pre-Reformation monastic choirs. The chancel was equipped with brass plaques inscribed with the Creed, the Lord's Prayer and the Ten Commandments. The community, alas, was short-lived, being first criticised by the Puritans and then in 1646 attacked and dispersed on the grounds that it was imitating popish practices.

The practice of regular hours of prayer, however, had been established before Christianity in the Jewish religion and was continued in the early Church. Indeed similar practices are common to a number of world religions. In Christianity such systems were central to pre-Reformation monastic life. Those who took up a professional religious life lived communally and their way of life and practice of worship determined the forms of their buildings. This in turn has left its traces in a number of parish churches. The earliest rule was that laid down by St Benedict of Nursia in the early sixth century, after which Benedictine monasticism spread throughout the western Church. Benedictine monasteries were established in England with the help of the Anglo-Saxon kings, and several of our cathedrals, including Winchester and Peterborough, were originally Benedictine foundations. A number of their monasteries were converted to parish use at the Reformation, such as Sherborne, Tewkesbury and Great Malvern. However, it was in the century after the Norman conquest that monasticism had its greatest period of expansion in Britain. By then the Benedictine Rule had been revised and adapted under Bernard of Clairvaux (1090–1153), who founded the Cistercian order. They established a number of large monasteries in remote places such as Rievaulx, where it was felt they could live a devout life undisturbed by the cares of the world. The Cluniac order, founded a century earlier, also had considerable influence in Britain through its connections with powerful baronial families and the royal court.

In the thirteenth century the Franciscan and Dominican Friars appeared. These were the so-called mendicant orders, an association of individuals who relied for their keep on their employers or the generosity of the community in which they worked. As itinerant preachers they had more impact on the life of the average parish, though their own churches were not parochial and so have generally not survived. The Augustinians, who established some 140 houses in England and Wales in the century after the Norman conquest, had the greatest impact on the fabric of parish life. Unusually for a monastic order, they were subject to Episcopal visitation, which brought them into closer contact with the hierarchy of parish priests, and they were

allowed to undertake parish duties. They were also closely involved
with caring for the sick, and thus with the establishment of churches
such as St Bartholomew the Great in London which was linked to the
hospital from the start. Their involvement with parishes meant that
their churches were frequently converted for parish use at the time of
the Reformation, as was the case with the choir and transepts of the
twelfth-century structure of St Bartholomew the Great.

All the orders lived under a Rule that regulated every hour of the
monks' life, whether it involved worship, work or sleeping and eating.
Monks undertook regular services of prayer in their churches, covering
the whole twenty-four hours. These were known as the offices (from the
Latin word *officium*, meaning duty) and began with the night office of
Mattins. Lauds followed at dawn and there were six further offices,
Prime, Terce, Sext, Nones, Vespers and Compline at dusk, before the
monks retired to bed. They were known as the Canonical Hours and the
names of four of them still recall the old divisions of daylight into twelve
'hours', Prime meaning first, Terce third, Sext sixth and Nones the ninth
hour. This pattern of daily services had some impact on the way that
monastic churches were designed and some of the evidence survives.

The need to keep a timetable of worship has left its trace in the
clocks that adorn most parish churches. Initially, most churches had
either a sundial or a mass-dial scratched on the outside wall in which
a twig could be used to indicate the hour at which mass would be
offered, and such things can still be seen in rural churches such as
St Mary at Hanbury in Worcestershire. The monks required a more
exact and efficient system, and the first mechanical clock was
installed at Canterbury in 1292. The clocks of this period were large
weight-driven affairs, usually sited in turrets, from which they took
the name turret clock. They had no hands or dial, but merely struck
a signal when the service was due. It was the bell rather than the
hour which mattered in announcing the offices. In the fourteenth
century striking clocks were developed and by the end of the
fifteenth century most major churches as well as all monasteries had
a clock. In parish churches, especially town churches, these were
usually sited in the tower and sounded every hour and its quarters.

In a few places more elaborate clocks were developed in which the
bells were set in full view and the strikers were carved in the form of
people. The combination of clock and striking figures at St Mary Steps
in Exeter or at All Saints in Leicester are particularly fine examples. Dials
to indicate the precise time were extremely rare before the sixteenth
century and generally had only an hour hand. However, advances in
mechanical engineering in the seventeenth and eighteenth centuries
allowed church-builders such as Wren to incorporate fine large clocks,
often in elaborate projecting cases. In the nineteenth century commercial

manufacturers of public clocks, such as Gillet & Bland of Croydon, helped in the spread of good quality timepieces, but by then the church clock often had to compete with the town hall or the railway clock, and its original purpose of announcing the canonical hours was long forgotten.

Most of the monasteries were gone too, swept away at the Reformation. The Dissolution of the Monasteries in 1534 saw the abandonment of an extraordinary amount of 'church plant' that was decreed redundant. Because they were usually sited outside towns the great churches were of little use to parishes after the Reformation, but the subsidiary buildings and rich monastic estates were very attractive to the king and powerful local men who competed to buy them. The remote Cistercian houses were left to decay until the Romantic movement of the late eighteenth century adapted the ruins as an element of the Picturesque, and they are now a key part of our medieval heritage. In most cases the building materials were far too valuable to waste, and in areas

Clock and sundial are both provided on the tower of St Mary, Putney Bridge in London. The tower is of Kentish ragstone, typical of London. (Church of England Record Office)

where the stone could be easily transported, the ruins were busily quarried for ready cut stone that was built into substantial houses in the vicinity. Fragments of finer work can occasionally be found in modest parish churches as well. It was, however, more profitable for the crown to sell redundant monasteries and their buildings were often converted into colleges, as at Jesus College in Cambridge, or schools, as at Sherborne in Dorset. Several were turned into grand houses, with the cloisters making a fine courtyard. However, conversion was much easier to effect in the ancillary buildings, and the churches were often left to rot alongside the new development, as at Newstead Abbey in Nottinghamshire.

There were a substantial number of monastic churches in which the local congregation had already worshipped, as well as abbeys that had taken on parochial responsibility. Their churches were regularly adapted for parish use and they form a significant group in which the traces of monastic life can be read. In the first place monastic churches needed to be large, in order to accommodate not only the ordained monks but also the lay brothers (who were typically twice

The west and crossing towers, nave and parts of the aisles – the remains of Wymondham Abbey, Norfolk – make a massive parish church. The ruins of the monks' choir are to the right. (Crown Copyright RCHME)

as numerous as the choir monks). It was the regular arrangement for the ordained monks to say or sing their offices in the choir, while the laity worshipped in the nave of the church. After the Dissolution this left structures that were generally too large for their congregation. Since congregational worship had been confined to the nave, it was common to abandon the eastern parts of the building, with the western arch of the crossing becoming the frame for a new east window. The parish church of St James Freiston in Lincolnshire, founded as a subordinate house of Crowland Abbey, has just such an arrangement. The entire eastern end of the church has been demolished, and only rough humps in the ground indicate its extent. More often there is not even that indication, though blocked archways at the eastern end of the aisles may indicate the former presence of transepts, and such churches will be without a distinct chancel separated from the nave by a major arch. There may also be blocked doorways that once led from the nave into the cloister.

The offices left their mark, too, and not only in the size of the choir. The pattern of choir seating, with rows of stalls facing each other, was devised for the saying of the offices. The monks would say or sing alternate verses of the psalms, and it was easier to manage this if both halves could see and hear each other clearly. Where the monastic choir survives the medieval benches may also be present. It is interesting also that this pattern of seating has more recently been revived, mainly by the evangelical wing of the church, as a means of improving the involvement of worshippers with one another – which was exactly the intention of the monks who first devised it. Such arrangements are based on an understanding of the body of the church as a crucible in which the faithful are all equal, rather than as the symbol of a journey towards salvation. The pattern can be seen in many recently reordered parish churches, such as St Andrew the Great in Cambridge.

In addition to seating in the church medieval abbeys were designed to cope with the twenty-four hour cycle of prayer, and there was regular provision for access direct from the monks' dormitory for the night office of mattins. A blocked high-level doorway in the south transept, sometimes complete with 'night stairs', may survive as evidence of this. But in general the change from monastic abbey to parish church was simply a matter of shrinking to a manageable size. Fortunately, a number of the houses with parochial responsibility were in towns and the large churches that the parishes inherited proved suitable for the growing prosperity of the area. Malmesbury, Selby and Romsey are all examples of substantial former abbeys converted into effective major churches in towns that were prosperous after the Reformation. Not all parishes were so fortunate, and smaller communities who had to cope with large churches sometimes took even more drastic action. The small hamlet of South Kyme in Lincolnshire coped with their grand Augustinian priory by walling off a small section of the west end of the south aisle, together with a strip of the nave. The rest of the building was demolished. The presence of substantial piers in the west wall indicates the fragment of the original west front that has been incorporated into the little church that was only finally tidied into a single hall in 1888. Nearby at Sempringham the nave, north aisle and north transept are all that survive of a much larger structure, to which, in the nineteenth century, was added an apsidal chancel.

Another occasional survival from the monastic world are some of the small chapels that were a regular part of the larger monasteries. There might be a separate infirmary chapel or a private chapel for the abbot or prior and there was frequently a *guesten* chapel, usually near the gate, for visitors. These more modest and separate buildings were easier to reuse. Prior Crauden's chapel at Ely, for instance, now forms a small chapel for the school that developed in the former monastic buildings. One of the most evocative is the church of St Leonard at Kirkstead in Lincolnshire, a tiny chapel, only 40 ft by 20, of the finest thirteenth-century workmanship, which is all that remains of a grand Cistercian abbey. It was almost certainly the chapel *ante portas* (that is, outside the gate) intended for visitors. Today it stands isolated in the midst of fields without either abbey or village but it is still occasionally used for services.

There is one final way in which the monastic orders, with their life centred on the daily offices, have affected parish churches. The ancillary buildings have gone, though they may have left traces on the outside of the church, perhaps in the form of blocked doorways or capitals of what was once a cloister vault. However, the site of the buildings has had some effect. They were usually on the south side of the abbey church, and thus the church will not have the usual relationship with its churchyard. Where the buildings survived or were converted the south side may be occupied by what are now barns or parts of a substantial house. The area would in any case not be suitable for a burial ground. So parish churches like St James Frieston may end up with a graveyard unusually laid out to the north of the church on account of the monastic ruins to the south.

Equally the monasteries were not built, as were the parish churches, as the natural focus of their community. The daily passage of the parishioners to and from work did not, as it generally would with a parish church, take them past or through the abbey church. It stood secluded behind its wall, reserved for the monks or for special occasions. Indeed many of the abbeys were not even in the towns, but outside them. Thus a converted abbey may have a different relation to its community. St Mary's Abbey in Shrewsbury, for instance, stood outside the medieval town

St Andrew the Less, Cambridge, was originally a chapel of Barnwell Priory; a parish church after the Reformation, it was abandoned as too small in the nineteenth century. It is shown used as a school in this engraving from Le Keux's *Memorials of Cambridge*, 1842. (Courtesy of the Syndics of Cambridge University Library)

across the Severn bridge. When it was still an operational monastery it would have been surrounded by a cluster of dwellings, but the abbey alone occupied the space on that bank of the river, the focus of an annual fair. Now, however, it is the parish church of a district that grew up around it after the Reformation. It is difficult today to recover the original relationship of such a structure to the community it currently serves. The absence of a complex of medieval streets or pathways may indicate the presence of a monastic church before there was a community around it. In some cases, such as Bath, the development of the town in the years since the Dissolution has been such that the abbey church has no churchyard round it at all. Yet the monastic way of life was widespread in England in the Middle Ages, with perhaps one per cent of the population committed to it, and many more involved as benefactors and supporters. The resulting buildings were numerous and often of high quality, and though the number of abbeys currently serving as parish churches is relatively small it needs to be recognised that there was scarcely a church in medieval England that was not to some extent influenced by their example.

CHAPTER FOUR

The Church and its Festivals

The Liturgical Year

The primary influence on church-building should be the requirements of regular services, the Eucharist and later the daily mattins and evensong that have formed the common pattern of Anglican worship. Yet there is no good evidence to show that all parishioners always went to church in the centuries before industrialisation. It was an obligation, backed by legal sanctions, but it seems that backsliders were numerous and generally enjoyed considerable leeway. However, major festivals attracted large numbers, and the very size of a church may be a reflection of its popularity as a place for such celebrations. The buildings should be understood as theatres for the staging of often quite elaborate ceremonials before a large congregation on a variety of different occasions throughout the year.

The Church recognises a cycle of major festivals reflecting the life, death and resurrection of Christ that shape the liturgical year. This cycle begins with preparation for the coming of Christ in Advent, celebrates his birth at Christmas, and passes through a period of penance in Lent to the festival of Easter with rejoicing at his rising from the tomb. This is succeeded by the festival of his Ascension into heaven after which comes Whitsun (literally white Sunday) which commemorates the gift of the Holy Ghost. After Whitsun comes the longer season of Trinity, which acknowledges the nature of the Christian deity as God the Father, Son and Holy Ghost. These are the major festivals which the Church keeps. In addition, the 1662 Book of Common Prayer listed no fewer than twenty-five Feasts that are to be observed in the Church of England, as well as all Sundays and the two days immediately after Easter and Whitsun. There were also sixteen vigils before major feasts, specified days of fasting and abstinence and, originally, four groups of Ember Days (the name probably derives from the Latin *tempora* and relates to the four seasons). These were sets of three days of fasting, in December, after Ash Wednesday, Whitsunday and in September. They have long since lost any connection with the seasons, but are still the times when priests are ordained. Finally, following the issuing of the standard prayer book of 1662, there were special solemn days to commemorate the gunpowder plot, the martyrdom of King Charles I, the return of Charles II, and the day on which the king began his reign. The last four reflect the ties between the Anglican Church and the State, and it is clear that not all festivals were celebrated with equal enthusiasm or regularity in every parish. However, all the major occasions were, and still are, marked by special festivities.

The festivals themselves have left little permanent trace but churches acknowledge the sequences of the Christian year in the colours of the cloths with which the building is dressed. These consist of altar frontals and pulpit falls (the short hangings in front of the reading desk on the pulpit), and are supplemented by coloured vestments. These touches of colour act as a visual reminder of each moment in the cycle as well as highlighting key places in the church. The altar frontal is usually the most prominent element and consists of a flat cloth, often richly embroidered, hung from the edge of the altar. An alternative form is simply a large table cloth reaching to the ground all round, a type made fashionable by Archbishop Laud in the seventeenth century and now increasingly popular once more.

The use of colours to mark the stages of the Christian year was established as early as the twelfth century among the Augustinian canons, but an agreed sequence did not become accepted until much later. The present use derives from the efforts of the ritualist revivers of the nineteenth century. Only five colours are recognised. White signifies both purity and joy and is used for most of the major feasts, such as Christmas and Easter. Red, recalling Christ's blood shed for the sins of the world, is associated with fire and with martyrs and is used on Palm Sunday and (confusingly) on Whitsunday. Green is the colour seen for the longest period since it is used when no other feast is being kept as well as for the feast of the Trinity and for Epiphany. Purple is used to indicate penance while black is reserved for Good Friday, the remembrance of Christ's death on the cross, and for funerals.

Along with the use of coloured hangings goes the need for appropriate places to keep them, and this is compounded by the occasional use of other items for specific feasts. Most churches have some sort of storage problem. The more valuable objects, such as altar cloths, are kept in the vestry, and it is no surprise that the nineteenth century, with its revival of ritualism, saw the widespread erection of vestries. Other ephemeral items, such as flower vases and stands, may be more bulky, and many churches end up with one area left as a sort of junk room. The casual visitor, confronted with the sorry appearance of such places, needs a determined imagination to see how glorious they may make the church when they are in use.

Advent, Christmas and Epiphany

The ecclesiastical year begins on the first Sunday in Advent, a few weeks before Christmas. The altar is dressed in penitential purple as a reminder of the need for Christians to repent before celebrating the arrival of Christ who will redeem the world from sin. But the festival is one of anticipation and leads into the Christmas celebrations so this is not a time of gloom. The events that accompany it reflect both the time of year, with services commonly held after daylight hours, and the joy of the season. One feature that is used in many churches is the advent wheel, a ring or wreath of greenery set with four candles for the four Sundays of the Advent season. These are lit in turn, marking the approach of Christmas as first one then two then three and four candles are lit to shine during services.

There is usually also a Christmas tree, something that was introduced to England by Prince Albert in the nineteenth century. Its use is so widespread that it is now seen as an essential part of the festive season though it is not directly a Christian symbol at all. Many churches go to some lengths to find a suitable place for the tree, and it tends to dominate any decoration arranged in the church for the festival. Trees are, however, a link with secular life, since the same symbol is equally widely set up in homes. The modern fir tree in its pot is, if anything, a relative of the Yule log, symbolising the warmth and cosiness of a good fire at midwinter; Yule, the medieval title for Christmas-tide festivities, means clamour or noise, and refers to celebrations of pagan origin in which communities feasted as a way of keeping up spirits in the dead of winter. The concept is closely linked with the week-long festival of the Lord of Misrule rather than with the advent of Christ. Now tamed, the Christmas tree, topped with a star, has acquired a new symbolism, referring to the star which guided the wise men to Bethlehem. Another even more recent import, though fully Christian, is the Christingle service. This was developed by the Moravian Brethren, a Lutheran Protestant church refounded in Bohemia in eastern Europe in 1722. The Christingle, which is given to children at the service, consists of an orange tied with a red ribbon, with a candle in it. The orange symbolises the world and the candle represents Christ as the light of the world. The red ribbon symbolises his redemption of the world by the sacrifice of his life. In the days before refrigerated transport, of course, it was also a considerable treat for the children.

Perhaps the most characteristic element of present-day services at Advent and Christmas are the carol services. These also derive from the nineteenth-century Ritualist revival, in particular from the employment of trained surpliced choirs, so they are of a piece with the ordering of a church with a chancel, and their music is some of the most popular. However, carols have a much longer ancestry, the first English collection being published in 1521. The word is derived from an Italian word meaning a ring dance, which makes carols ideally suited to Christmas festivities. They were originally popular songs, only semi-religious in nature, and were not a part of the formal liturgy – that was reserved for the more formal hymns. Since the nineteenth century that distinction has been largely lost, and carols now form a regular part of both Advent and Christmas services. What has survived in most parish churches is their popular nature, which is linked to the importance of congregational involvement, something that is oddly at variance with carol services where highly trained choirs sing for a congregation to listen to like an audience at a concert.

At this time of year services also demonstrate the importance of artificial lighting in establishing the character and quality of the spaces. The practice of holding evening carol services, quite often by candlelight, greatly enhances the romantic aspect of the festival. Perhaps also it reinforces the pathos of the Christmas story, with the holy family denied lodging at the inn, with the contrast between the worshippers in the candlelit warmth of the church and the winter night outside. Few churches today are regularly lit by

St Margaret, Ditchling, Sussex, at Christmas in about 1960. The nave, crossing and chancel are all decorated. (Church of England Record Office)

candlelight, though some remote churches are still not wired for electricity. The quality of candlelight, however, is softer than electricity, and those churches, such as St Mary Wissington, and those that are lit by paraffin (a warmer but still soft light) have a particular atmosphere that is only shared by other churches when they are lit by candlelight alone. The survival of large candelabra or individual candle stands on pews, choir stalls or by the pulpit serves as a reminder of what was previously a universal quality of churches. Because of the size of most churches it was inevitable that large numbers of candles would be needed, and these were often set on *coronas*, large wheel-like structures, usually of iron, that could illuminate a wide area. Since these were being made specifically for churches, there was generally an attempt to make them as fine as possible, and those that survive are generally richly decorative examples of the blacksmith's art.

The advent of electricity is relatively recent, well within living memory in many country churches, bringing with it the problem of brightly coloured wires, large fuse boxes and so on, which do not always fit easily into a building designed before such technology was born. The full potential of lighting as a part of the architecture is something that is seldom realised in older parish churches. On the other hand, many modern churches were carefully designed for artificial, as well as natural, light. There is considerable

A choir is an important element in a procession: this is a candlelit procession at Christmas. (Church of England Record Office)

potential for making the building appear dramatic as well as inviting. In general architects have tried to avoid harsh light or visible spotlights that shine directly on the viewer. Concealed lighting, especially up-lighting, is used to draw attention to impressive roof structures in both new and old churches.

Medieval roofs are often wonders of carpentry. The more expensive stone vaulting was generally reserved for high status churches, such as abbeys and cathedrals, and the presence of a stone roof, even if only over the chancel, was something of an achievement for a parish church. However, cheaper timber could be assembled to make a dramatic and functional covering. A whole variety of different forms can be identified, with different structural systems popular at different times or in different parts of the country. Some of the richest are the so-called hammer-beam roofs that abound in Suffolk. Probably more important to the worshippers was the way most roofs were decorated with painted texts, stars and painted or carved angels, as though the whole heavenly host was in attendance. These have to be considered in the context of the faithful assembling to celebrate

The fifteenth-century double hammerbeam roof of St Mary Woolpit is set with carved angels. The canopy below the window was inserted during restoration in 1875. (Colin Cunningham)

the festivals of the Christian year. The dim appearance of gilded angels in the light of hundreds of candles on a dark Christmas evening must surely have been particularly evocative.

One reason why church lighting has an added interest at Christmas is that this great festival, like others, was regularly preceded by a vigil, a nocturnal act of prayer and fasting that ended with a mass. Such vigils were subject to abuse in the Middle Ages, and so were generally moved to daylight hours, making the whole of Christmas eve a part of the festival. During the Commonwealth the Puritans even banned the ringing of church bells, and urged the suppression of midnight services. However, some trace of the public vigil survives in the popularity of the midnight mass (one of the few occasions when the Anglican Church regularly uses that title for the communion service) which has become a regular part of the Christmas liturgy in the last generation or so. Those who attend this service can feel that their very first act of the feast was one of worship.

A final element of the Christmas decoration of a church is the provision of a crib. Some continental Roman Catholic churches have quite large permanent structures complete with stone or clay statues.

The cribs used in the Church of England are much rougher and less substantial models of the stable in which, according to the gospels, Christ was born. Because Christmas celebrates Christ's birthday there is a strong association with children, and the making or setting up of the crib is often left to them. Since it is a three-dimensional model, a good deal of space is often required. Frequently this is found at the west end of the nave near the font, though there is no liturgical justification for this. It is one more example of a space in a church being used only for certain festivals. When the festival is over, all that is left is often no more than a few boxes containing figures and the dismantled structure that housed them.

The Christmas crib, however, lasts slightly longer than Christmas itself. The stable can be set up in advance, though the Christ child obviously does not arrive until Christmas day, when the shepherds also come to worship, as does the congregation. The addition of the wise men, the Three Kings, takes the story on to its next stage when Christ was revealed to the wider world. This has its liturgical place in the feast of Epiphany (literally, the Showing) that follows on 6 January. This, the twelfth night after Christmas, officially marks the end of the Christmas season, and follows minor feasts such as Holy Innocents' Day, which recalls Herod's attempt to suppress Christ by murdering all new-born boy babies in the kingdom. Epiphany also follows the feast of the Circumcision of Christ, which recalls the first stage in his growing up, a reminder, too, that Christ grew up in the traditions of Judaism. None of these events requires any special construction, and so they leave little trace in the church, except that after Epiphany the altar frontals and other hangings are replaced by the green ones signifying new life and hope.

Parishioners at work erecting the Christmas crib over a statue of the Holy Family. (Church of England Record Office)

The open chancel survives even in this eighteenth-century church, and makes an ideal space for a nativity play at Christmas. (Church of England Record Office)

Lent

Lent, the period of six weeks before Easter, is observed as a time of penance in preparation for that great feast. It is therefore a time when simplicity is more important, and it leaves even less mark on the structure of a church than the great feasts. In fact, because it is officially a time of fasting, activities such as weddings are proscribed for the season. It is marked by the use of purple hangings, the penitential colour, and continues until Easter Sunday, perhaps the greatest of the Christian festivals.

In the early centuries the fast was very strictly kept, and Lent for Christians was as tough as Ramadan is for Muslims now. By the fifteenth century, however, the rules had been somewhat relaxed, so that the one meal that was allowed was taken at midday, and fish was permitted. Even so, it was a long period of regular abstinence, accompanied by prayer, and Vespers, the evening service, was held every day in the church after the meal. The fast was not abandoned at the Reformation, indeed it was specifically ordered in the new prayer book, but in the eighteenth century Lenten observance became very lax and it was not revived until the Tractarians of the nineteenth century brought back the old liturgy.

The fast was supposed to last forty days, recalling Christ's forty days of temptation in the wilderness. However, because the Sundays in Lent were not counted as part of the fast, it was extended to the Wednesday before its first Sunday, and begins with the solemn service of Ash Wednesday. At the Reformation a special service was written that involved both congregational prayer and the solemn reading of what the prayer book called 'the general Sentences of God's cursing against impenitent sinners' from the Old Testament.

That service of Commination survived in all the editions of the Book of Common Prayer, and even in the 1920s Ash Wednesday was mentioned as a special fast day. However, a more recent practice, revived in the last decade or so, has been that of 'ashing'. By about the tenth century it had become common practice for the congregation to undertake a general penance which was symbolised by marking the foreheads of priest and people with ashes in token of mourning and penitence. Still ordained in the Roman Catholic Church, this practice is now finding favour among Anglicans, and affords a visible symbol of the particular season and its purpose.

Another activity connected with the fast is cooking and eating pancakes. Originally this Shrove Tuesday practice provided one last good meal before the fast began, but it had its place at home rather than in church. Now, when the link between everyday life and religious observance has become tenuous, pancake cooking and pancake racing have survived as popular expressions of the time of year – an example of an originally religious activity taking on a secular life, yet it is another connection between the church and the community around it. The first pancake races may well have been run in churchyards.

The culmination of the Lenten fast leads directly into the festival of Easter through the events of Holy Week. Palm Sunday recalls Christ's triumphal entry into Jerusalem, which for centuries was recalled in the practice of processing with palms, usually from one church to another and then back again to celebrate mass. This direct linking of different churches was unusual, and reinforced the understanding that all congregations were a part of one wider flock. It must have been something of a spectacle since the whole congregation would be carrying palms and led by the priest and acolytes carrying a crucifix, or in some places a figure of Christ on a donkey. Since the Sunday was not part of the

Small crosses made from strips of palm leaf are still handed out on Palm Sunday, recalling Christ's entry into Jerusalem. (Church of England Record Office)

Lenten fast the colour for the procession was the crimson red of sacrifice, though purple was still ordained for the mass. The rite for blessing the palms was rich and complex, but that made it objectionable to the reformers and it was specifically abolished in 1549. None the less it is still common for congregations to take small palm crosses and have them blessed during the communion service of Palm Sunday. Sometimes whole branches of palm trees are carried by the choir and these may be left on display during the succeeding Holy Week. They are yet one more item for which storage space is needed for the other fifty-one weeks of the year.

Lent reaches its climax on Good Friday when Christians recall the crucifixion and death of Christ. On Good Friday, and often during the whole of Holy Week, many churches cover all images and crucifixes with a purple veil. For that period the church is deliberately made to look sombre, before the return of the light at Easter. Good Friday was always a time of particular sadness for Christians, but Easter Eve was a day of vigil until the festival of Resurrection began at midnight. As we shall see, the drama of this was not lost on the pre-Reformation congregations, and the impact on the church is the same as that described for midnight mass at Christmas.

Easter eve was also a time when families would dress the graves of their ancestors with flowers. It is a spring festival, coinciding generally with the first appearance of wild flowers, and when working people were able to take time off to visit their native village. The practice is described in the diary of the Revd Francis Kilvert, the curate at Clyro on the Welsh borders from 1865 to 1872:

> When I started for Cefn y Blaen only two or three people were in the churchyard with flowers. . . . But now the customary Easter Eve vigil had fairly begun and people kept arriving from all parts with flowers to dress the graves. Children were coming from the town and from neighbouring villages with baskets of flowers and knives to cut holes in the turf. The roads were lively with people coming and going and the churchyard a busy scene with women and children and a few men moving about among the tombstones and kneeling down beside the green mounds flowering the graves. . . . I found a child wandering about the tombs looking for her father's grave. She had found her grandfather's and had already dressed it with flowers. The clerk was busy banking up and watering the green mounds not far off and I got him to come and show the child where her father's grave lay. He soon found it for he knows almost every grave in the churchyard. And then I helped the child to dress the long narrow green mound with the flowers that remained in her basket. . . . More and more people kept coming into the churchyard as they finished their day's work. . . . Water was in great request for the ground was very hard and dry and wanted

softening before flowers could be bedded in the turf. The flowers most
used were primroses, daffodils, currant, laurel and box. A pretty wreath
of greenhouse flowers lay on the high flat tomb of Mrs Williams of
Pipton but no one seemed to know who had placed it there. . . .

[Kilvert made flower crosses for the graves of his friends] I am glad
to see that our primrose crosses seem to be having some effect for
I think I notice this Easter some attempt to copy them and an advance
towards the form of the cross in some of the decorations of the graves.
I wish we could get the people to adopt some little design in the
disposition of the flowers upon the graves instead of sticking sprigs
into the turf aimlessly anywhere and with no meaning at all . . . I am
thankful to find this beautiful custom on the increase, and observed
more and more every year. . . . As I walked down the churchyard alone
the decked graves had a strange effect in the moonlight and looked as
if the people had lain down to sleep for the night out of doors, ready
dressed to rise early on Easter morning.[1]

Easter and Ascension Day

The celebration of Christ's rising again and his redemption of the world is
a key moment in the Christian year. Although it is accompanied by a
bank holiday, this festival does not have a large secular dimension, though
it is the one festival that has left a substantial mark on the structure of
churches. Probably the most splendidly decorated element in the
medieval sanctuary was the Easter sepulchre. This took the form of an
empty tomb, and was an important element in Easter ceremonies, which
recall Jesus' crucifixion, the removal of his body to the tomb and his
resurrection on the third day. It was the practice to keep the bread and
wine for the mass, from Good Friday until the Sunday, in this Easter
sepulchre. Quite a number of churches actually built permanent
sepulchres, usually in the north wall of the sanctuary, for the purpose.
They are almost all elaborately carved with scenes of the resurrection and
ascension, and their survival is an indication of the huge importance of
the festival. A group of churches round Navenby in Lincolnshire have fine
examples from the fifteenth century, and they may all be the result of the
efforts of a dynamic local priest. But there are examples from all parts of
the country, stone survivals of what was more commonly temporary.

Quite often these Easter sepulchres include a carved figure of a
Green Man in their decoration. He is one of the most striking
examples of the way in which Christianity absorbed pagan symbols
into its own iconography. The Green Man is a particularly ancient
pagan fertility symbol, often equated with the terrifying horned god
who lived in the forest and controlled all living things, and was the
focus of a number of spring festivals. Christian iconography translated

him into a symbol of Easter and the Resurrection, and he is therefore usually depicted as smiling and benevolent.

In most churches today Easter sepulchres resemble Christmas cribs, though with a model of the tomb. They likewise require open space and again are frequently positioned at the west end. This is appropriate since it was originally at Easter that new catechumens were baptised. Nowadays such Easter sepulchres are decorated with flowers and often described as Easter Gardens. The use of flowers is also appropriate in that Easter falls as spring begins, and the Christian festival was almost certainly grafted on to older pagan rituals celebrating the return of life. However, it was only in the late nineteenth century that the practice of bringing flowers into church for Easter was widely adopted. Francis Kilvert describes one early example:

Mrs Morrell has been very busy all the morning preparing decorations for the Font, a round dish full of flowers in water and just big enough to fit into the Font and upon this large dish a pot filled

Christ rising from the tomb, depicted on a bench end from St James, Hatch Beauchamp, Somerset, of about 1485. (Colin Cunningham)

and covered with flowers all wild, primroses, violets, wood anemones, wood sorrel, periwinkles, oxlips and the first bluebells rising in a gentle pyramid, ferns and larch sprays drooping over the brim, a wreath of simple ivy to go round the stem of the Font, and a bed of moss to encircle the foot of the Font in a narrow band pointed at the corners and angles of the stone with knots of primroses. . . . At 11 [on Easter eve] I went to the school to see if the children were gathering flowers and found they were out in the fields and woods collecting moss, leaving the primroses to be gathered later in the day to give them a better chance of keeping fresh. . . . Found the schoolmaster and a friend staying with him . . . carrying the East window sill board from the church to the school to prepare it for tomorrow with the text 'Christ is Risen' written in primroses upon moss. . . . When it was done the board was taken to the church and left there all night in a cool shady place where the morning sun would not touch it, for if it were laid in its place in the East window over night the early morning sun would wither the delicate fragile beauty of the primroses.[2]

The altar of the church at South Seale, dressed in white for Easter, pictured in 1898. On this occasion a cross in electric lights was set up on the rood beam. (Church of England Record Office)

The mass of flowers makes an obvious visual impact, though different in colour from harvest thanksgiving (see page 117). The use of flowers also led to the need for vases and flower stands. Some of these were made of fine materials and decorated for use in the sanctuary and on the altar. The whole paraphernalia of flower arranging is one more of the backstage elements of a working church that put pressure on storage space.

Two other symbols have an impact on what the Easter visitor sees in most churches. First, Easter is one of the six great festivals for which white is ordained as the liturgical colour, and after the six weeks of dark purple the sudden appearance of white frontals and pulpit falls makes a dramatic change. Secondly, it is at Easter that the old practice of keeping the vigil is most often observed. The Church of England has no ceremony to match the Orthodox Easter at which a single candle is lit at the altar of a darkened church in a darkened village at the first moment of Easter. From the one light, flame is passed to candles held by each worshipper, and then carefully taken home to mark the doorway of each house with the sign of the cross in candle smoke before the feast of Easter begins. In some Anglican churches, as we have seen, this practice is effectively transferred to Advent. However, it is increasingly common to light a candle at midnight on Easter eve. The whole church is darkened as a reminder of the death of Christ, then one candle, the paschal (Easter) candle, is lit to celebrate the return of the Light of the World. This forms the focus of a vigil service, and may be carried round the church in procession. Because of the solemnity of the occasion paschal candles were often elaborate affairs with rich decoration on the surface of the wax. A very few examples of medieval candles survive in museums, but the holders, the paschal candlesticks, are more common objects. Since only a single candlestick was needed, they were often made with especial elaboration, and are richer than the pair of candlesticks usually set on the altar. Such things were mostly destroyed in the years after the Reformation, but the nineteenth-century Tractarian revival led to the production of a number of fine ones, mostly of brass, and generally confined to churches with a strong ritualist tradition. An exceptionally fine one, set about with angels and pinnacles all in brass, was designed for the Roman Catholic seminary at Ushaw in County Durham by Augustus Welby Northmore Pugin.

The principal focus of Easter Day is, of course, the Eucharist, a service that directly recalls the death and resurrection of Christ. Even during the period of Puritan ascendancy in the mid-sixteenth century Easter was one of the three or four occasions during the year when the communion was celebrated. The Easter

The Easter Sepulchre (*c*. 1325) in St Peter, Navenby, Lincolnshire. Beneath are carved three Roman soldiers, recalling the regime under which Christ was crucified. (Colin Cunningham)

mass was (and still is) celebrated with particular ceremony. In the Middle Ages, especially in churches with a ritualist tradition, this required the provision of full sets of vestments and also of space within the sanctuary for all those assisting. All churches, however, needed space for the communicants, who at Easter were supposed to include all those eligible in the congregation. It is very difficult for a large congregation to use a small medieval church for this purpose and the same was true in the Middle Ages. In some churches the mass was celebrated at more than one altar. To ensure that the various celebrants were properly coordinated they were sometimes provided with squints – holes in the pillars against which their altar was set – allowing them to see what was happening at the high altar. Today, concelebration of that sort is rare in Anglican churches (partly through lack of staff) but the bread and wine are regularly distributed from secondary altars whenever the size of the congregation requires it.

In Protestant churches of the sixteenth century much less attention was paid to Easter communion, though the retention of a small sanctuary meant that communicants could usually stand or kneel at the altar rails. In the Middle Ages, when communicants passed through the rood screen to take communion, Easter must have been one of the rare occasions when the average villager came close to the splendour of candles and vestments. When Leeds parish church was rebuilt in 1839–41 a wide open space was provided to the east of the fixed pews to enable communicants to come forward. In most parish churches the survival of the pre-Reformation chancel affords room enough for this, just as it did when first built.

The festivals of Easter come to an end with Ascension Day, which falls on the Thursday forty days after Easter, thus giving a symmetry to the whole season. Again the church is dressed with white hangings, and the ceremonies used to include a procession. The festival recalls the final appearance of Christ after he rose from the dead at Easter and his passing to heaven. This had its symbolic counterpart in the extinguishing of the Paschal candle after the reading of the appropriate scripture at the Ascension Day Eucharist. Thereafter the candlestick was put away and, apart from the Easter sepulchre, all direct evidence of these specific festivals was gone. Yet they form the core of the Christian year, and it must have been a principal intention of the designers and builders of churches that these celebrations could be properly accommodated.

Whitsunday

Whitsunday has red as its liturgical colour, and the association here is with fire rather than blood, for Whitsunday commemorates the descending on the Apostles of the Holy Spirit which is described as coming with 'tongues like as of fire'.[3] It ranks second after Easter among the festivals of the Christian year, and was, from early times, another occasion that was regarded as especially suitable for baptism. Whitsunday falls fifty days after Easter, and its other name, Pentecost (meaning fifty) is derived from the Jewish celebration held fifty days after the Passover. From the early centuries of Christianity Whitsun was celebrated as one of the Octave feasts (that is, feasts which involve eight days of special celebration), with the last day falling on the same day as the first.

There were usually processions to accompany the Whitsunday liturgy, and one has to make a conscious leap of the imagination to recapture their effect on the community. They were important in linking the church as a structure with its community and, since there were special hymns sung at the various feasts including Whitsunday, the sight and sound of such a procession moving through the village or town were a regular part of the impact of religion on the community. Today, in contrast, few churches do more than process round inside the church, but there is a wider connection in the whole meaning of Whitsun. The apostles were commissioned by Christ to preach the word, and it was the descent of the Holy Ghost that enabled them to speak in tongues, and gave them the strength and the ability to do so. This pattern has been emphasised by the Pentecostal churches where baptism in the Holy Spirit is accompanied by speaking in tongues, and where a charismatic Christianity is emphasised. Their movement began in the United States and first appeared in Britain in about 1907. In the 1920s and 1930s there was a considerable growth of Pentecostalism, and the movement now includes a number of very large congregations. This type of worship places much less emphasis on the nature of the worship space than on the activity of the individual in communing with God, and many charismatic congregations worship happily in converted warehouses or cinemas. The impact of the architecture on their liturgy, and vice versa, are less close, and thus form no part of this study.

Another parallel with the meaning of Whitsun can be seen in the missionary church, where the act of bringing the gospel to other races is a continuation of the work of the first apostles. Anglican missionary work was very much a product of the later eighteenth and nineteenth centuries as the British Empire expanded, leaving visible remains in the shape of vast numbers of English-style churches in places that were once colonies. In India it is significant that churches in the hill stations are like so many English village churches, even in their setting as centrepieces of the community, usually at the opposite end of the main street from the town hall or government offices. Their builders were, perhaps unconsciously, trying to recreate the English village life that was 'home' to the British community for whom the resorts were developed. More truly missionary were the churches set up to bring the new religion to the natives, but here, too, the traditional spaces of worship were carefully replicated. St John's Church at Colabar in Bombay is a close copy of the typical large Gothic church, complete with soaring spire. The only concession to the locality is the provision of a large *porte cochère* to shelter worshippers during the monsoon. For the most part the missionaries of the Anglican Church, trained as they were among churches built in the medieval period or in the revived Gothic style, carefully repeated the high nave, with or without side aisles, the bell tower (less frequently the spire) and the spacious chancel if possible. The only concessions to the actual situation tended to be in the use of local materials, and the size of the windows, where hot sun called for small openings rather than the broad openings needed to light the interiors in the gloomy climate of Britain. Even so, the longer established or wealthier a congregation overseas the more effort they seem to have put into creating replicas of the structures that had been developed over centuries of the western and then Anglican liturgy. Even so the many Anglican churches of the wider communion can be seen as continuing the legacy of Whitsunday, a major festival that leaves no visible trace in the churches in which it is celebrated.

The Season of Trinity

Originally celebrated only as the octave of Whitsun, Trinity Sunday did not become a separate feast until the fourteenth century. It marks the end of the festivals of the life of Christ and so is appropriately a celebration of God in all three persons, Father, Son and Holy Ghost. This difficult concept found a ready symbolism in the triangle and groups of three, and leads on to the issue of symbolism in churches. The visual language has probably been more popular with artists than with church builders, and there are even occasions when God the Father is depicted with a triangular halo. Initially, artists seem to have refrained from depicting the Trinity naturalistically, since God the Father, being unseen, was also unknowable. It was more common to use ideograms. However, it is difficult to be sure whether any given triangular form was deliberately chosen for its symbolic value. Some people have even identified the triangular form of the steep gable as symbolic, but the low pitch of most church roofs in the fifteenth century suggests that at that period at least no such symbolism was recognised. Among artists it was more common to depict God the Father as an all-seeing eye, such as appears in the ceiling painting of St Mary Abchurch in London, and there are a number of stained-glass images which show him only as a hand reaching down from the clouds. It was principally the revivalists of the nineteenth century, fascinated by visual symbols, who really chose shapes such as the trefoil for this purpose. Three-light windows could be seen as Trinitarian symbolism, but the plethora of five- and seven-light windows makes it unlikely that there was any such intention in the minds of medieval designers.

None the less there undoubtedly were people for whom symbolism was hugely important. The best known Trinitarian example is the triangular lodge or summer house of the 1590s at Rushton in Northamptonshire, where every detail and dimension is governed by the number three. This is a secular building but its owner was a zealous Catholic, passionately interested in precisely this symbolism. Other Trinitarian symbols are sometimes found in churches. A formal version is the shield with three circles at its corners linked to a single circle at its centre. This sets out very precisely the difficult doctrines of the Trinity, for when fully detailed it has lettering identifying the centre circle as God, and the three around the rim as Father, Son and Holy Ghost. Between these outer circles are the Latin words *Non est*, giving the meaning 'The Father is not The Son is not The Holy

Ghost', while the bands linking to the centre bear the Latin word *est*, explaining that each of the three is God.

However, the whole language of Christian symbols was much more varied.[4] A more common representation of the Deity is to be seen in the letters A and Ω (alpha and omega, the first and last letters of the Greek alphabet), referring to God as the beginning and the end of all things. Many churches have carvings or paintings of the vine and ears of corn, usually in the sanctuary, which refer to the bread and wine of the Eucharist and to Christ's claim 'I am the vine, ye are the branches'. From the Greek we have drawn the common Chi-Ro symbol, looking like an X with a tall P drawn on top of it. The Greek letters stand for Christos, the anointed one, or Christ. The use of this symbol became particularly popular in the later nineteenth and early twentieth centuries, and is frequently found on hangings as well as in carvings. Even more recent is the popularity of the fish sign, the secret sign of the early Christians, whose letters in Greek are the initial letters of the words 'Jesus Christ, Son of God, Saviour'. This is now often found on the covers of service books, on hangings and carved on items of church furnishing. It is also regularly adopted by committed Christians as a personal badge and worn as jewellery and even on car stickers, in something approaching the medieval blurring of the boundary between religion and everyday life.

A still wider symbolism identifies saints and the hierarchies of the church in paintings and carvings. The range is enormous, but it is clear from detailed studies that those who commissioned the carvings and paintings usually had very precise meanings in mind. The modern viewer will need to research the precise meaning of the choice of scenes or symbols depicted in any given church or at any specific time. However, it is equally unlikely that any one congregation would have been able to understand more than a fraction of the symbols available. The crossed keys of St Peter, for instance, are well enough known, as are the unicorn as a symbol of the Virgin Mary and the scroll as that of the five books of Moses. The nails, crown of thorns and lance may be recognised as instruments of the Passion, drawn from the New Testament account of the crucifixion. But the tooth in pincers, for instance, as the symbol of St Apollonia will be meaningless to almost everyone except those who know who St Apollonia was.[5] Even with a scene as familiar as the Annunciation there were nuances of emphasis in the pose of the Virgin, popular at different points in the Middle Ages, which depended on whether she was shown surprised by the sudden appearance of the angel or meekly accepting after he had delivered his message. There is not the scope here to unravel the immense richness of medieval iconography, or even that of the Gothic revival. Besides, the whole arcane business of symbolism was suspect in the eyes of the Puritans, with the result that most churches were subject to deliberate vandalism in the seventeenth century, leaving paintings obscured and carved symbols so disfigured that it is difficult to see what the symbol is, let alone understand what it represents. It is hardly surprising then that there is a good deal of doubt about Trinitarian symbolism.

The feast of Trinity, however, marks the beginning of the long season from the end of Pentecost to Advent, and uses the liturgical colour green. All the remaining Sundays until Advent are numbered as 'after Trinity', a practice that appears to downgrade Pentecost, but in fact was instituted by Thomas Becket to remind the Church of what he considered the momentous day when he was consecrated as Archbishop. The length of the period from Trinity Sunday to Advent means that green is most commonly seen in frontals, and, however attractive the colour is, the visitor needs to remember that the adoption of different colours for the focal points of the church can make a substantial difference to the appearance of the whole. (This is the same problem that faces the occasional visitor to an empty church in peopling it with congregations of the different periods in which it was built.) The empty and superfluous space may be a real problem for the smaller congregations of today. Yet the apparently wasteful space was a vital part of the church's accommodation for elaborate festivals such as Trinity. The buildings were not designed simply for people to sit or kneel in one place during the whole of a service, be it a Eucharistic mass or mattins with a two-hour sermon. The activity of worship in the centuries before the Reformation was closely involved with actual movement, designed to show the world at large the stages of the Christian year; the churches accordingly included space for ceremonial use on great occasions.

Corpus Christi

One final feast, celebrated on the Thursday after Trinity Sunday, is that of Corpus Christi (Latin for the body of Christ). This commemorates the institution of the Eucharist in which Christians consume bread and wine in remembrance of the body and blood of Christ as he commanded on the day before he was crucified. There is no biblical justification for the feast, and it was not adopted until the middle of the thirteenth century. After all, the memorial was also the key focus of the regular masses. In fact the festival should most properly be celebrated on the Thursday of Holy Week, the day on which Our Lord instituted the feast. That, however, was felt to be too intrusive in a week devoted to the Passion, or suffering, of Christ. So the festival was set for the first free Thursday after Easter-tide.

The resulting festival in early summer proved a fine opportunity for a celebration that spilled outside the church, and in towns it became the occasion for the so-called Mystery Plays. In these the various trade guilds each presented a short play in a series which together told the story of Christ's life, his death and resurrection. Corpus Christi was not the only occasion on which the gospel stories were dramatically re-enacted, but it was certainly the greatest and most elaborate. In a medieval town it was one occasion that brought all the churches together, though each play was rooted in the particular church adopted by each guild. Almost certainly they would use their guild chapel or an aisle of their church for the preparation, and one can imagine their float setting off from their church, accompanied by friends and relatives of the performers, to join the procession of carts ready to perform the various plays in sequence. This was obviously a festival confined to the larger towns, and the surviving texts of the Mystery Plays are the York and Wakefield cycles. The very large number of performers required ensured that almost any member of a congregation who wished would be able to play a part, and the plays were a powerful and hugely enjoyable means of familiarising participants with the details of the gospel stories. The floats and the performances were apparently extremely elaborate. Such scenes as the Harrowing of Hell, in which Christ in the day between Good Friday and Easter passed through Hell and rose again, afforded plenty of opportunity for extravagant display as well as caricature of townspeople who it was felt should rightly be in Hell. The surviving texts are sadly incomplete, but it is clear that this was a festival that was hugely popular in the later Middle Ages. The impact on the churches was, however, ephemeral, as the props would only be used for a short period each year. Yet the importance of the guilds in relation to churches is significant. One has to assume that in the weeks before Corpus Christi the aisles of each guild church could have been filled with the sets and props, even perhaps used for rehearsals.

Harvest Festival, Rogation and Beating the Bounds

The Christian year was also linked to the cycle of the seasons, and thus built directly on much older pagan festivities to do with crops, fertility and so on. Such festivals multiplied the calendar of Christian feasts, and some have remained popular to this day. Harvest Festival is one that is celebrated in all churches, though the connection between town churches and produce is now pretty distant. This did not achieve a real status as a Christian festival until the nineteenth century, but since then both town and country churches have regularly been decked with produce. Sheaves of corn, fruit, vegetables and flowers are carefully and laboriously attached to every shelf and bracket in a display that can transform the building utterly. In some churches there is even a tradition of baking a special harvest loaf, typically in the shape of a sheaf of corn or a platter with loaves and fishes recalling the miracle of the feeding of the five thousand. This loaf is then kept carefully, to be brought out and shared (rather stale, it is true) at the Easter communion.

Harvest Thanksgiving effectively took over the older secular feast of Harvest Home. On the continent it is still quite common to come across the last load of corn being carted back to the farm behind a tractor decked out with bunches of whatever has been harvested, and for those involved in agriculture the harvest safely gathered is very much a thing to be thankful for. In the 1960s there was a fashion, still followed in a few town churches, of trying to celebrate an appropriate 'industrial' harvest. Thus a manufacturing community may bring the products of the local factory into church for blessing and thanksgiving. Yet the service is still an autumn one, held at a time that coincides with the harvest of nature.

A lavish display in the chancel for Harvest Festival. The door leads to a small side chapel. (Church of England Record Office)

The cycle of growth, of course, covers the whole year, beginning with ploughing. The first Monday after Epiphany is accordingly kept as Plough Monday, and many country parishes still celebrate Plough Sunday when a plough may be taken in procession through the village and into the church for blessing. In these days of multiple ploughs it is becoming difficult to find a single plough, with the result that an old plough may be kept specially for this purpose, and this too, often gets stored in the church, adding to the museum-like aspect of the building.

Rogation-tide is another festival that has long links with the cycle of the year. It was regularly held on the three days preceding Ascension Day (that is, in early summer), and its Christian intention was fasting and prayer for the harvest-to-be. This naturally linked it to earlier pagan fertility festivals such as the pagan *Robigalia* (from which the name derives) and, like that festival, there were processions through the cornfields with prayers at appropriate spots. Apart from prayers for a good harvest the procession also had a practical purpose in checking the boundaries of each settlement, and it is worth remembering that in the Lenten service of Commination the Old Testament sentence, 'Cursed be

A Rogation-tide service at St Mary, Newington, Kent, in the early 1950s. The choir and congregation process out into the parish. (*Kent Messenger*)

he that removeth his neighbour's landmark' was read out as a part of the diatribe against impenitent sinners. When the rich and riotous processions of the medieval Rogation days were proscribed by the Reformation of 1547 it was soon felt that the practical purpose of beating the bounds of the parish should be continued, and this was the subject of a special royal injunction under Elizabeth I. Occasionally the activity is revived, but more as a parish social activity than as a key religious act. However, the occasional survival of names such as Gospel Oak is a reminder of the places at which the Rogation processions stopped to mark a spot by prayer. They are invariably set on the original parish boundaries, and the procession to them emphasises the important link between the church and its services and the whole of its parish.

All Saints and All Souls

The tail of the year also saw two key festivals, the linked celebration of All Saints and All Souls. All Hallows Eve (or Hallowe'en) precedes 1 November, the Church's celebration of the whole communion of saints on All Saints' Day. The following day is the Christian celebration of All Souls, when all the dead are remembered. Both are ancient festivals, though All Souls' Day was not added until the tenth century, some six hundred years after All Saints was first recorded. Hallowe'en is widely enjoyed as an evening of spooks and pranks, with children demanding trick or treat, and there is a strong pagan element in these activities. The Christian feast of All Hallows Eve was in fact superimposed on the Celtic

The redundant church of St Mary, Stocklynch Ottersey, Somerset, still stands at the centre of its vanished village. (Colin Cunningham)

The high altar of a large town church, St Mary Magdalen, Newark, Nottinghamshire, was given focus in 1937 by a large reredos (designed by Sir Ninian Comper) depicting Christ in glory flanked by scenes from his and the Magdalen's life, and images of saints. The outer wings close like doors but are kept open on festival days. (Colin Cunningham)

The late fifteenth-century chancel of St John, Thaxted, Essex, is hung with banners bearing symbols of saints. A nave altar is to the right. (Colin Cunningham)

At St Mary, Whitton, Ipswich, the priest – controversially – distributes the consecrated bread to children in 1998. The altar rails and sanctuary floor date from 1852. (*East Anglian Daily Times*)

The fifteenth-century pulpit (restored in 1868), a rare survival and taller than many Gothic revival examples, in Holy Trinity, Long Sutton, Somerset. (Colin Cunningham)

The glowing pink sandstone of the imposing church of The Holy Cross, Crediton, Devon (site of an early bishopric), is a reminder of the rich variety of building stones in Britain. (Colin Cunningham)

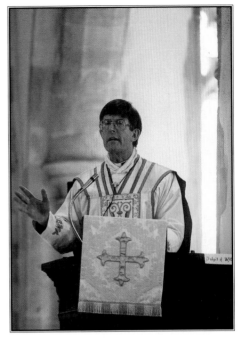

The Easter Sermon in 1997 was given from the seventeenth-century pulpit in the thirteenth-century church of St Mary, Mendelsham, Suffolk. (*East Anglian Daily Times*)

Completion of the Christmas decorations in St Andrew, Great Finborough, Suffolk, 1997. The Christmas tree stands in front of the screen. (*East Anglian Daily Times*)

Bright stained glass in 1869 in St Mary, Fowlmere, Cambridgeshire, represents the Te Deum. The altar is dressed for Lent in penitential purple. (Colin Cunningham)

Easter Eucharist in St Mary, Mendelsham, Suffolk, with spring flowers on every pew. (*East Anglian Daily Times*)

A Plough Sunday procession in the streets of Burwell, Cambridgeshire, in 1994. (*Cambridge Evening News*)

St George and his dragon, a detail of the screen in St Mary, Wellingborough, Northamptonshire (1908–30), one of the last Gothic revival churches and Sir Ninian Comper's masterpiece. (Colin Cunningham)

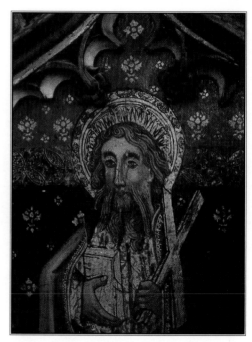

This image of St Andrew was painted on the screen in St Agnes, Cawston, Norfolk, in about 1460. (Colin Cunningham)

Scenes from Christ's life in the east window of St George, Everton, Liverpool (1812–14, by Thomas Rickman). The delicate tracery is of cast iron. (Colin Cunningham)

The large town church of St Mary, Long Sutton, was built by Castle Acre Priory in 1180. Festival banners provide a dramatic note of colour in its dark and massive interior. (Colin Cunningham)

Brick, flint and a variety of stones give a patina to the fourteenth-century tower of St Mary, Lawford, Essex, and reveal centuries of maintenance. (Colin Cunningham)

The recently restored limewash makes All Saints, Witley, Surrey, stand out brightly as many medieval churches must have done. (Society for the Protection of Ancient Buildings)

An angel corbel by William Burges in St Mary, Studley Royal, Yorkshire – a recreated medieval dream of 1871–8. (Colin Cunningham)

St George, Shimpling, Norfolk, a remote thirteenth-century church, is now in the care of the Churches Conservation Trust. (Colin Cunningham)

festival of Samhain at which the dead were propitiated and bonfires lit to express the hope of survival through the long dark winter. For centuries the Church was uneasy about this festival, eventually abandoning its opposition and sanctioning All Hallows fires. This had a useful practical function in the later medieval church, since it became the occasion when the bones which had accumulated in parish charnel houses were removed and burned to make way for new ones. As graveyards became crowded or where there was insufficient depth of soil to allow for more burials this was an essential action, and one that fitted well with the old pagan meaning of Samhain. One presumes that such fires were lit in the churchyard, probably on the unconsecrated north side. The effect of the leaping flames throwing the tracery and pinnacles into sharp light in the darkness and the silhouette of the church lit from behind must have been intensely dramatic. It was a curious foretaste of the floodlighting that is becoming more common today, but the more dramatic because it was done with moving flames and happened only on one day in the year.

The pagan origins of All Hallows and its link with the dead was particularly lasting, and some would argue that it survives still. Even in the late eighteenth century there are records of parishioners waiting in the church porch on All Hallows Eve to hear ghostly whispers from inside the church naming those people destined to die in the next year. But that was Hallowe'en, the evening before All Hallows Day, which became known as All Saints' Day. Where the previous evening had celebrated the departed, All Hallows Day, sometimes called Hallowmas, celebrated all Christian saints, a more hopeful as well as a more firmly Christian celebration.

This festival centred on the usual Eucharist and was an annual reminder to the congregation that they, too, were a part of the communion of saints. It was an opportunity to affirm that the well-known saints, as well as less widely known saintly bishops or local visionaries, and the congregation assembled for the mass were all part of the same tradition and shared the same aspirations. Though the Puritans of the sixteenth century were unhappy about too many references to saints, and despised the idea of miracles and the intercession by saints, the Church of England continues to recognise many saints.

The point of All Saints' Day is to celebrate saints known and unknown, and it should be no surprise that many saintly Christians of the early centuries are now forgotten or their life stories confused and exaggerated. St George of England was the object of much romantic attachment as recently as the nineteenth and early twentieth centuries. He appears regularly on war memorials as well as in plays such as *Where the Rainbow Ends*, now almost forgotten. Current studies suggest that he is largely mythical, and if he did exist he was probably more in the nature of a Turkish warrior, even if he did convert to Christianity. St Andrew of Scotland is directly attested in the Bible, and both St David of Wales and St Patrick of Ireland have a direct link with the development of Christianity in their countries. However, these four saints still have a symbolic meaning that is widely understood and appreciated. There are many other saintly Christians whose existence is well attested and whose spirituality securely documented. St Francis of Assisi, who lived from 1181/2 to 1226, is a prime example, and we have already mentioned St Birinus, Bishop of Dorchester, who died around 650 CE. Individual saints have special festival days; but a few surface more widely in prayers and writings; St Francis, for instance, is recalled in the regular use of the hymn based on the Canticle of the Sun which he wrote in the last years of his life. But mostly they are recorded in the dedications of churches and, as we have seen, their images are carved about the church or painted on the window glass.

While the Roman Catholic Church gives most recognition to saints, and indeed still regularly considers candidates for canonisation, all Christians can recognise the example set by particular individuals who have followed the faith. Pastor Bonhoeffer and Cardinal Romero, one a Lutheran and the other a Roman Catholic, are only two examples from the twentieth century who would be seen as inspiring by most Christians. Attention to their work may well suggest to present-day users of churches what Christianity is about. By the same token the anonymous parishioners who are commemorated by All Souls' Day, and who over the centuries have used and adapted a given parish church, also have something to say. Their witness, however, is mute and can only to be read from the stones they have left behind as reminders of what they did to foster worship in their time.

CHAPTER FIVE

The Parish Church in the Christian World

Dedications and Patronal Festivals

The most widespread recognition of saints in the Church of England is in the dedication of churches. Many are dedicated to Christ, the Holy Trinity or the Virgin Mary, and there are a few named after places such as the Holy Sepulchre in Jerusalem, such as the Holy Sepulchre Church in Cambridge. A substantial number, too, are dedicated to All Saints. However, the practice of dedicating churches to individual saints goes back at least to the fourth century CE, and the dedication may very well be the oldest thing about a church. This might seem of little importance, but dedications take us back to the original intentions of the founders of the church, and may well be significant.

A good many churches are dedicated to St Michael and All Angels, associating them with the archangel who fought with the devil. Quite a few of these are on hill-tops, and it has been suggested that they may occupy former pagan sites, in which case the dedication to St Michael would be particularly appropriate. Churches may also be linked with the events of the life of the saint. Thus it is no surprise to find a church dedicated to St Thomas the Apostle in Madras, since he was supposed to have travelled to India. Not unnaturally, the fashion for a particular dedication was generally in response to events outside the parish. For instance, after the assassination of Archbishop Thomas Becket, a number of churches were dedicated to him; not surprisingly, many of these lie on pilgrimage routes to Canterbury.

Certain saints were considered more effective or were more popular at different times. St George, for instance, is not a major character in the list of western saints but his position as the national saint of England made him particularly popular at times when nationalism was strong. Thus a number of eighteenth-century churches in London, such as St George in the East (1714–29) or St George Hanover Square (1716–31), are dedicated to him. Dedications were particularly useful in towns where they helped to distinguish between churches. Norwich, for instance, had about fifty churches in medieval times. Even so it was often necessary to distinguish churches by location as well as by dedication. Norwich has two St George's and there are also St John Timberhill, St John Maddermarket and St John de Sepulchre. In this case, there is more than one St John, just to confuse matters. Then there are a good many joint dedications, with Sts Peter and Paul, two of the first apostles, being a particularly popular pair.

In other cases there are associations of experience. St Nicholas, a fourth-century bishop from Asia Minor, became the patron saint of sailors, so it is no surprise to find major churches dedicated to him in medieval ports such as Yarmouth, King's Lynn or Old Shoreham. The Church of St Nicholas in Bristol is a particularly apt example, for it was built over the town gate where the road led out to the river and Bristol Bridge. Other dedications may reflect the experience of a given parish and its relationship with the wider world. For example, in the heart of East Anglia stands the little church of St Nicholas Thelnetham. The dedication is unusual inland, yet it has a special meaning here since the village stands close to the source of both the Ouse and Welney rivers, which reach the sea close to St Nicholas' Church King's Lynn and St Nicholas Great Yarmouth respectively. There is a link in the life of medieval England here that deserves pondering, and it is entirely possible that the dedication at Thelnetham reflects actual contact with the two towns.

Finally there are a number of unusual dedications. Some of these are newer churches, such as St Elisabeth of Hungary, built in 1883–5 in Reddish near Manchester, where the dedication was presumably chosen either by the mill owner W.H. Houldsworth or by the priest he appointed to his new industrial suburb. Presumably St Elisabeth was chosen because she was seen as the female symbol of charity, and the church, along with the school, was a charitable donation. Churches dedicated to her are rare in England, though they are common in much of northern Germany. Another English rarity is St Cyriac, to whom one of the two medieval churches at Swaffham Prior in Cambridgeshire is dedicated. St Ethelbert at Fakenham in Suffolk is equally unusual. In each case, however, the choice must have been deliberate and the link with the saint may explain either the siting or the date of the church. Some unusual medieval saints had a particular popularity which led parishes who may have had individually minded priests or patrons to choose them for the dedication. St Margaret of Antioch, a fourth-century martyr, would be one such. She was popular

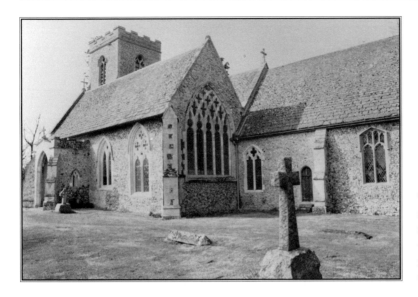

The splendid south aisle of St Nicholas, Thelnetham, Suffolk, with Decorated windows added in the fourteenth century. (Colin Cunningham)

in the later Middle Ages as patroness of women in childbirth, and the church at Leiston in Suffolk is one of those dedicated to her. The present structure is entirely Victorian, but the present dedication is a hint that it replaces a late medieval original, as in fact it does.

More often obscure saints are associated with a particular area, and churches dedicated to them tend to be restricted to that area. They are more common in remoter parts. Wales, for instance, has more than its fair share with dedications to St Ishmael in two villages of that name near Carmarthen and Milford Haven. St Crallo at Coychurch, near Bridgend, or St Teilo at Llandeilo are equally little known, though both villages have fine churches dating back to the thirteenth century. Cornwall has a number of similar rare dedications, such as St Melan at Mullion, St Materiana alone on the clifftop at Tintagel, St Sampson at Golant near St Austell, and St Austolus, with one of the finest towers on Cornwall, in St Austell itself. The north of England has a fair number of churches dedicated to St Cuthbert or to St Aidan, monks from Melrose and Iona respectively, both of whom became bishops of Lindisfarne.

Any saint could, of course, be easily commemorated in sculpture or stained glass, and it would be unusual to find a church which did not have some image of the saint to which it was dedicated. For the visitor to identify them is a harder task since there are a great many, often more than one with the same name, and the number of their attributes is even larger. A dictionary of saints or of signs and symbols is essential. The image might be in the form of a sculpture set in an external niche. Most commonly, the niche over the main door was reserved for the Virgin and Child rather than a saint, but there was always space for other saints in a decorative scheme that might well call for groupings of saints. Sets of window lights or panels on a screen require multiples of images, and the design could be accommodated accordingly. The grouping itself will also have a meaning particular to its church, since that too will have been deliberately chosen. The four evangelists, for instance, form a common group, as do the twelve disciples, and the number of panels or niches may be an indication of the group that filled them. Equally the choice of male or female saints may indicate the gender of the original patron, and hence something of the nature of the church.

Unlike the eastern Christians, the western Church never developed the strict hierarchy of placing that allows a visitor to almost any Orthodox church to work out from the position whether a particular figure was a martyr, a holy warrior, a bishop or a monarch. However, the practice of depicting particular saints in appropriate places was a part of the western tradition. The setting of two figures, St John the Evangelist and Mary, on either side of the cross on the rood screen was simply a depiction of what is described in the Bible. It is also common to find the four evangelists carved on pulpits, a position appropriate to their role. Similarly fonts are often decorated with an image of John the Baptist in addition to other symbols. Many of the surviving images date only from the nineteenth century, because so much had been destroyed before then. The nineteenth century saw the first scholarly interest in iconography, the study of symbols, and it is no surprise that Victorian decorative schemes such as the tile panels of saints inserted in the north wall of All Saints Margaret Street in London display the results of this scholarship with carefully depicted symbols for each image. However, although the Puritans generally removed the heads of images they seem to have been less concerned with the objects the figures held, and these now remain to identify the battered figures that are left.

All churches pay special attention to the patronal festival, the feast day of their particular saint, which is celebrated either on the particular saint's day or on the first Sunday in October. It is a reminder of the founding of the church, and also of its link to the history of Christianity as a whole. There will be, for instance, a recognition of other churches with the same dedication, while reference to saints relates a church to the whole communion of saints, an article of belief regularly repeated in the Apostles' Creed. The patronal festival in pre-Reformation times was a major event, involving a candlelit procession to the church the evening before, and on the day itself a mass and a variety of celebrations that would very likely include a drama and always a feast. These last activities took place outside the church in the unconsecrated ground on the north

During the consecration of this new church, a fairly simple suburban structure, the bishop beats with his staff on the west door. (Church of England Record Office)

side of the church. In towns such occasions would be an opportunity to display the strength (and wealth) of a congregation to the neighbouring parishes. A few developed further into major fairs, such as that associated with the abbey of St Mary and St Helen, a parish church since the Reformation, at Elstow in Bedfordshire. There was some attempt to bring order to this revelry at the time of the Reformation by requiring that all such festivals, known as Wakes, be held on the first Sunday in October. However, the attempt to control a festival so close to the heart of each individual parish was doomed to failure and the order was widely flouted. It was not until 1840, in response to Victorian middle-class sensibility, that the announcing of Wakes from the pulpit was forbidden by Act of Parliament, and the separation of local enjoyment from its religious origin was secured.

The dedication of a church is also linked to the moment at which it was set aside for religious use. Naturally this was a particularly solemn event, and involved the local bishop in blessing the outside and the inside of the church, the procession of the relics (without which it was felt no church could be effectively consecrated), and the blessing of the altar and the altar vessels. One element of this survives today in the consecration crosses. Set just out of reach of vandals, three of these were carved in each of the walls outside and inside, and there was a further set of five on each altar. They were individually anointed with oil by the bishop as he blessed the church. Once consecrated a church could be enlarged, repaired or restored as much as was needed, but it required a special act of deconsecration to remove its special nature. However, there have been so many centuries of rebuilding that few of the original crosses survive, and there is no church with its complete set of twenty-four. The beautiful late fourteenth-century church at Edington in Wiltshire probably has the highest surviving number with twenty-one. They make little impact on the church building, and the exterior ones must have eroded easily, yet those that survive are important reminders of the special nature of these buildings for Christians.

If individual saints were popular in different parts of the country, the geographical area is also important in studying churches, especially medieval churches. As we have seen, the locality gives the physical structure its principal character. There is a strong regional flavour about the medieval parish churches of England that affects not only their form but also their colour, texture and detailing. Fine limestone allowed the building of substantial and richly carved churches from the Cotswolds to Lincolnshire. East Anglian flint allowed richly decorative flint flushwork, while in Yorkshire and parts of Lancashire the hard gritstone of the Pennines produced churches without delicate mouldings or fine carvings whose solidity seems entirely appropriate to the rugged land. The same is true of Cornwall, though there the colour is the lighter grey of the local granite, a marked contrast to the more easily carved strongly tinted sandstones of the softer country of Devon and Dorset to the east. Brick walls and tiled roofs are widely used in the southern counties, but hardly at all in the north of England, where stone slates, often massive like those on the church at Bellingham in Northumberland, protect their buildings from severe weather. Rubble-faced ragstone is common in the churches of London and Kent. Such a list could be easily extended. It is always useful to compare the materials of a church with those of the older walls and buildings around. This regional variety is one of the delights of parish churches in England and Wales. It was only the rise of international classicism in the eighteenth century and the ease of transport in the nineteenth that put paid to the vernacular charm of our churches. Fortunately the architects of the Gothic Revival were fairly quick to appreciate the value of local materials and frequently made careful provision for their adoption, especially in village churches. By the nineteenth century this approach, a central tenet of the Arts and Crafts movement, led architects to produce some carefully vernacular buildings, using traditional methods and giving craftsmen a freedom they had not enjoyed for centuries. Herefordshire has several such churches, such as All Saints at Brockhampton by Ross and St Edward the Confessor and St Mary at Kempley nearby. On the other hand, it is also worth noting that a great many medieval churches, especially those that were built of rough stone or a mix of brick and flint, were regularly plastered and limewashed externally, so that they stood out like beacons against the green of the land. The regular repainting of this lime coating would have been done by parishioners in the same way that they

The outstanding Arts and
Crafts church of All Saints,
Brockhampton by Ross,
designed by W.R. Lethaby in
1901. (Colin Cunningham)

limewashed their cottages and barns. It probably formed a more or less
regular part of the pattern of yearly work, perhaps even being a part of
the preparation for the patronal festival. The Victorians were responsible
for the widespread scraping of surfaces, by then admittedly failing, back
to natural stone or replacing them with hard grey cement render. In the
last decade or so, under the guidance of the heritage authorities, a
number of church architects have begun to return to limewashed
exteriors with striking results.

Martyrs, Saints and Pilgrimages

The publication in 1563 of Foxe's *Book of Martyrs* commemorated,
within a few years of the events, the execution of almost three
hundred[1] people who had supported the Reformation against Queen
Mary. The book was a startling, largely politically motivated,
demonstration of what was perceived as a threat to the Protestant
Church of England, and it was regularly set out in churches along
with the Bible as a vivid, even blood-curdling, reminder of the
terror. Today we are perhaps less ready to look for martyrs, though
the experience of Christians, such as Jergei Popeiuscko, in
communist Poland or even more recently in the Sudan, is a reminder
that Christians may be ready to die for their belief.

   The newly established Church of England in the sixteenth century
was ready to acknowledge martyrs, but the physical evidence for this
was largely in the presence of Foxe's book, which is no longer found in
churches. In the early centuries of Christianity there had been much

more awareness and more widespread experience of martyrdom. Roman emperors such as Diocletian regularly required their subjects to demonstrate loyalty by sacrificing on the altar of the emperor, or of Rome and Augustus. This was unacceptable to Christians, though they protested they were fully loyal to the empire's political establishment. For many, refusal to sacrifice meant death, and the example of these men and women was highly prized by early Christians. Martyrs were ranked before all other saints in pre-Reformation times (as they still are in Roman Catholic liturgy), and their memory was recognised by the colour red for vestments and altar hangings on their annual festivals. Their relics and their names were used in the dedication of many early Christian churches, but that was before many churches were built (or indeed before there were many Christians) in Britain. Some early martyrs, however, are commemorated in the dedication of medieval churches. One of the most widely venerated was Catherine of Alexandria, and her torture on a spiked wheel is illustrated in a number of churches of the later Middle Ages. In Britain the historical event of the martyrdom of the Roman St Alban probably had more impact than the many more distant early martyrs. Not only did he give his name to the town, with its cathedral on the site of his execution, but there are a number of churches dedicated to him. Rather later, the established nature of the Church saw the execution of Charles I as an act of martyrdom, and after the Restoration a few churches, at Tonbridge Wells in Kent and Falmouth in Cornwall, were dedicated to Charles King and Martyr. There was even a special service in the 1662 prayer book to commemorate the execution. But the building of a new church with such a dedication, even more the re-dedication of a new or completely refurbished structure, as at Shelland in Suffolk, marks a considerable show of loyalty on the part of the congregation. Martyrs, like other saints, were a ready source for the decoration of pre-Reformation churches and their images occur in numerous stained-glass windows. They are usually shown with the instrument of their martyrdom, but it requires an iconographical dictionary to recapture their story, and hence the link to the church containing their image.

In the great age of missionary work in the nineteenth century, there were also many priests who lost their lives in remote parts of the empire. A host of eager young men and women travelled in the wake of the empire builders to bring Christianity to the natives. Some were killed in natural disasters, crossing flooded rivers, some died of disease, and a few were actually executed. Most Victorian Anglicans felt unable to recognise them as martyrs, although it could be said that they had given their lives for their faith. There is an interesting chapel in the Anglican Missionary College of St Augustine in Canterbury[2] where the initials of these eager young priests cover the walls, together with a record of how they died. Those who were actually killed have their initials picked out in red, the martyr's colour.

Thomas Becket's murder in Canterbury gave him the status of a martyr and, as we have seen, churches dedicated to him, such as one at Capel near Tudeley in Kent, often lie on pilgrimage routes to Canterbury. The phenomenon of pilgrimage is common to many religions. The Haj in which Muslims make the journey to Mecca probably has the widest draw among pilgrimages today. In the Christian life, pilgrimage was hugely important in the pre-Reformation period; along with its religious function, it had the effect of linking parishes in different parts of the country. The focus of any pilgrimage was the shrine or relic which the pilgrims intended to venerate, and we have already seen the effect a shrine might have on a given church. Pilgrims might travel many miles on their way, and in so doing would visit churches as they passed. The churches along the pilgrim routes would be a continuing reminder of the aim of the pilgrimage, while for each local congregation, the passage of pilgrims would be a reminder of the wider Christendom of which they were a part. The rewards of pilgrimage were supposed to be either a cure or the forgiveness of sins. Pilgrimage was often undertaken in fulfilment of a vow, and votive crosses, recording the vow, can often be found scratched on the churches from which pilgrims set out. Traditionally a pilgrim travelled unarmed, and relied on local charity on the way; most pilgrims also journeyed on foot. The badge of the pilgrim, then, was the staff as an aid to walking and a scallop shell, which could be picked up from the seashore and used as a basic drinking vessel on the way. These symbols are carved on some churches, and may be shown in images of pilgrims.

Of course, the greatest pilgrimage was to Jerusalem, and, as we have seen, there were organisations such as the Knights Templar, who were dedicated to protecting pilgrims on their journeys to the Holy Land. Another very popular destination was the shrine of St James at Compostella in Spain, to which pilgrim routes converged from all over western Europe. However, there were a number of sites of pilgrimage in Britain which have left their mark in churches and the remains of shrines. In many cases the shrine was in the guardianship of an abbey or monastery, such as the relic of the True Cross, or Holy Rood, at Broomholm in north Norfolk. The advent of pilgrims would, however, also bring prosperity to the neighbouring parishes, which may well explain the substantial fifteenth-century parish church at Bacton close by. Similarly, at Little Walsingham in the same county, the Priory of our Lady of Walsingham was guardian of the Holy House of Mary, one of the most popular pilgrimage sites of medieval England. The parish church in the town is also dedicated to Mary, and is a fine large structure of the fourteenth and fifteenth centuries. It is even possible that this richness, deriving from the pilgrimages they condemned, is one reason why the parish church was so badly damaged by the Puritans of the seventeenth century. Its beautiful font, carved with images of the seven sacraments, had its carvings defaced, and no medieval glass survives. It is difficult to tell how far such prosperity might spread in the neighbourhood of an important shrine. The neighbouring church of Great Walsingham is also notably fine, and one might guess that it, too, benefited from the pilgrims in the area. However, it is dedicated to St Peter, and thus would not have been of the same interest to pilgrims.

The effort involved in making a pilgrimage is not easy to recapture, but it is significant that some churches today still organise pilgrimages, to Walsingham among other places. The practice is not common in the Anglican Church, but parishes that do undertake pilgrimages often make contact with others along the route; thus the pilgrimage is a way of linking churches and congregations in different towns and villages, even in different dioceses, at the end of the twentieth century, just as it was for centuries before the Reformation.

Special Festivals and Memorial Services

The Church of England accommodates a wide range of special services, some of which are common to a number of churches. These recognise particular needs or activities in the local community, and the requirements of the services may leave their mark on the church, or churches, involved. Some of the services are constructed specifically to build on a particular association in order to reach a wider congregation. A series of 'Oranges and Lemons' services at St Clement Danes in London was derived from the nursery rhyme. The

In the 1950s an annual 'Oranges and Lemons' service was organised at St Clement Danes in London, aimed principally at attracting children. (Church of England Record Office)

intention was to draw children and young people to the church, and, of course, the success of such ventures leads in turn to the need for more or different accommodation in the building.

One of the most widespread forms of special service is the civic service, and in most towns and cities there is some historic link between the Corporation and one of the older churches. We have already seen the effect of the ancient links between trade guilds and churches, and the connection between a particular church and the local Corporation usually means an access of wealth and a degree of rich embellishment. Traces of these links may be seen in such items as mace rests, or special pews set aside and usually cushioned. However, in our multi-racial society attendance by mayors, aldermen and councillors is becoming rarer and the connections are less visible. In any case cushioned pews are also a relic of the days when individual parishioners might rent their own pew and equip it with cushions for their own comfort.

The front pew in St Mary Abchurch, London, is reserved for civic dignitaries. It is marked by the city's badge of a unicorn with a shield and boasts a handsome iron sword rest. (Crown Copyright RCHME)

In Northampton the civic church is All Saints, which was burnt down in a fire of 1675. The rebuilt church is a splendid classical edifice, reflecting the prosperity of the late seventeenth-century town. It was arranged to provide the maximum seating with galleries, which have since been extended, and a fine pulpit that originally stood in front of the altar. All this dates from the 1680s, and from the same period is a splendid mayor's seat. There is also a grand throne with a coat of arms that was originally designed for the Consistory Court, one of the institutions of the Church's administration and control, that was held in the west vestibule of the church. This is a fine example of a civic church, and, like many civic churches, was at its peak of splendour in the late seventeenth and early eighteenth centuries, when towns were becoming increasingly wealthy and independent. In Ipswich the civic church is St Mary le Tower, a medieval church that was extensively rebuilt in the nineteenth century in response to a period of considerable prosperity in the town. None the less it retains two eighteenth-century sword rests that are relics of its older civic ceremony. The mayor of a borough is

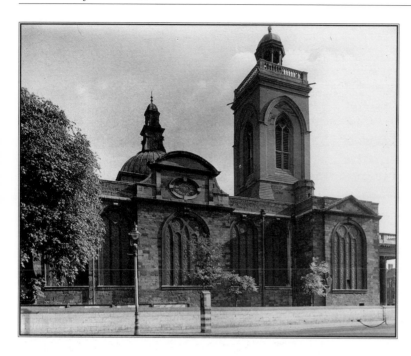

All Saints, Northampton, rebuilt in 1676–80, has a grandeur to match the prosperity of the town. (Crown Copyright RCHME)

always accompanied by his mace and often by a sword, the emblems of the authority of the Corporation. In every civic church there needs to be a place to lay these during civic services. 'Mace rests' seldom date back beyond the eighteenth century, the time when urban organisation and commercial self-confidence became widespread. However, they are often fine examples of ornamental ironwork, and their presence indicates the chief church of any town.

In Cambridge, Great St Mary's, between the market-place and the senate house of the University, acts both as the civic church and the University church. The mace rest is a movable item, which is fitted to the front pew for civic services. The connection with the University left a more permanent mark. There are still regular University services, and in former times it was a requirement that the students attend, so in the eighteenth century galleries were added to provide extra seating, fitted with a pair of special stalls for the Proctors, the University's disciplinary officers. Following the Reformation the church had been reorientated, and the pulpit set at the west end; accordingly the Proctors' stalls are at the east end, allowing their occupants a clear view westward over the congregation, to supervise the young men's behaviour. Oxford, too, has a University church in St Mary's, which is sited close to the University Library. It was where the University library was kept in the early years, and was the site of all University ceremonies until the Sheldonian Theatre (where degrees are awarded) was built in 1663.

There are many other reasons in local industry why a church may become special. In smaller towns along the coast, for instance, there is often a connection between a parish church and the fishing community or the lifeboat crews. Lifeboat Sunday is still a regular part of the year in such places, and may bring together congregations from a number of churches for a special service in the lifeboat station. In such places, tragedies such as the Penlee lifeboat disaster are recorded in memorials, which are linked naturally to memorial services. There are also often other reminders of the local way of life in maritime relics as well as memorials of those lost at sea. Elsewhere the whole church may be a sort of commemoration of a local trade, as in the case of the eighteenth-century church of St George on the Isle of Portland. Built to serve the scattered hamlets of the quarrymen at a time when the export of stone was a major industry, it stands isolated on its hill-top, a large classical edifice built entirely of Portland stone.

The view eastward in Great St Mary's, Cambridge, shows the chancel arch blocked with a massive gallery, and the nave seating largely by means of movable benches. From Le Keux's *Memorials of Cambridge*, 1842. (Courtesy of the Syndics of Cambridge University Library)

Other churches may acquire a special character some time after their original building. St Paul's Covent Garden in London, for instance, which was designed in 1630 to complement the Duke of Bedford's new urban development, has more recently been adopted by the acting profession and is the site of the annual Clowns' service. Its walls are filled with memorials to actors and actresses of the last hundred years or so.

Where an existing church acquires a special function, this will frequently be acknowledged in the adornment of the church. The more important the connection, the richer the adornment – and in some cases the whole church becomes virtually a commemoration of the particular association. In those cases the whole church may become a sort of commemorative artwork. St George, Portland, is almost a work of art in itself in the way it displays the virtues of the local stone. In a similar way, though at a different level, the small parish church at Sandringham in Norfolk became important when Edward VII, then Prince of Wales, bought Sandringham House in 1861. Since that date it has been gradually filled with costly ornaments that reflect its standing as a church

Lifeboat Sunday in Kent. Combined choirs meet for a service outside the lifeboat station. Note the banners of the different churches. (*Kent Messenger*)

regularly attended by royalty. The pulpit, for instance, is made of oak and silver, and the marble font from Florence was a gift from Edward VII himself; the church, though dedicated to St Mary Magdalene, contains an aluminium and ivory statuette of the national saint, St George.

A royal church is a natural focus for costly ornament and artworks, and as a state institution the Church of England has many connections with royalty. From 1688 onwards the celebration of the king's birthday was a major festival that linked secular jollification, often on a huge scale, with a thanksgiving service. The monarch is regularly mentioned in the Sunday services of mattins and evensong set out in the 1662 prayer book, and there were also special services to commemorate the martyrdom of King Charles I, the Restoration of Charles II and the day on which each king began his reign. All this reflects the monarch's position in the Established Church as Defender of the Faith, though this has left little mark on the buildings of the Church beyond the ubiquitous royal arms. These are generally carved or painted on wood, though Puddletown in Dorset has the arms of Elizabeth I painted on the wall of the nave. Under Henry VIII the royal arms were regularly displayed on the rood screen. These were promptly removed under the Catholic Mary I, but after 1614, on the direction of the Archbishop of Canterbury, royal arms were set up in all churches 'with helmet, crest, mantell and supporters in due form as they ought to be, together with the nobel young princes'. The result was a series of often grand coloured boards, many of which can still be seen. There is less evidence of other thanksgivings ordained by the 1662 prayer book, such as for the preservation of Parliament. Today, 5 November is celebrated as an entirely secular firework spectacle, though there was originally a religious element. It is also significant that the controversial fireworks display and bonfire at Lewes in Sussex involves burning an effigy of the Pope, recalling the execution of five Protestant men of Lewes under Mary Tudor.

Services are also regularly arranged for local organisations with some church connection. Most numerous are the Founder's Day services held by the many schools with a church foundation. In many cases, as at Christ's Hospital Horsham, the service takes place in the school's own chapel, and private chapels of that sort are a widespread sub-class of the Anglican Church. Most are of the nineteenth or twentieth century, since the Public School movement, to which most of them belong, was to a great extent a development of the nineteenth century. One of the most dramatic is the chapel built by Richard Cromwell Carpenter at Lancing in Sussex. This soaring Gothic edifice perches on the edge of the Downs as a dramatic assertion of the commitment of its ritualist founder Charles Woodard. At Holbrook in Suffolk a huge cold classical chapel declares the establishment position of the Royal Hospital School for naval cadets.

Many schools, however, have a strong connection with their local parish church, and at Bath, for instance, the Abbey is filled once a year with uniformed pupils and gowned staff from the King's School. In Leeds the grammar school still arranges an annual service in the parish church, and thus maintains a link, although the nineteenth-century rebuilding provided a separate chapel on the school site.[3]

Closely akin to school commemorations are the occasional thanksgiving services arranged by local hospital trusts. These reflect the way in which many of our hospitals had some charitable element in their foundation, which links them to the work of the Church in earlier times. There is also a link in the universal provision of hospital chapels, themselves mostly nineteenth-century constructions, which form part of many hospitals today. Sometimes, as at St James's Hospital in Leeds, the chapel forms a major element in the facade of the hospital. In other cases the chapel is squeezed in among wards and other facilities, as in the old Royal Infirmary at Liverpool where it was fitted beneath the operating theatres. The need for chapels in the workplace continues to be felt, and modern hospitals still set aside space for this. So, too, do airports, and even Stansted, London's newest terminal, has a chapel tucked under Sir Norman Foster's airy steel canopy. The Houses of Parliament have their own splendid chapel in the crypt of St Stephen's hall. Gorgeously decorated with paint and gilding, this is a chapel of the Established Church at the heart of the political establishment, although members of parliament also regard the parish church of St Margaret Westminster as a sort of parliamentary parish church. A very few commercial organisations have also arranged chapels. The Prudential Assurance Corporation, for instance, set aside a room in the tower of its great headquarters in Holborn as a chapel, and equipped it a with lectern and other fittings designed by the architect of the building. Such places are akin to the chapels of ease that we have already discussed, and are in themselves evidence of the religious dimension felt appropriate by the founders or managers of the various organisations. However, any tangible evidence of a connection with a parish church is rare in this sphere.

Partly this is because the services occur only rarely. The same absence of permanent reminders is to be found in the many other special services that are arranged. The Church has organised national days of prayer in times of trouble, and on occasions parishes have arranged special services in response to deeply felt local needs; there are also occasions, such as services for family pets, which acknowledge the cares of groups of parishioners. But for these, all that is needed is the space and the presence of priest and people. The very invisibility of such things after the event is perhaps a reminder that the essential elements of Christianity do not necessarily involve a church building at all. A church is certainly a special place, and it usually bears traces of the activities for which it was designed, but few churches are designed for special occasions only.

The promise of resurrection to eternal life, however, is for many people a driving force in the practice of religion. As we have seen, this is related to the pattern of the sacraments and it focuses attention on the remembrance of those who have gone before. As with the concept of the communion of saints, it links the worshippers of today with previous generations. Individual memory, however, does not last much beyond a generation, which is why the church has always been a focus for memorials, whether of saints or other souls. It has become common, particularly in cases where a person has made a particular mark in the community or in his or her professional life, to arrange a memorial service after his or her death. This may well take place in a different parish from the one he or she lived in, typically in a church near or related to his or her work. The liturgy of such a service is often designed for the one occasion, and a common feature is an address or eulogy on the deceased. This leaves little mark on the fabric of the church, however important the personage or however frequent the use of the church for memorial services. The linking of the home parish church and one near the place of work may also have its importance, but is barely acknowledged in either structure unless there is some form of permanent memorial.

Much of the effort of church builders has, however, been devoted to the memorialising of either events or individuals. Individual memorials are a feature of most parish churches, and are usually funded by a single family or individual. Among the most common are those which record the dedicated service of a parish priest. These are very frequently related to a campaign of restoration in which the priest left his mark on the church. A few may record other aspects of the priest's career, for example missionary work, in the form of items such as crosses of native manufacture brought back from overseas. In London the church of St Mary Woolnoth records the place where William Wilberforce worshipped and was inspired to begin his fight against slavery. There is also a plaque in memory of the saintly vicar who inspired him, John Newton, slave ship captain turned preacher and author of 'Amazing Grace'. The tablet also reminds readers of the link between London and Newton's previous parish at Olney in Buckinghamshire. A more recent memorial, in St Stephen Walbrook, London, commemorates the founding of the Samaritans by the Revd Chad Varah, who was vicar there. The range is enormous and may relate merely to dedicated service in a single place or to a career that affected the whole nation. In almost all cases there is an inscription recording at least the date and the name; these may be in the border of a stained-glass window or on a brass plaque.

This habit of memorialising has, however, brought its own problems. We have already seen how widespread funerary memorials are, and at worst a church may be so full of such things that it is difficult to appreciate the space as an entity. They may even affect the ability to concentrate on worship, and may lead a congregation to clear them away to some obscure corner. At Great St Mary's in Cambridge, for instance, the proliferation of plaques in the nineteenth century resulted in the placing of specially curved brass plaques here and there on the piers of the arcade. Another problem has been that of choosing words that are adequate to recall the individual, but economic enough to be fitted on a plaque. These two difficulties have led Church authorities in this century to restrict the number of memorials that can be allowed. A case needs to be made that the contribution of an individual really represents a major element in the religious life of the parish, and wording may be closely scrutinised. One Suffolk parish wanted to record a life of support for their church from one parishioner with the words 'He Gave His All'. The claim was felt to be extravagant until it was demonstrated to the visiting archdeacon that it was precisely the truth, and the plaque was promptly installed. Such devoted service by anonymous individuals is not infrequently the reason why a particular church survives at all.

Another common way of memorialising, particularly in the nineteenth century, was by dedicating a stained-glass window.

Stained glass had been common in the medieval period, but, because many of the windows contained images of saints, they proved offensive to the Puritans of the seventeenth century, and most churches were re-glazed throughout in clear glass. Although there are a few examples of eighteenth-century glass, it was the Gothic Revival of the nineteenth century which really revived this habit. The craft was virtually reinvented, with small pieces of coloured glass held together by special strips of shaped lead called *cames*. The best designs were drawn in such a way that the cames followed the outline of individual parts – a face, a wing or a hand – of the figure. A window may commemorate parishioners who have died far away, perhaps in one of the many wars that Britain fought, or who simply moved away from the parish they were born in. Alternatively, they may simply commemorate a benefactor, not even necessarily one dead. A great many commemorate the clergy, since the insertion of a stained-glass window is often the final stage in the beautification or restoration of a church, which was often the life's work of an incumbent. The vast majority of windows carry an inscription, usually in almost illegible Gothic script, which records this.

By their very nature windows can be filled with a huge range of images and most were carefully designed to remind church users of aspects of their faith and to assist the liturgy. There may be scenes from the Bible; there was an ancient tradition that scenes from the Old Testament were set in windows on the north side, and scenes from the New Testament on the south. Where this happens, the New Testament scenes are inevitably appreciated as brighter since it is through them that the sunshine enters the church. Other windows may depict saints, particularly the saints to whom the church is dedicated, and there may even be scenes of the building or founding of the church in which the window is set. Others show acts of charity, especially if they can be associated with the person commemorated, and some churches

A fragment of medieval glass set in the restored chancel window of St John, Stanton St John, Oxfordshire. (Colin Cunningham)

contain windows depicting the virtues, even the vices. Of course, since the iconography was so varied, the meaning could be related to the particular opinions of the vicar or his patron. Images of saints were a great deal less popular with Low Church clergy and even the crucifixion was less acceptable than the Last Supper in churches where ritualism was suspect. Sometimes a whole church would be fitted out with windows at the same time, so that the entire set could tell a consistent story. More often, however, one or two windows were given over a period of time, and a great many parish churches have some windows that remain clear glass. It is a reflection of the fact that not all parishes were able to call on major benefactions even in the nineteenth century when so much attention was paid to religious observance.

Memorials of any kind are closely allied to funerary monuments, which we discussed in the context of burial. Indeed it can be argued that memorials separated from the place of burial have effectively taken the place of laudatory funeral inscriptions for all but a few. One widespread form is a Book of Remembrance which contains the names of parishioners who have died, but who, in what is now a common response to the problem of burial space, have been cremated elsewhere. Such books are regularly displayed in a case, and often an area of the church is set aside nearby for private prayer and reflection. An extension of this practice is that of memorialising individuals or groups in their parish church with a plaque or inscription. An inscription can record something of the career and commitment of the person, and may take a variety of forms. They may also demonstrate a particular congregation's reaction to events in the world around. They are, however, widespread and recall a good deal of the history of worship in any church. It would be impossible to detail the whole range of events or acts recorded in this way. They can be divided into individual and group memorials, and among group memorials there are such things as records of large-scale loss of life in shipwrecks, or more unusually, at the river port of Outwell in Norfolk, the arrival of cholera in the early nineteenth century and the havoc it wreaked among the congregation.

Some churches commemorate a link with a particular regiment, and their memorial often incorporates the display of standards that have been laid up in the church. When a war memorial or regimental memorial is placed in a church it is almost invariably set in the nave or aisles, rather than in the chancel, and it is often accompanied by regimental or British Legion banners set alongside it. A few churches, such as St Clement Danes in London, are dedicated in their entirety to a branch of the armed forces, in that case the Royal Air Force. More recently there have been a number of memorials recording the presence of American forces in the Second World War. The presence of an airfield and the arrival of large numbers of allied airmen would have been a major event in the history of the small villages where the wartime airfields were hurriedly laid out, and some permanent record of the impact on the congregation is important in reflecting their contact with events in the wider world. These memorials often take the form of a stained-glass window which may actually show the events recalled. Over the centuries some churches have acquired a number of such things, which adds to the museum-like quality of the space; but it is important to remember that the effort and expense involved in setting up each memorial does reflect a serious concern on the part of the congregation at the time to show their involvement in whatever catastrophe or achievement is commemorated.

There is usually some sort of war memorial in a church, and this is still the focus of a Remembrance Day service. Such services involve the presence of the armed forces and the British Legion who will process into the church with their banners. The occasion also used regularly to involve other organisations, like the Boys' Brigade or the Scouts, and the connection of such groups with a given church may leave its mark in the dedication of banners in the same way as commemoration of regiments. Frequently these banners are kept in the chancel, and in some parishes there are regular parade services at which the banners are brought to the chancel in procession.

The presence of banners is an echo of the pre-Reformation practice of carrying such items in procession, and banners can make a considerable impact in a church, whether carried in procession or merely hung along the arcade. They are generally temporary, being brought out for special occasions only, but they may make reference either to national organisations and identities or to specifically religious ones. One of the most common religious banners today is that of the Mothers' Union, frequently to be found leaning by the altar. In that 'storage' position it does not have the same impact on the church as when carried in procession, and it is the use of such things as a part of the liturgy that really justifies their existence.

The most widespread form of memorial is the war memorial itself, and that, too, is associated with burial, though few of those who gave their lives in service were buried in their native parish. A few churches, like Great St Mary's in Cambridge, contain memorials of earlier conflicts such as the Boer War. However, the experience of the First World War touched every parish in Britain, and that 'war to end all wars' led to an interesting approach to memorials. Officers and other ranks were buried with identical tombstones, and there was no

A range of organisations attend parade services and dedicate their banners in the parish church. (Church of England Record Office)

distinction of social status in the shape of the stone, as had been common in earlier centuries. The communal reaction to the cataclysm recognised the fact that all were equal before God, and the sacrifice was the same whether it was made by an officer or a private. Most of the war dead are, of course, buried near where they fell, but in a few churchyards one can see one or two low white stone tombstones of the standard Imperial War Graves Commission design marking the graves of men who returned to 'Blighty' to die of their wounds.

The horrors of two world wars have also given rise to another commemorative offering, the war memorial window. This may be in memory of an individual or simply dedicated to all those from the parish who fell. Most depict angels, often St Michael in full armour, and there are a few with curious illustrations of warfare, such as St Mary Swaffham Prior in Cambridge, with its pale portraits of a Zeppelin and a fortified trench. Relatively few have strictly biblical scenes, such as the resurrection, which ought to be appropriate. Of course, stained glass is by no means the only type of memorial, and many fittings in churches were added in memory of those killed. One of the most touching is the side altar in St Mary Burgate in Suffolk. There a returning army chaplain installed (in the face of some Episcopal disapproval) an altar entirely furnished with candlesticks, vases and so on made from used shell cases in a casualty clearing station by wounded soldiers. The chaplain's own tin helmet is stored beneath it to this day. More frequently some major item was made for the church, and since the fashion for the ritualism of the nineteenth century was on the wane by 1918 a new reredos or new altar is quite a common form of First World War memorial. Thus the corporate commemoration of the dead is linked to a modernisation of the liturgy that arose from the controversies over ritualism and sought to bring services such as baptism, communion and marriage into closer touch with the twentieth-century world. They belong with the compromise prayer book of 1928.

In many towns the main war memorial is not even in the churchyard, and it is important to remember that those who were being commemorated were by no means confined to the Anglican Church, nor even to the Christian faith. None the less there was a deeply felt need at the time for the sorrow to be recognised in some form of ritual on the part of the establishment. The actual memorials vary. Some parishes commissioned their own, with sculptures of varying quality, but the national memorial – a tall octagonal cross set with a sword, designed by the architect Sir Reginald Blomfield – stands in many churchyards and links parishes from all parts of the kingdom. These memorials, too, are part of the focus for the annual Armistice service at the eleventh hour of the eleventh month.

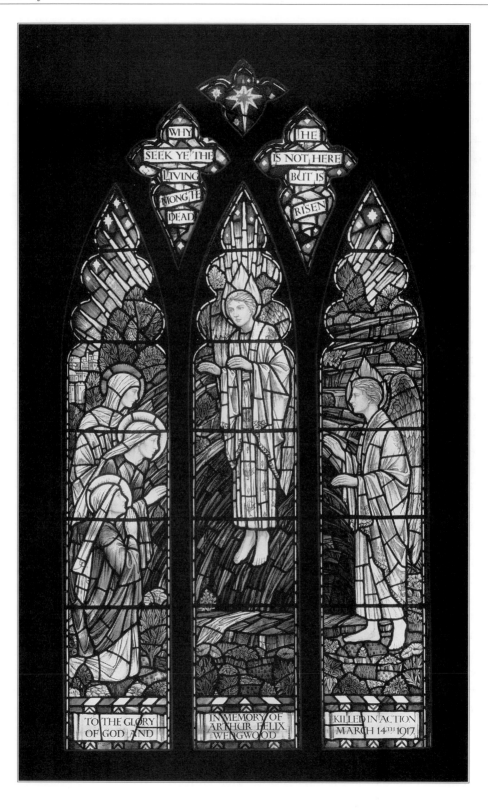

WHY
SEEK YE THE
LIVING
AMONG THE
DEAD

HE
IS NOT HERE
BUT IS
RISEN

TO THE GLORY
OF GOD AND

IN MEMORY OF
ARTHUR FELIX
WEDGWOOD

KILLED IN ACTION
MARCH 14TH 1917

Much rarer is the memorial of thanksgiving for escape from disaster. At Rodney Stoke in Somerset, for instance, a stained-glass window records the safe return of all the men of the village from the First World War. Only thirty-two parishes in the country were able to give thanks for such a safe return.

The installation of a memorial inevitably involves some creative effort, and it is in the whole range of memorials that we see most clearly the insertion of artworks into churches. The practice of giving works of art to churches has a long history. Effectively, all ornaments can be seen as works of art, and it is clear that the beauty of the various objects was an important consideration in the minds of the donors, alongside their function. Some of the most individual medieval works of art are the gargoyles that drain water from medieval roofs, or the rows of heads that ornament string courses. These

A nineteenth-century gargoyle on William Burges's church of Christ the Consoler, Skelton, Yorkshire (1871–2). (Colin Cunningham)

seem to have offered medieval craftsmen a much freer hand in imaginative design, and include a whole range of terrifying, surprising, and even obscene human and animal figures. The presence of such features on churches is generally considered to be a matter of warding off evil spirits, and such sculptures are always on the outside of churches. They were seldom defaced by the seventeenth-century Puritans and thus there are more survivors, and we tend to value them as works of art because they demonstrate originality. However, this was probably not a priority for the masons who carved them, though happily the tradition of allowing masons a free hand with such things is very much alive, and there are modern replacement gargoyles with caricatures of sextons or of local worthies. The tradition was, in fact, recovered in the nineteenth century by the architects of the Gothic Revival, and there are splendid modern examples such as the dachshund atop a gargoyle on the church of Christ the Consoler at Skelton in Yorkshire.

There are a few occasions when a whole church is actually conceived as an artwork. One of the best known is the War Memorial Chapel at Burghclere in Hampshire, whose walls and vault are entirely painted with designs by Stanley Spencer. The building is not a parish church, but a private chapel; what makes it interesting is that

(Opposite): The Resurrection makes an unusual, but appropriate subject for this war memorial window of 1926 by Donald Milner, formerly in the Ivy Hatch chapel of ease in the parish of Ightham, Kent. (Courtesy of Mr K.F. Cunningham)

the architect, Lionel Pearson, worked with the artist and incorporated his suggestions as to structure and the outline of mouldings to make the whole building a frame for the remarkable series of First World War paintings. Significantly the chapel is dedicated to All Souls, and the commission incorporated a set of almshouses as well as the chapel. It is now in the control of the National Trust.

Similarly the addition of an extensive range of artworks may make a dramatic impact on a particular church. The Norman church of St Michael at Garton on the Wolds in Humberside was dramatically altered when the entire interior was covered with decorative paintings in the 1870s. It is at least likely that the provision of schemes for wall paintings made the same dramatic impact in the Middle Ages. Today the recovery and restoration of medieval wall paintings can also change a church radically after years of concealment under whitewash. The insertion of stained-glass windows can have a similar effect, and there are a number of examples where a consistent design is followed throughout the church, creating a single artwork out of the whole. The tiny parish church of St Nicholas Moreton in Dorset, for instance, was entirely fitted with windows of plain etched glass designed by Lawrence Whistler in the years from 1955 to 1984. At Tudely in Kent the parish church was refitted with a complete set of windows by Chagall. Such major schemes are, however, uncommon and usually represent the particular interests of a major patron or some special function of the church.

It was always more common for a part of a church to be set aside for receipt of an artwork than to be an artwork in itself. Many medieval chantry chapels could be described as works of art, and there are numerous examples of chapels being entirely redecorated as such in the nineteenth century. The Coleridge memorial chapel designed by Butterfield in 1879 for St Mary at Ottery St Mary in Devon is a good example, where the mosaic and tile panelling are foreign to the medieval church, but typical of the nineteenth-century passion for polychrome decoration.

Sometimes artworks were bought as antiques and then installed in a church. Two churches in Bedfordshire, St George at Cockayne Hatley and St Leonard at Old Warden, are filled with fine ornamental woodwork, mostly from medieval churches of the Low Countries, which was bought by the local landlord or vicar and reassembled in his church. A little later, committed Christians, such as Athelstan Riley, used to purchase works of art and make gifts of them to churches with which they or their family had some connection. At Cavendish in Suffolk a sixteenth-century Flemish alabaster sculpture, which was originally in Athelstan Riley's personal chapel, was given by his descendants to the church; it was set in a special frame, carved with its own sculptures, and painted and gilded by Sir Ninian

Comper. More recently Henry Moore was commissioned to design a Madonna and Child for the Church of St Peter, Northampton.

The list of fine additions conceived as objects of beauty in themselves, as well as being useful or functional, is almost endless. The south doorway of St Mary the Virgin in Oxford, a splendid baroque structure with barley sugar columns, stands out in contrast to the medieval fabric of the church but it is an exceptionally fine doorway and was undoubtedly intended to be an artistic embellishment of this important church. More widespread are smaller items such as the tiny medieval bronze figure of the crucified Christ that was found near the church and set on the processional cross of the parish church of North Leigh in Oxfordshire. The little church of St Mary at Thornham Parva in Suffolk boasts a fine fourteenth-century reredos that was actually a retable for a much grander church, lost presumably at the Reformation and built into some corn bins. At Tardebigge in Worcestershire the lectern was a late nineteenth-century gift in the Art Nouveau style, inlaid with mother of pearl. Similar fittings are found in the new parish church of St Mary at Great Warley in Essex. This replaced an earlier church, Christ Church, in 1904, and was filled with what Pevsner describes as 'an orgy of the English Arts-and-Crafts variety of the International Art Nouveau'. The font is supported by standing bronze angels, the walls are decorated with panels of lilies, and the screen has flowering fruit trees in copper.

Paintings are almost the only type of artwork to be uncommon in Anglican churches today. Before the Reformation, as we have seen, it was common for walls to be painted, and the few surviving examples are highly valued. Most were painted over by the Puritans or later restorers, but occasionally a modern campaign of repair will uncover new designs. From the eighteenth century it became common to hang pictures in churches and some of Constable's first commissions were for such works. By and large these have now been removed to art galleries where they can be better conserved – but it has to be admitted that many such paintings were copies of late Renaissance paintings of the Italian school, more suited to an Italian baroque church. In the few churches that retain paintings, often in conventional gilt frames, they tend to contrast awkwardly with the medieval architecture; moreover, since many of them are eighteenth-century copies their colours have often darkened somewhat. Occasionally a modern artist is commissioned to paint the walls of a church or of one chapel. Hans Feibusch is one artist who has undertaken such work, for instance in the rebuilding of St Alban Holborn after the war. Occasionally, too, a local artist is commissioned, as in the case of the pre-Raphaelite painting of Christ and the little children by Miss Curtois in St Mary Whaplode in Lincolnshire. Here, the models were local schoolchildren. At Huntingfield in Suffolk the vicar's wife painted the entire roof of the church with brilliantly coloured angels in a glowing recreation of a medieval concept. Today there are a large number of artists designing for churches, and stained-glass windows are still regularly being inserted. Etched glass is also increasingly popular and there are letter carvers of distinction designing both plaques for church interiors and tombstones for the churchyard.

Outreach and the Mission Field

One rare type of church that was designed to fulfil a special function is the memorial church. Perhaps the most famous in its time was the Crimea Memorial Church. This was another war memorial, recording the nation's grief at the tragedies and thanksgiving for the eventual end of the Crimean War, but instead of an empty monument it took the form of a complete Anglican church designed by George Edmund Street. It belongs effectively to another category of Anglican building, the church overseas. In the years after the Napoleonic wars, the British travelled abroad in increasing numbers, and many settled in warmer climes. They generally remained loyal to their Protestant faith and a number of Anglican churches were built for expatriates and visitors. They are to be found in all the places where the Victorians regularly holidayed, such as the Alps, Italy and Greece. In Florence, where there was a sizeable expatriate community (which even had its own cemetery), the stables of a renaissance palazzo were converted to form the church of St Mark. In the baroque city of Rome, G.E. Street designed a redbrick Gothic church that announced Anglicanism in the heart of the Roman Catholic

A wedding in the nineteenth-century Anglican church at Grindlewald for a couple on holiday in about 1955. The richly carved woodwork is about the only concession to local craft traditions. (Canon W.E. Purcell)

The Anglican (Episcopal) chapel at Pompion Hill, near Charleston in South Carolina, is a neat Protestant hall with its entrance in the centre of the south side. The pulpit occupies the centre of the east wall in an arrangement familiar to Nonconformists. (Colin Cunningham)

world, and which would not have looked out of place in any English nineteenth-century town. Even classical Athens has its Gothic church, complete with stained-glass windows in memory of a party of tourists assassinated by brigands, that looks adrift in comparison with the Orthodox Byzantine churches that are the norm in that city.

Anglicanism was a natural export into the British Empire, and Anglican churches survive in most places where the British claimed territory. Among the less well known, but a tribute none the less to the Establishment nature of the Church of England, are a few churches built around Charleston in the eighteenth century. The little chapel at Pompion Hill (1708) or the later St James at Goose Creek attest by their size the smallness of their congregation, but their neat completeness, with box pews and fine woodwork, displays the status of the Established Church in what was still then part of the British Empire; their pulpits, centrally placed at the east end, demonstrate the Puritan nature of the worship they were designed to house. Later, such structures were succeeded by a whole host of Episcopal churches which continued the same liturgy in an era of independence. Canada, Australia, New Zealand and, to a lesser extent, South Africa can all show similar buildings for their congregations of British emigrants.

These, of course, were all churches built for established congregations that had moved to new territories. There is yet another type of structure that needs to be considered: the mission church. True, there were mission churches in England, designed, mostly in the later nineteenth century, to take the established religion into the slums of industrial towns where it was felt the Church had failed. Many of these were erected by evangelising clergy of the Tractarian movement, and they are often richly decorated in an attempt to bring some colour to lives that were altogether starved of visual beauty. Churches such as St Benedict in Gorton in Manchester or St Philip in Wapping are good examples, and even All Saints in Margaret Street was richly decorated to bring a sense of the numinous and the Glory of God into a slightly run-down area of central London. Many of these churches were in districts that were later organised as separate parishes.

However, it was the overseas empire that really led to missionary building in the sense of taking the Church of England to native populations. The history of Christian missions is not without controversy, but it was a phenomenon that followed closely in the wake of empire building; some missionary priests, such as Bishop Colenso of Natal, were not only deeply loved by the people to whom they preached, but also widely, if controversially, known in England. The heyday of colonialism was effectively from 1850 to 1914, and many missionary churches were built in that period, particularly in Africa but also in other parts of the empire and in lands with which Britain was trading. After 1914, though colonialism was disappearing, the missionary effort continued, and Anglican dioceses became a part of the life of newly independent countries. To serve this the process of church building has continued in many countries of Africa and elsewhere. However, two characteristics seem to stand out increasingly. In the first place most of the native congregations were poor, and their churches are correspondingly plain and undecorated. Secondly, there was a growing awareness of the need to respect not only local climatic conditions, but also local traditions of building. This means that many African churches are built with low walls and small windows to keep out the heat. Thatch is a common roofing material and most of the structures are of brick rather than the more expensive stone. On the other hand a good many churches built in the mission field still house active and committed congregations, and there are a number of spacious churches which make their English village cousins seem small by comparison. Another feature of these churches is that they are almost all built in one go, whether they are the older churches of the nineteenth century or newer ones of the twentieth. Sheer size witnesses to the vigour of the congregations, and the general simplicity is in keeping with the present fashion for less decoration even when the liturgy itself is rich.

Anglican churches overseas are, as we have seen, often determinedly derivative of what was the norm 'at home' when they were built. They served an expatriate community who sought to retain the modes and practices of their own civilisation, often at considerable cost, wherever they were. India has a particularly rich crop of such structures. Under the British Raj (1858–1947) the Church of England was the established church in India as well as in England, though few Indians adopted Christianity, and not all of those Anglicanism. Since they belong to the period of the British Empire, Anglican missionary churches are all more recent structures, and not an amalgam of constant alterations from a medieval original. This often makes them clearer statements of a particular liturgical position. The churches built in India were largely designed for the expatriate community, which meant in most cases for the military. One of the most impressive is the garrison church of St Martin just outside Delhi. A huge gaunt pile of brick, pierced only by small windows to keep the interior cool, it is a bold landmark, a traditional cruciform shape with a central tower, but plain in keeping with the twentieth century in which it was built, and arranged for a large congregation of ordinary soldiers rather than for any elaborate ritual. In the cities of the empire the nineteenth-century colonisers built and rebuilt churches in much the same way as was happening at home. St John's Church in Colabar, Bombay, has already been mentioned, but the permanent British presence in India went back well before the nineteenth century, and in Calcutta, Madras and Delhi there are a number of fine neo-classical churches that echo the forms that were being erected in the cities of England at the time. The Church of St James, Delhi, for instance, commissioned by Colonel James Skinner, is a sophisticated piece of classicism with an octagonal nave and three pillared and pedimented porches. St Mary's Church in Madras, the oldest surviving example of Anglican building in the sub-continent, is a simple classical rectangle with small chancel to the east and tower to the west. Begun as early as 1678 it is an architectural cousin of the churches in the City of London in which the Directors of the East India Company worshipped.

A familiar classical style for the expatriate community at St James, Delhi (1820–36). (Colin Cunningham)

CHAPTER SIX

The Parish World

The Church in a Place: Church Sites

A church serves the spiritual needs of its congregation, yet religious belief sees no firm divide between activities in church and daily life. As a building a church is in the world but not of it, and so its site and surroundings are often as important as the building itself. In the same way that movement through the varying spaces of the church has meaning in relation to the act of worship, so movement around the church and in its vicinity, though part of the normal pattern of life and work, acknowledged the church and its site as a focus. As places of Christian worship churches were almost invariably laid out with their sanctuary to the east. This acknowledged the symbolism of Christ, the Sun of Righteousness, rising to heaven just as the sun rises in the east. It was also the case that for most Christians, since the faith developed round the Mediterranean, east was the direction of Jerusalem, which in the eyes of medieval cartographers was the centre of the world.

Many of the first churches, however, were built on the site of older, pagan holy places, such as groves or wells. Pope Gregory in the seventh century wisely decreed that such places should not be destroyed but furnished with altars so that they might 'become temples of the true God'. Many such sites are marked by circular churchyards. Other churches were built to accompany new farms or *vills*, as the Norman lords established their rule. Where such places developed into lasting communities the church was already there as a physical focus, and the various routes though the place would be focused on it. This was not merely because the building was there, but because it was the locus of so many events in the life of the people. Baptisms, weddings and funerals all brought them to the church, as did the festivals of the Christian year. But worship was a great deal more than an occasional or weekly visit to the church. Although the laity took little active part in the liturgy, it was common to attend and hear mass daily. There are numerous records of people, not always conspicuously devout, hearing

This aerial view of Swaffham Priory, Cambridgeshire, shows the two churches, St Cyriac (left) and St Mary (right), in one churchyard. They are orientated to the east, rather than aligned to the street. The graveyard has been extended. (Crown Copyright RCHME)

mass three or four times a day. It did not mean that all their time was spent in worship, for it was also accepted that the church was the meeting point of the community. It was perfectly common to go to church to conduct business during the mass, merely falling silent for the most sacred moments.

As each community grew and prospered, so the building would not only be enlarged and beautified, but it would also become accepted as the principal focus of the place. It is for this reason that many town churches stand at the head of a market-place, and they were often the background to markets and fairs. The annual hiring fairs, crucial in the pattern of agricultural employment, were linked to Candlemas (2 February), and many fairs were announced by the display of a stuffed hand hung on the church as a sign of contracts to be made. It is usually only the open space nowadays that indicates this crucial role of a church. The little church of St Giles in Oxford, for instance, standing today at the head of a wide area of parking and four lane highways, is a reminder of the great medieval fair that was held just outside the walls of the city. The vast majority of our country or small-town churches, however, still dominate their surroundings. They act as landmarks along the main street, while the churchyard often provides one of the principal open spaces of the town or village. In fact churchyards have been used as meeting places since the arrival of Christianity, and often before.

Some churches were set apart from their village. Villages in the flood plain of the Wye, for example, often built their churches on high ground, whereas the people lived lower down where it was convenient for their work, only moving uphill in times of flood. A number of churches are in apparently uninhabited places, a reminder that the building and its churchyard may outlast the community for which it was originally constructed. There are cases where a village has ceased to exist altogether, leaving only the church standing. Not all such churches are abandoned, however, since the care of them often passed to a neighbouring parish, and there might be special features, the presence of a relic or holy well for instance, that kept alive an interest in the place. In other cases the village might have been moved, though it was clearly not so easy to move the consecrated church. The Black Death in 1348, for instance, reduced a number of communities to utter desolation. When the inhabitants returned after the plague they preferred to rebuild on a different site away from their original plague-ridden dwellings. In such cases, as at Comberton in Cambridgeshire, the parish church often stands a little out of the village, though still fully functioning. Later still, when many great lords were busy rebuilding manor houses and embellishing parks, it was a common practice to resite the village at a decent distance from what might once have been simply a large house in the village centre. In many such cases the church survived as an ornament in the park, and the villagers would still worship in the traditional space even though their new homes might be a mile or more away on the edge of the park. The process continues with the movement of town dwellers to further and further suburbs, often leaving city centre churches stranded in a weekend desert of uninhabited commercial property.

If the regular pattern of medieval life took many members of the community past their church during the week, worship and special festivals brought them into the building as well. The routes into the church are thus as important as its site, and as its several parts. There is a deep symbolism in thresholds, and the act of passing from one space to another through doorways was always considered important in the use of churches. Thus in addition to the complex edifice, its site and its surroundings, there was a liturgical element in the way it was approached and entered. Such was the power of this symbolism that not only were doors regularly ornamented, but they were also frequently preserved when a church was rebuilt and refixed in the new wall. There are, for instance, a great many more doorways surviving from the Norman period than there are churches where much else from that period is visible. The west door was most frequently used for processions, since it gave an immediate view right through to the altar. Worshippers would usually enter through the south door, which thus became associated with their secular life and became a sort of halfway house between the sacred space of the church and the secular world in which they lived and worked.

The obvious sense of value that earlier generations found in their church buildings, and the creative energy that they lavished on their construction, is a constant reminder of the key role these places played in their lives. In our secular age it is less easy to appreciate the close involvement of the religious dimension with the normal pattern of living. Yet for the vast majority, throughout the Middle Ages and after until local communities began to break down in the industrial period, the church (or chapel) was the physical focus of an accepted spiritual need. It was to meet this need that the Church developed patterns of worship that changed, even passed through revolutions, as society developed, but which always recognised something for which there is no better term than holiness. In accommodating that concept and finding agreed methods of responding to it the Church as a body devised step-by-step these complex and varied buildings. Each one is different, but all bear mute witness to the faith and the practices of worship of their various builders.

Extravagant Norman carving on the south door of St Mary and St David, Kilpeck, Herefordshire. (Colin Cunningham)

The Church as a Secular Focus

It is a truism to say that each church became the focus of its community, and that it is a special place both in the world and not of it. But that reality embraces the sense in which each church building reflects links with the secular world it served. As communities grew over the centuries, so their churches developed to accommodate secular as well as spiritual needs, and the medieval church was very far from being merely a place of prayer reserved for the 'sacred mutter of the mass'. For a start the church was the physical focus for secular management of the parish. It was usually the largest building in the place, and provided satisfactorily neutral ground for meetings. The lord of the manor was naturally the effective ruler of the community, and dispensed justice from his own hall, but, if there was a need for discussion between parishioners over such things as the markers that divided their strips of cultivation, the church was often the most convenient place for it. Indeed supervision of that area of village life was, as we have seen, one of the purposes of the Rogation processions. In towns where there were more people and a number of different parishes in the same large community, it was easier and more effective to manage local affairs through the trade guilds, from whose meetings developed our town councils. But in most of the kingdom the practice of holding meetings open to all the congregation in the church was the only possible forum for local government, and these became known as vestry meetings. In the early Middle Ages, however, the incumbent may well have been the only literate (or half-literate) inhabitant outside the lord's household. As such, he would have been the natural co-ordinator of secular meetings in the parish. It is probably from this that the system of administering parochial affairs through vestry meetings began.

After the Reformation the legal rights of the parish priest became more important, but he was not in sole charge of the parish. He was assisted by two churchwardens – a post that survives in parishes to this day. Until the nineteenth century the churchwarden was almost more important in the parish at large than the vicar or rector. Until that date the vestry meeting was the body responsible for local government as well as for the management of the church, and the churchwardens would be responsible for appointing parish constables, poor law overseers, for overseeing the local school and administering local charities. In many parish churches painted boards record the extent of charities that were in the control of the church. Many give directions for bread to be given to the poor, often out of the rent from a field or two. Where the money or property left was profitably invested the charity could amount to a substantial one, and a number of churches, especially in market towns, had responsibility for a set of almshouses where the elderly could live when they had to leave homes that might be cottages tied to employment on the local estate.

The primary responsibility of the churchwardens is, of course, now directed to the church, although this always formed a major part of their role. They were required to draw up accounts, and to keep records which (now mostly in County Record Offices) provide invaluable sources for historians. They kept such records in the parish chest, a substantial lockable object, many of which survive from the medieval period. Churchwardens were, by virtue of their role, leading members of any parish. They were expected to uphold standards of morality and to report offenders. They also represented the views of the parishioners to the church authorities. For this reason there were always two churchwardens: a vicar's warden, whose badge of office was a staff topped by a silver mitre, and a people's warden, whose staff was topped by a crown. Such staffs frequently survive in churches, though they are no longer so widely used. They are usually set in holders beside the pew in which the churchwarden sits; in some churches there are even special pews reserved for the churchwardens, usually at the back of the nave, giving them a clear view over the congregation in front of them.

The vestry of St Mary's, Dover, is the place for the record-keeping that links Church and State. The curate and a churchwarden are pictured at their work in about 1940. (Canon W.E. Purcell)

Two other officials assisted the vicar in the post-Reformation period. The parish clerk was a layman whose duty it was to assist with the services, reading the gospel or epistle, leading the responses and announcing the metrical psalms. The sexton was officially the assistant to the parish clerk with the duties of digging graves, looking after the churchyard generally and ringing the church bell when necessary. The whole team not only involved different people under the parish priest, but also established a complete hierarchy for organisation of both secular and religious life in the parish. Much of the secular role has now passed from the church, but traces of the hierarchy can often be seen in the furniture and regalia of a church, special seats, staffs and so on. And, of course, the duties relating to the church still have to be carried out.

Both parson and churchwardens had an important role in vestry meetings, and the connection of those meetings with the church needs to be examined. Today the word vestry is used to refer to a usually small room tacked on to the north side of the church, full of cupboards and storage space, where the vicar puts on his surplice before the service. In larger churches there may also be space for a choir to robe as well. This reflects the true meaning of the word as a place where the clergy donned the vestments required for the mass, and where such vestments were stored. Another term for this is a sacristy, which sounds more solemn, a place where sacred things are stored. Many cathedrals still have sacristies, and sacristans to look after them, but the religious importance of such places in ordinary churches is really only understood by a visit to a large Roman Catholic church such as Sta Croce in Florence, where the sacristy is a splendid room furnished with its own altar and finely worked cupboards around the walls to hold the vestments and service books that are still required for such a major centre of worship. Such a space would have made an ideal place for solemn conclaves. The average village church was a different thing altogether, and it may well be that the 'vesting place' in a small medieval church was no grander than the curtained corner of the nave that still serves as a vestry in a few small country churches. The presence of a small door, known as the priest's door, in the south wall of the chancel in many churches is evidence that he usually entered directly into the sanctuary, and so presumably donned his vestments at home. In such cases a parish meeting would most probably have been held in the nave.

The sacristy or vestry, if there was one, was nevertheless a useful place for small meetings and during the seventeenth century, when the importance of churchwardens as leaders of the laity was increasing, it began to assume its role in secular management of the parish. The churchwardens, together with the incumbent, formed the nucleus for the system of managing local affairs, whether religious or secular. Though many meetings were held in the church with the participants seated round the Lord's Table, the vestry was generally the most convenient place to gather. It was warmer and would also contain a table and writing equipment. Thus the vestry meeting became the core of local government in parishes.

The vestry came to mean the place, the parishioners and the gathering at which they discussed affairs, and was the only form of local government outside towns; even in towns it controlled most local affairs until the nineteenth century. As local services became more complex, the work was taken up by various committees – Improvement, Poor Law or Highway Commissioners – and the role of the vestries waned, but it was not until 1894 that their secular power was finally removed. A generation later, in 1921, elected Parochial Church Councils were established to administer church affairs, and vestry meetings ceased to have any function. The word has survived, however, in the various Protestant Episcopal churches, where vestrymen are responsible for the church financing, together with the vicar and wardens.

Another mixing of sacred and secular took place in the church itself. The nave of a medieval church, free of pews, was the largest covered area in the district and so was ideal for occasional secular meetings. We have already seen that trade guilds might appropriate an aisle for their own functions, where religion and secular life joined. This sort of activity made the medieval church the natural storage place for all the items that a community might need occasionally, particularly if they had to be shared or were too large to fit in a private dwelling. Very occasionally a parish helmet or suit of armour survives as a relic of the periods in the fourteenth and fifteenth centuries when parishes were expected to help defend the realm. Full armour was, however, the prerogative of knights, and the presence of items of actual armour in churches was probably always a rarity. The few bits that survive are more often parade pieces, insufficiently strong for use in battle, that were made for the funeral cortège of a great lord. The Church of St Mary at Redgrave in Suffolk has one that presumably decorated the bier of a member of the Bacon family.

There is better authenticated evidence for the link between churches and archery, since it was a legal requirement in the fourteenth and fifteenth centuries that parishioners should practise archery on a regular basis. The churchyard was one of the few suitable open places, and many were used for this. It is possible that some had more or less permanent butts, with mounds against which the targets could be set. There is a popular tradition that churchyards were planted with yew trees to provide the wood for longbows. Alas, they are the wrong sort of yew, and it is more likely that they belong to an even older tradition of planting yews around ancestral burial grounds. Since each individual had his own bow, there was no need for them to be stored in the church, and almost the only evidence of this secular activity around the church are occasional long grooves in exterior stonework where archers sharpened their arrows.

The occasional hazards of more peaceful times have, however, left their trace in a few churches. Until the later part of the nineteenth century bucket chains were the only means of fighting fires, and there are a few churches where a row of old leather buckets hangs, often in the tower, as a reminder that parishes made provision for this. The buckets were certainly not only for church use, but it was a building that was always open, and a place to which all could hurry in the desperate effort to save something from a neighbouring conflagration. With open fires for warmth, candles for light and thatch as a common covering in many parts of the land, serious fires were a constant risk. A fire in a thatch roof was difficult to put out by merely throwing water, and so parishes often equipped themselves with a long pole and heavy hook that could be used to drag off the burning roof material in the hopes of saving the walls at least. Such a thing could only be stored in the church – there would be no other building big enough in a village – and a few of these monstrous objects still hang in the side aisles of village churches. There is a splendid example at Outwell near Wisbech.

Sacred and Secular Structure: the Porch

Every church had its connection with the secular world, and two areas of the church are particularly associated with this: the porch and the churchyard. A porch was frequently built over the door used by the congregation. Grander churches might add a north porch as well. Their original purpose was simply to provide shelter, but they have brought the fortunate benefit of preserving many older carvings in the tympana above older entrance doors. However, these extra spaces were soon used for particular activities that either were not appropriate for the body of the church or were felt to be particularly appropriate in the porch. These functions might be religious or secular.

The lighting of the new Easter fire on Holy Saturday was always done in the porch. This fire symbolised the renewal of spiritual life and was an important element of the celebrations of Easter Eve. It had to be carried from the church to each house in the community, and so the porch as the place where sacred and secular space met was particularly appropriate. It was, as we have seen, the place where marriage contracts were regularly exchanged before the bride passed into the church to her wedding. In some places the practice arose of calling the banns in the porch. This announcement of a forthcoming marriage, and the call for anyone knowing a reason why the marriage might be unlawful to say so, effectively needed to be made to the whole community, and again the porch, open to the world at large, was especially suitable.

Porches were the natural start and finish point for the many processions that were a regular part of pre-Reformation worship. Thus they became the focus of special decoration, and a few were even provided with temporary galleries that could be set up just for the purpose of hanging garlands on festive days such as Palm Sunday. There were also occasions when it was considered unsuitable for a person to enter the church proper or for an activity to take place inside the church. One practice that has fallen almost entirely out of use is the churching of mothers. The old belief that childbirth was a defiling act meant that after giving birth a mother would come to the church porch and there give thanks (and what the prayer book described as 'the usual offerings'!) before coming into church to take communion. The practice survived certainly till the middle of the twentieth century, but is not thought appropriate in today's world and has been dropped. It is, however, one reason why a few porches were supplied with altars; no doubt the benches that were regularly found in larger porches would have been particularly welcome.

From very early times church porches were connected with the right of sanctuary. As early as 431 CE the right of sanctuary had been extended to churches, and the fugitive merely had to reach the church, or a defined area round it, for his forcible removal to be a sacrilege. Some churches even provided a sanctuary knocker for the fugitive to grasp so that his contact with the place of sanctuary would be clearly established. (A rare survivor is that on the north door of Durham Cathedral.) The fugitive had then forty days in which to take an oath, usually on the altar in the porch, by which he confessed his sin and agreed to leave the country. Porch altars, like the Saxon porches they stood in, seldom survive but the porch became associated with solemn obligations.

By extension porch altars became a place where other oaths might be sworn

This handsome porch was a fifteenth-century addition to the church of St Mary, Kersey, Suffolk. (Colin Cunningham)

and contracts agreed. This gave the church a particular link with the judiciary, and made the porch into a place of some importance in the whole business of medieval commercial life. The practice was widespread, and it was soon accepted that it was not necessary to swear on an altar. The church porch itself was a sufficiently symbolic place. The secular importance of the porch that this use secured was one of the reasons why porches, particularly in town churches where a good deal of business might be contracted, were often substantial structures.

The religious functions, however, made the gift of a porch to a church an attractive proposition for a parishioner anxious to secure salvation or the hope of it through an endowment. As a result many churches have porches that are among the most splendid parts of the building. Fine stonework and rich carving make them, in some cases, almost little buildings of their own. Perhaps the most splendid is the three-storey structure provided for the church of St John the Baptist in Cirencester. This richly decorated porch dates from 1490 and was used for the secular business of the Augustinian abbey. It was later used as the town hall before being transferred to parish ownership in the eighteenth century. A good many porches were built of two storeys with a room over the porch itself. The functions of these rooms are difficult to recapture, and few have any regular use now. It seems that some may have been used as dwellings for a priest. Others appear to have been more in the nature of a study, and a porch at Newark, for instance, was for long used as the parish library. One or two seem to have been used as schoolrooms, and they would certainly have been convenient places for the teaching of catechumens, that is, for training new members of the congregation in the doctrines of their church, which was about all the schooling that was available to most people in the Middle Ages. A room in the porch secured space for this, that was a part of the church, yet symbolically not a part of the liturgical space.

Sacred and Secular Space: the Churchyard

The space outside the church but inside the boundary of the churchyard had a similar ambiguous relationship with both religion and secular life. However, as it was fully outside the church the activities there were generally still closer to the secular. Where a church stood in the centre of its churchyard, the land to the north of the church was frequently unconsecrated and generally free of burials, and formed a convenient open space for all sorts of parish activities. Archery, as we have noted, may well have been practised there, and the churchyard was certainly an informal gathering place, though one would assume that it was preferable to meet on the sunny southern side. In fact there is often more space on the southern side of the churchyard, possibly because the preaching cross was the first thing to be erected on a church site, and when the church was put up care was taken to site it to the north so that its shadow did not fall on the cross.

There are records from the Saxon period of moots (local parliaments) being held in churchyards, but the most frequent use was for social and recreational purposes. This often distressed the church authorities, but activities such as wrestling, ninepins and quoits were all apparently held in churchyards, and the game of fives was easily played against the church wall with its buttresses. In a few places rings survive in the wall for the shutters to protect the windows when fives was played. Some churchwardens' accounts even record the provision of benches for spectators. (Churchyard benches nowadays are more likely to be given in memory of former parishioners.) For the most part churchyard games were far removed from religion and even included cockfighting, which, together with fives, led to widespread gambling. King James, noticing that some clergy were attempting to curtail these activities, issued a declaration in 1619, known as 'The Book of Sports', which was intended actually to encourage traditional English churchyard sports 'in due and convenient time, and without impediment or let of Divine Service'. Clergy were supposed to read the declaration from the pulpit of every church. Many refused, or read it and immediately preached against it. Those seventeenth-century Puritans doubtless disapproved but they seem to have been totally unable to limit these games, and some continued well into the nineteenth century.

There was a serious intention behind some of these practices. The ritual year with its many festivals allowed a variety of means of raising funds and it is important to remember that the construction and maintenance of the church was the responsibility of the parish. Funds were needed then as now, and the medieval practice was to lay on a festival of dancing and sport, accompanied by drinking, in order to attract customers. The present-day village fête is a more genteel descendant of these Church Ales, which were often fairly riotous, though one hopes successful, fund-raising events.

Of course, the principal purpose of a churchyard was to provide a space for burying the dead of a parish, and the effect of constant contact between previous generations and the continuing life of the parish must have had its effect on the community. The patterns and customs of funerals and gravestones have already been discussed. Today, churchyards are seldom the only available open space but they have become increasingly appreciated as havens of peace and quiet removed from the bustle of the community. This is perhaps even more necessary in towns, but the idea that a churchyard is principally a garden of remembrance ignores one half of its original purpose as a locus for the continuing life of the present.

Other Ecclesiastical Structures

In the fifteenth and sixteenth centuries in towns and larger villages it was not uncommon for the parish to erect a parish room, often a free-standing structure separate from the church, for the storage of equipment and occasional entertainments. This was easier for those parishes who took over monastic buildings at the Reformation. The parish of Elstow in Bedfordshire, for instance, acquired what was probably the outer parlour of the former Benedictine Abbey as a supernumerary space. Sometimes a room was reserved in a private house, but by the fifteenth century many urban parishes had built their own parish house which was maintained by the churchwardens. There was a considerable range in both the pattern of provision and the function of these additional structures in the medieval period. Some of the structures had very specific functions. At Higham Ferrers in Northampton the church is flanked by two such, which, though not in matching styles, were clearly designed to fit with and enhance the approach to the church. They were both the gift of Bishop Chichele in the 1420s and housed a school and a bede house (or almshouse). Each one is a fine building in its own right but they were emphatically subsidiary to the parish church.

Archbishop Chichele's school of the 1420s beside the very grand church of St Mary, Higham Ferrers, Northamptonshire. (Colin Cunningham)

Many older parish rooms have now passed into other hands or been demolished. However, a similar current concern is the building of church halls. The church hall was a regular feature of the late nineteenth-century village, and quite a few memorial halls were built after the First World War to fulfil the same function. Some villages even bought prefabricated huts for the purpose after the Second World War. These are usually on another site, often near the recreation ground. More recently there has been a tendency to erect halls adjoining the church, which can be used for a whole range of both secular and sacred activities, and usually include facilities such as toilets and kitchens. The problem has been that congregations are now reduced, and funds accordingly at a premium. Few parishes have the courage or determination to build a church hall of the same quality as their medieval church, and, to be fair, it is a difficult task for an architect to design a set of modern rooms that will match or blend with the old. Success in attaching a church hall to a church is no mean feat, and such buildings are generally (and deliberately) less impressive than the church they serve.

The Victorians had rather more success in this field when they built new churches in the growing industrial towns. They were often able to build a church hall, or at least plan for one, that would match the church. There was always a clear hierarchy of architectural richness, and the parish hall was built with similar materials and to a similar design as the church, but more plainly.

This provision of a complete centre for worship matched the aims of the Tractarians. In their intention to return the Church to what they saw as its proper pre-Reformation ministry, they often provided clergy houses as part of a new church development. Perhaps the best-known example is All Saints Margaret Street, where the church is set at the back of a small courtyard, flanked on one side by the clergy house and on the other by the choir school. Both these have now lost their original function, but it has been easier to adapt such elements to new uses. Other examples survive more or less intact. At St Peter's Wapping the church is entered under an archway leading to a courtyard; the clergy house fills one side and the top of the arch, and still houses the rector, though no longer the seven curates. The other side of the arch still has the rooms built for the Anglican nuns whom the rector assembled to help with his slum mission.

The Tractarians were deeply concerned to bring religion – and a colourful religion at that – into the dreary slums, and their priests were expected to live in those slums, however much time they spent in wealthy drawing-rooms raising funds for the good work. An example of this closeness

The matching clergy house of All Saints', Margaret Street, London (William Butterfield 1849–53), flanks the church. (Colin Cunningham)

to the work is in the clergy house of St Benedict Gorton in Manchester which is actually built on to the north aisle of the church, with a window from the dwelling looking directly into the church. Yet the crowded slum parish was not the normal experience of Anglicanism, and most Anglican vicars had better living conditions in the nineteenth century. Town rectories are often substantial, though few are now left as single-family dwellings, and the size of rectories generally indicates the status of the parson at any period. In the hierarchical society of the Victorians, the clergy had a distinct social position and were expected to live comfortably.

Medieval parish clergy often lived very simply. A few actually lived in a single room over the porch of their church. For the rest conditions would have been little different from those of their parishioners. It was only the greatest prelates who lived in palaces, though it is worth remembering that Hampton Court was built for one. A pre-Reformation parish priest gained his living from tithes. If he was lucky there was also glebe land, which he might farm or lease to others. This, of course, made him like the bulk of his parishioners, since, in addition to his priestly duties, he was regularly engaged in the same labour. But neither tithes nor glebe necessarily made him wealthy, unless it was good land. A few pre-Reformation parsonages survive, with medieval barns as an indication of the produce expected; the occasional Glebe Farm is also an indication of the way a priest made his living. Sometimes these suggest some substance, as, for instance at Little Snoring in Norfolk, where the old rectory is a building of considerable size, but there are also other indicators of unusual status in the structures of the church. Little Snoring is one of those rare instances where two churches were built in the same churchyard. An early eleventh-century church, probably developed from an earlier structure, was left unfinished or demolished a bare fifty years after it was begun and replaced with a larger new structure. Clearly it was a place where someone had enough power and money to indulge in substantial church building at an early date. It is hardly surprising that whatever priest was employed to serve the church was well supported.

The widespread rise in the status of the clergy can probably be dated to the seventeenth century. If the pre-Reformation priest was made special by the sacrament of Ordination, the Puritan priest was made special by his ability to preach. This required a degree of learning, and so emphasised the professionalisation of the clerical life. Along with learning went status of the sort that had previously been possible only with appointment to numbers of livings and by climbing the Church hierarchy. In the eighteenth century the potential status of the ordinary parish priest reached considerable heights, since the younger sons of the gentry, who would not inherit their father's estate, were encouraged to consider the Church as a suitable alternative to the army for a career. The new vicarage built by Lord Scarsdale at Kedleston, where his younger brother was the parson, is a good example. It is a sizeable and elegant Georgian building of brick, well matched to the elder brother's grand palace in the park nearby.

This high social status ran parallel to an interest on the part of landlords in seeing 'their' parish church as an ornament or architectural set piece. There was little of Christian worship about this, but the effects on the buildings could be considerable. In the first place the eighteenth century saw the resiting of a good many villages as manor houses were rebuilt at the centre of extensive parks. The church, however, was never moved; isolated from its community, it became attractive as an ornament in the park. The villagers would then come into the park to their landlord's church to worship, though they might live a mile or more away. In these cases the first benefit for the church building was that the structure would be kept in decent repair. More interesting architecturally are cases where the estate church was rebuilt to make a feature. At Wimpole in Cambridge the surviving fragment of the medieval church was given over to the monuments of the noble family, the Yorkes, who owned the estate and employed the villagers. The rest was entirely rebuilt with a smart classical facade towards the house and a west doorway that led only to the family pew in its gallery. Examples of such magnificent display are widespread. At Croome D'Abitot in Worcestershire the Earl of Coventry engaged Robert Adam to refurbish his church in a delicate Gothic style as an eye-catcher on the hill in front of his new house. At Shobdon in Herefordshire the church was completely kitted out with new pews, new pulpit and so on in delicate white painted Gothic woodwork. The medieval parish church of Kedleston was so close to the old manor house that Lord Scarsdale was actually unable to build the whole house that Adam designed for him. The church was left to stand in its own small garden close against the side of the house. At Great Witley in Worcestershire the Earl of Dudley's mansion was so hugely enlarged that it was actually joined on to the parish church of St Michael, built close by barely a hundred years before. Later in the nineteenth century a grieving mother at Newby Hall in Yorkshire engaged the architect William Burges and spent a fortune constructing a new parish church at Newby cum Skelton dedicated to Christ the Consoler as a memorial to her son and heir who had been killed by brigands in Turkey. But not all these park ornaments were ideally suited to worship, and the changing fortunes of a great landlord might call the whole edifice into question. Robert Adam's extraordinary church at Mistley in Essex, with its twin towers at east and west ends, was without doubt a splendid setting for the family monuments, but it was less than ideal

The elegant west front and entrance to the family pew of St Andrew, Wimpole, Cambridgeshire, designed by Henry Flitcroft in 1749 as an ornament in the grounds of Wimpole Hall. (Colin Cunningham)

At Lydiard Tregoze in Wiltshire the medieval church of St Mary stands close behind the mansion that was rebuilt for Viscount St John with a palatial façade in 1743. (Colin Cunningham)

for the revived worship of the nineteenth century. It was therefore demolished and replaced in the 1860s, leaving the two towers as paired landmarks facing each other across a small garden.

The fashion for splendid building was, however, a matter for landlords and patrons. The work of the Church was in the hands of the parish priest, though where he was resident in his parish, the parson ranked as one of the more important inhabitants throughout the eighteenth and nineteenth centuries. It was generally expected that he would provide for all the support that we now take for granted from the various social services. Parson Woodforde, who had such a lively reputation as a *bon viveur*, regularly visited his parishioners, and expected to feed the needy from his own kitchen. However, it was only rectors who had enough wealth or security of tenure for this, and so it was common for parish priests to accept appointment to more than one living and appoint a curate to stand in for them. These high-status clergy often lived outside their parishes in towns where they could find smart houses to accord with their social position, and enjoy the company of others of their rank. So it was a common experience to see the parish priest arrive in his carriage for the Sunday service and depart immediately afterwards for his elegant but distant home. In 1777 it was argued that 'many of the parochial clergy, for want of proper habitations, are induced to reside at a distance from their benefice, by which means their parishioners lose the advantage of their instruction and their hospitality'.[1] The result was two-fold. An Act of Parliament made it easier for parish priests to borrow money, and in the first decades of the nineteenth century there was increasing pressure, some of it legislative, to force priests to live in their parish. They were also discouraged from taking more than one benefice. Architecturally, the outcome was a surge of rectory and vicarage building, and many elegant regency mansions, now sold off and smartly labelled The Old Rectory, once housed the parish priest as the leader of local society. The process continued throughout the nineteenth century. Sometimes it was a matter of repairing and adding to an old building, sometimes a vicar was determined to start from scratch, and a few were even driven to bankruptcy in their efforts to house themselves in decent splendour. The rectory at Long Melford, in Suffolk, for instance, was enlarged in 1878 to include five reception rooms, sixteen bedrooms, and three dressing-rooms. The rectory of Hanbury in Worcestershire of much the same date, one of the richest livings in the diocese, still required a staff of four indoor servants and several gardeners in the opening years of this century. At much the same time Sabine Baring-Gould, author of the well-known hymn 'Onward Christian Soldiers', as vicar and squire of Lew Trenchard in Devon used to visit his parishioners in a carriage driven by liveried footmen.

Holy Trinity, Ryde, Isle of Wight, a new church in a resort town that was growing in 1873, pictured in a contemporary photograph with the house to be purchased as the parsonage. (Church of England Record Office)

But it was not all splendour, and by the end of the Victorian era more clergy were resident in their parishes than before, or since. With residence came more and better organised service to the community. In addition to relieving poverty the Church had long been involved in education. In the earliest centuries that meant simply the catechism which allowed individuals to be confirmed as full members of the church. The teaching took place in the church, with no special provision made for it, or occasionally, as we have seen, in a room over the porch. It was one of the hopes of the Reformation that the money recovered from the monasteries and destroyed shrines would be redirected into education. Edward VI did indeed found, or refound, a number of schools such as Sherborne, using monastic buildings as well as finances but the bulk of the money stayed in the royal treasury. None the less the Church did involve itself in education, and some parishes made increasing provision for it. Church reordering in the seventeenth century found occasional use for redundant chancels, especially those separated from the nave by partitions, as schoolrooms. In the eighteenth century the Lady Chapel at Long Melford was fully equipped as the village school, and the benches for the scholars survive there to this day. The eighteenth century also saw the foundation of a number of charity schools, often in the control of the local parish church. Their pupils, often dressed in uniform, were regularly seated together in the church. Occasionally special charity pews were made, though usually these poor children sat on benches or in a gallery; their obvious presence was simply the bottom end of the rigid social scale that also encompassed the elaborate family pews.

Education in the faith is an important part of the ministry, and in early times this was all the education available to most. Here children of the 1950s learn about the prayer book in church. (Church of England Record Office)

The same century saw a new development with the birth of Sunday Schools after 1780. Their originator was Robert Raikes in Gloucester, and, though he was not himself a parish priest, his movement was supported by the local vicar. The schools taught both the Catechism and reading, and took their name from the day on which they operated – the one day when pupils might not be working. In the nineteenth century an increasing care for education, and the gradual restriction of child employment, led to schools that were open during the week and taught a wider curriculum. Until the advent of secular State education after 1870 these were mostly provided by various denominational organisations. The National Society was the one most closely tied to the Church of England, and their National schools inevitably involved the local priest as a member of the governing body. The buildings were usually in the Gothic style, and often close to the church. In rural areas these church schools were little affected by the arrival of State education, and many still operate as the local primary school. When the government finally took over financing of schools and teachers in 1944, many Church of England schools opted to continue their links with the Church and took what was known as voluntary status. This usually continued the involvement of the clergy in the governing body as well as the buildings, though many have now been closed and converted to domestic use. Quite frequently the school and teacher's house were designed by the architect who built the vicarage and altered or restored the church, so they form a grouping of religious buildings in many parishes. At Denstone in Staffordshire the Church of All Saints together with its rectory and school were all designed by George Edmund Street

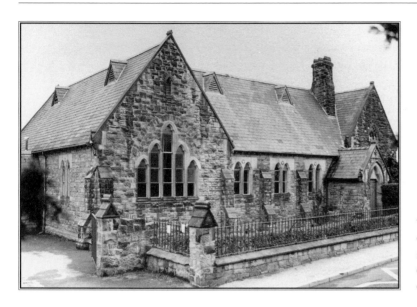

The church school at Gresford, Clwyd, built across the road from the parish church in a Gothic style (1873–4). (Colin Cunningham)

around 1860 to a unified Gothic livery. The church is the richest building, with bands of coloured stone, and the school the plainest, but there is no mistaking the uniformity. The provision of schools was also linked to the patrons, who so often paid for the beautification of the church. Funds for each church school had to be raised locally and inevitably a wealthy landlord would be expected to contribute handsomely. In a good few cases they provided the whole school. The village of Steppingly in Bedfordshire displays the contribution of its landlord, the Duke of Bedford, in the row of completely rebuilt church, new school and teacher's house all of the 1860s and 1870s and all designed by the Duke's architect Henry Clutton.

Along with better services to the community went a greater attention to comfort and order in the church itself. The vestry, which was primarily for the use of the clergy, was a regular addition in the nineteenth century. These are usually in the form of a small structure at the north side of the chancel. They allowed vicar and choir to don their robes unseen by the congregation, but the nineteenth-century clergy attended to their comfort at the same time. Vestries are almost always provided with a fireplace, which, since they are close to the higher chancel, required a tall chimney to make the fire draw. With their usual attention to detail and love of ornament, Victorian architects often turned these chimneys into richly decorative external elements like the medieval pinnacles. And warmth was not restricted to the clergy. As soon as transport made it possible to move coal cheaply, it became fashionable to install heating in churches. In remoter areas this has never been done, and rural churches are still sometimes heated by portable calor gas stoves, or are left freezing. Richer churches installed great stoves of cast iron with ribbed bodies like overgrown radiators that created areas of heat all round them. (Not infrequently, these also set fire to the church when their flue, passing through the roof, became too hot.) The richest parishes even installed boilers and underfloor heating by means of great iron pipes beneath gratings. Along with underfloor heating, of course, went new tiled floors, and where many a medieval church still had a floor of worn flagstones or brick, the provision of coloured tiles around the new pews was a regular part of the nineteenth-century experience. They could even be organised to help foster the symbolic meaning of the whole structure, with a development from plain tiles in the nave and aisles to increasing richness in the chancel. The finest patterns and richest colours are reserved for the sanctuary and the altar step.

One last aspect of the parish world deserves mention. We have already seen that charitable giving formed a major part of the life of the congregation, and the various boards recording donations often make interesting reading. From the Middle Ages it had been common for the well-to-do to leave funds for the relief of poverty, and there were many such bequests in the seventeenth century when the Puritans argued that works of piety were more important than faith. Where such funds were managed by the Church, their control was in the hands of the churchwardens, who in the late eighteenth and early nineteenth centuries would often record the legacy and its conditions on a painted board. In most cases these are now stowed away or hung in the tower space. The majority record gifts of land, from the proceeds of which cash or fuel, or more often, bread was to be dispensed to the poor of the parish on certain occasions. A few churches, such as St Martin at Ruislip in Middlesex have handsome *dole* cupboards in which the bread could be stored before being distributed publicly on occasions such as Shrove Tuesday, and a particularly elaborate Jacobean poorbox survives at Outwell in Norfolk. In one church, Norton St Andrew in Suffolk, the benefactor determined that a handsome painted stone slab like a memorial should be built against the west wall. Its top incorporated a small canopy to house the charity bread, while the benefaction was recorded in a large brass inscription.

More palpable evidence of charity can be seen in the many almshouses that survive up and down the country. Many were established in the Middle Ages, either by monastic houses or by trade guilds, to provide homes for the aged and infirm, and shelter for wayfarers and pilgrims. These medieval establishments regularly had their own chapel, and the inmates were required to pray for the soul of their benefactor, just like the chantry priests. Most were closely linked with their parish church. However, the Reformation swept that aspect away, though the Elizabethan Poor Law gave some impetus to the provision of suitable housing for the deserving. Many new charitable almshouses were founded in the seventeenth and eighteenth centuries, and there were more in the nineteenth century. These places were occupied by people selected for their virtue, and that selection often brought a link with the parish church and its authorities. It was quite common for the vicar to have power of nomination to a place in these favoured retirement homes. A few medieval almshouses, such as those at Sherborne in Dorset, survive in whole or in part. Many of the later ones are built in the Gothic or Tudor style, and particularly handsome ones survive at Chipping Campden in Gloucestershire. A town such as Cambridge may have several sets each with some link to one or other of the churches in the town. Where a village boasts a set of almshouses – and that is generally only in the larger villages – they may be built near the church, and form yet another element in the local grouping of church-inspired building. They are evidence of the way in which previous generations managed their social services as an integral part of their religion.

The entire gamut of church-related structures can include other more purely functional buildings. A few churches which served scattered parishes built shelters or stables for the horses of those who had to ride to church. More common is the provision of a special stable or shelter for the parish bier, where that could not be conveniently stored in the church. At Hanbury in Worcestershire, for instance, where the church stood alone on a hill-top, and was entered by a flight of steps, a separate stable and bier house was built in the nineteenth century halfway up the hill. The arrangement allowed the bier to be readily available to parishioners, and avoided the rather gruesome reminder of mortality that might have resulted from storing it in the tower, through which the congregation passed each week to worship. The whole range of buildings is seldom found in any one location, for there was much variety of practice. However, all these structures need to be taken into account in considering the contribution of the church to its community. Church and parish room, vicarage tithe barn and school, almshouses and charities have all left their varying mark on their communities and though many of the structures have now passed out of Church ownership or control, their shapes are a lasting reminder of the outreach of congregations of earlier ages.

CHAPTER SEVEN

Continuity and Change

Introduction

The image of the country church, its tower peeping over the trees, or the town church standing proud at the head of a market-place or looming over an industrial cityscape, is deeply ingrained in our appreciation of the texture of Britain. Such buildings are a key part of our national heritage, and important for all of us. Whether we use them or not, we would certainly miss them if they were not there! Sometimes it is simply their age that we marvel at – a Saxon tower that has stood for more than a thousand years is a wonder in itself. Sometimes we marvel at the craftsmanship of the masons and carpenters who built them and carved their delicate tracery. Or, and this is especially the case with medieval churches that have been patched and repaired over the centuries, we find delight in the mellow quality of the stone or brick of which they are made. These are characteristics that all can enjoy, whether Christian or not, for they are integral parts of the heritage of Britain and marks of its civilisation.

However, there is a further value in the reason why these buildings are there at all. Each church is a statement of the Christian activity of its congregation over generations, and a reflection of spiritual values. Religion has been too easily engaged as a justification for the many violent conflicts that have beset civilisation, and the Church of England still suffers from its share of disagreements, though fortunately those seldom lead to violence these days. Yet the church buildings afford mute witness of the results of the often violent disagreements of the past, for instance in the defaced carving and empty niches. Churches bear witness also to periods of confidence and prosperity in which the faithful found it worth while to set aside money and to turn their energy to glorifying their God. Both the tribulations and the triumphs have left their mark, as has long-sustained devotion.

We can follow a chronological thread that links the earliest churches of this country to those of today, tracing a gradual modification of historic structures and various attempts to break away into new architectural forms. One thing is important. Whatever their state or doctrinal allegiance, the parish churches of England are the product of a developing theology and changing systems of Church organisation. They stand now as a continuing witness, and any Anglican can recognise a point of contact with each place that has a church. Though the practices of each parish church may differ widely, and visitors may dislike the arrangements of the church, there will still be this sense of contact, of worship rooted in the same tradition. Something of this is true for Christians of other denominations, too, though church buildings and the arrangements for Christian liturgy may be less intelligible to members of other faiths, or those who find an organised 'church' restrictive. Anyone who accepts the importance of a spiritual element in life, especially if he or she is willing to recognise that traditions play a part in most patterns of behaviour, will be able to trace some of the ways in which a parish church can capture the numinous. There is a curious power in the underlying unity of function, akin perhaps to the solidarity a Muslim must feel seeing a mosque in a foreign country whether it be in Bosnia or London, or a Jew finding a distant synagogue, whether in Poland or Los Angeles. It may be the same for a Hindu whether the temple is in Oldbury or Mathura. A part of this feeling is the knowledge that others have worshipped the same God in whatever church we are visiting as we worship in our own way at home. The church building identifies the faith as easily as the minaret the mosque or the gopura the Hindu temple.

What makes Anglican parish churches interesting, however, is not only their sharing in a single tradition, but the combination of ways in which each community has reacted to the shifting fashions and fortunes of Christianity over generations. There is a constant interplay between the influences of locality and local events and changes in liturgy and practice. Yet, in spite of the variety, all churches partake of a shared experience of worship that involves what is known as the community of saints. And it is, as we have seen, a long tradition and a wide community. For the first thousand years there was but one Christendom, though practices varied, especially between east and west; and that sense of a united Christendom lasted in Britain until the Reformation. But the many minor shifts and changes over the centuries all make up the rich patchwork of the history of each church.

Continuity and Conquest

It is at least likely that there has been actual continuity of Christianity in parts of Britain from the time the faith first arrived under the Romans. It is certain that there were Christians in Roman Britain,

Excavation lays bare the remains of Capel Maelog, near Llandrindod Wells, showing the largely thirteenth-century church, an earlier square structure and burials in the cemetery. (Clwyd Powys Archaeological Trust)

and influential ones at that, as can be seen from the Christian emblems on treasures such as that from Water Newton in Northamptonshire (now in the British Museum). The proximity of some churches to Roman sites may well reflect this continuity of worship and, though little now remains above ground, this is where archaeology can help to fill the gaps. In Colchester, the first *colonia* of the Roman province, a Roman church site has been identified just to the west of Holy Trinity Church. The Church of St Peter at Bailgate in Lincoln, demolished in 1971, turned out to be built over not one but three successive churches of the post-Roman period. These were in what had been the forum of Roman Lincoln, and the earliest may date back as far as the fifth century, arguing their importance in that centre of Roman occupation. Even in rural England, at Rivenhall in Essex, the Church of St Mary and All Saints stands on the site of a

Roman villa graveyard. The building was reconstructed in 1838, but it was an ancient church site, and it may well be that the first builders retained some recollection of its original function. Still more dramatic is the site of the twelfth-century church at Capel Maelog, near Llandridnod Wells in Powys. Excavations there revealed remains of a two-cell church to which apses had been added in the thirteenth century, and which had remained in use until the sixteenth century. It had been built to take account of features in an existing cemetery dating back to the ninth century (and possibly earlier), while the first structure on the site belonged to the fourth or fifth century. In this one spot in the countryside of central Wales there had been continuity of worship from the end of the Roman period to the Reformation.

Some of those Roman Christians probably stayed on in Britain when the Romans left, and they stayed on as Christians. The little post-Roman kingdoms of Wales and the west of England evidently included Christians, and the legends of Arthur paint him as a Christian king, as was the historical Alfred. In fact by the time of his reign, there may have been something like an Established Church in the lands of the west. There was, however, nothing like a complete parish system, and churches were few and far between, though such as existed were often richly fitted out. By the eighth century Britain was so far Christianised that British priests were acting as missionaries in Germany, and we must assume that the churches they came from were by then well appointed.

The eighth and ninth centuries saw the emergence of something approaching a parish system under the influence of Theodore, Archbishop of Canterbury from 699. There were several new smaller dioceses so that bishops could be in closer touch with their flock. Ramsbury in Wiltshire, Sherborne in Dorset and Crediton in Devon, for example, were all the seats of bishops, and, though the sees were later removed, their presence in those centuries may explain why those places later built substantial parish churches or abbeys. However, all that was swept aside by the Viking raids when churches were a target for looting. That in itself suggests their richness, and we can assume that they possessed jewelled chalices, embroidered frontals, richly bound service books and reliquaries. All those were carried off, and the churches, which were largely wooden, burned.

Not that the Viking raids meant the land was de-Christianised any more than it was depopulated. There was, however, poverty and it was not until the late Saxon period that many new churches were built. Some of these were substantial, but the surviving remains are relatively few and far between, since the Normans, as a part of their determined reorganisation of the whole kingdom, engaged in a great deal of rebuilding. And it was the Normans who really established the parochial system with a church for each community. By the end of the eleventh century the Church was served by a network of rural deans overseeing groups of parishes, and the number of archdeacons had been increased. The sees of bishops were transferred from villages to cities. Selsey lost its cathedral to Chichester, and Dorchester in Oxfordshire lost its to Lincoln. But there were examples of close contact between bishops and their parish churches. Wulfstan of Worcester was a regular visitor, travelling with a train of monks and priests, and with his chamberlain ready to give alms to all in need. They were famous for the way they sang psalms and litanies on the road, and the bishop made a point of entering the church, as soon as he reached any settlement, to preach and confirm the villagers. This sort of interest encouraged the building of structures designed to impress and large enough to house the whole village.

By the time the Normans arrived the practices of the Celtic church had been subsumed in the Roman, and new feasts such as All Souls' Day were soon introduced from Cluny. This commemoration of all the departed reflects an emphasis on congregational attendance which justified the building of churches large enough to shelter the whole community. There was a noticeable change of gear in the architecture of churches, and in the richness of the ornamental carving, which argues both a commitment on the part of the feudal and ecclesiastical authorities and a considerable increase in the opportunities for craftsmen. The vigour and quality of the carved ornament on the little twelfth-century church of St Mary and St David at Kilpeck in Herefordshire amply demonstrate the new richness, and the sheer size of churches such as St Michael at Melbourne in Derbyshire or St Mary le Haura (by the harbour) at Old Shoreham in Sussex demonstrate the economic resources that were now available to some parishes.

The twelfth and thirteenth centuries were a time of great vigour and prosperity for the Church in England. It was a period when Britain became perhaps the most densely monasticised country in Christendom, and significantly, in the mid-twelfth century, there was an Englishman, Nicholas Breakspear, as Pope in Rome. In every parish there was pressure on both priest and people for regular worship. Priests were forbidden to demand fees for baptism, absolution, visitation of the sick, communion or burial of the dead, but instead were expected to receive tithes to live on; parishioners were encouraged to receive Holy Communion at least once a year, and, after 1215, to make their confession at Easter at least. Relations between Church and monarch were not always smooth, and could affect parishes. At the beginning of the thirteenth century King John saw the growing wealth of the Church as a tempting target, and actually confiscated the goods of the see of Canterbury. The Pope tried to reassert his authority by placing the whole kingdom under an interdict, with the result that services everywhere were reduced to the bare minimum. No sacraments were allowed, except penance and extreme unction, and baptisms might be celebrated only with the immediate family present. Church doors remained shut, except for the principal festivals, when parishioners might be allowed in to pray. All Sunday worship had to take place in the churchyard. The effect on church maintenance can easily be imagined. King John, however, is better known for the Magna Carta, and it is in that document that mention is first made of the *Ecclesia Anglicana*, the Church of England. This simply meant that part of the Church which happened to be in England, but inclusion of clauses defending its freedom helped to secure the position of parishes and their clergy. In fact it was John's contentious Archbishop Stephen Langton who finally established the parochial organisation of the Church following the Lateran Council of 1215 and that in Oxford in 1222. The resulting decrees required priests to 'have everything orderly in their churches', and there are careful directions about the need to conduct the services with due decorum and the correct liturgy. They even specify that there should be two candles lit for the mass, and recommend that where a small parish needed only one priest, a large one should have two or three. The Council of Oxford gave archdeacons the duty to ensure that churches were well furnished, the consecrated bread and oil properly stored (which led to the need for aumbries) and the priest able not only to pronounce the words of the mass, but also to understand them. There were also instructions about behaviour in church, which enjoined the congregation to kneel and join their hands in prayer at the moment of consecration. That, however, does not seem to have stopped people industriously transacting business at other moments of the mass.

St John, Wantisden, a simple interior with a few medieval benches and plain seventeenth-century pews. The font is Norman, as is the narrow arch that separates the nave and chancel. (Colin Cunningham)

Secure in their organisation, the parishes of the thirteenth and fourteenth centuries began to flourish, and there was a great deal of building and extending. Fine churches of this period abound, such as St Patrick at Patrington in Yorkshire or St Andrew at Heckington in Lincolnshire; many more were partly rebuilt or extended, most often with a newly gorgeous chancel as at Tiltey or Lawford in Essex; the style is known as Decorated from the rich patterns of window tracery. There was, however, little development in liturgy, and little involvement of parishioners in worship, for all they saw to the maintenance of the body of their church. The *Layfolk's Mass Book* did not appear until the end of the thirteenth century and the *Primer*, or *Book of Hours*, in English, not until the fourteenth. There was a growing divide between the generally upper-class clerics of the monastic orders, who amassed considerable wealth and power, and the less distinguished secular clergy of the parishes who served the needs of each parish. They were often diligent, and Chaucer's 'povre Parsoune of a toun' is a good example, but they were frequently ignorant and occasionally a bad example.

Where that was the case, especially in smaller villages, efforts at building were modest, and the fabric of an older church would merely be patched and made to serve as long as possible. It is noticeable that the finest thirteenth- and fourteenth-century churches are almost all in larger centres where there was a degree of prosperity. That, of course, also meant more educated and influential parishioners. Such people who were prepared to demand greater freedom, like the townsmen who in 1327 broke into the Abbey at Bury St Edmunds and forced the abbot to grant them a charter. Significantly they were backed by no fewer than thirty-two parish priests. And that sort of discontent continued to fester wherever parish life came into conflict with monastic control. True, there were benefits for a few parishes, such as the conversion of parish churches into collegiate ones. Ottery St Mary in Devon, for instance, was reconstituted with eight canons, eight vicars and eight clerks, as well as a schoolmaster and eight choristers. However, the provision of an English Psalter in 1306, and Wycliff's English Bible around 1380, though suspect to the Church authorities, were symptoms of a growing pressure on the part of sections of the laity and clergy to see a wider involvement in worship.

This period was, however, one of increasing and increasingly widespread prosperity. Trade flourished, within and between countries, and crops such as wool brought wealth to East Anglia and the Cotswolds. The period has been described as the 'great rebuilding', a time when many houses were reconstructed and enlarged, and many mansions greatly enriched. Church-building shared in the general confidence, and in the late fourteenth and early fifteenth centuries most were enlarged, rebuilt or modernised. New windows were a common addition, but new aisles, clerestories, porches, and a number of new towers were added to make the parish churches of the Perpendicular style some of the grandest in the land. Architecturally the style was as imposing as it was widespread, with its easily recognisable pattern of shallow four-centred arches and pairs of tall mullions rising through the tracery the full height of the windows.

It is often said that churches of the Perpendicular style are more monotonous than those of the earlier Decorated period. Certainly they are more ordered and uniform, but they are also more elegant. However, although there was much church enlargement and refurbishment, relatively few churches were entirely rebuilt, like St Mary at Burwell in Cambridgeshire. Generally speaking, more work was done in enlarging and adapting, and the finest craftsmanship is as often found in new fonts or new screens as in the structure of a church as a whole. In fact by about 1450 there was considerable concern, among those who wished for reform, that churches were being allowed to fall into disrepair, and the glory of surviving Perpendicular churches has to be set against a more widespread lack of care. Many parish priests of the time did not meet all the aspirations of developing congregations, and their churches began to be seen as part of an increasingly outdated and corrupt organisation. In 1414 Oxford University actually compiled a list of complaints and suggestions for reform,

Large windows of the Perpendicular style at Holy Trinity, Long Melford, Suffolk. The south chapel is of 1484 and the clerestory of 1481. (Colin Cunningham)

which might have had a considerable effect on churches had they been acted on. Preaching was still effectively in the hands of itinerant preachers, especially the friars, and there were scandalous tales of their importunate begging in church the moment their sermon was finished. Too many parish clergy were non-resident, and the practice of holding numbers of benefices in plurality meant that some churches were not well cared for. There was far too great a disparity between rich and poor clergy. The same could be seen in their churches, with remote or small parishes, such as St George, Shimpling in Norfolk, continuing to use the simple church their ancestors had built a century before. As dissatisfaction with the clergy grew, there was less will to see that the buildings were made glorious for God.

Iconoclasm and Reformation

The pressure for reform grew slowly and most strongly in towns where there were more educated clergy and laity. In rural parishes, even in the early years of the sixteenth century, the church operated largely on the model that had been established at the outset of the Middle Ages. Plough Sunday at the start of the year and Lammas (Loaf Mass) around harvest time were easily understood festivals, there was a ready empathy with Christ as the poor carpenter's son, and traditional practices were continued largely because they were hallowed by usage. The Henrican Reformation, when it came, was no radical revolution, at least as far as parish churches were concerned. It was monasticism and the legal rights of clergy that were swept aside, and there was little desire to reconstruct churches in their entirety. New developments in liturgy were slow to be adopted, and in most parish churches the pattern of worship in the years after the establishment of the Church of England was very little changed. The king approved Ten Articles of religion in 1536, which, together with the set of Episcopal Injunctions of 1538, confirmed the seven sacraments and approved the continuing celebration of 'honest ceremonies' such as Ash Wednesday and Palm Sunday, provided they were done without superstition. What was proscribed were merely the more extreme examples of rapidly repeated responses in processions, and the adoration of shrines. The famous rood of Boxley in Maidstone, for instance, was demolished because it was constructed with 'certain engines and old wires with old rotten sticks at the back of the same which caused the eyes to wink'. In other churches rood screens and stone altars were removed as the years passed, though the work was never universal. A more positive move was the instruction that a large English Bible should be set up in every church, which must have led to commissions for lecterns. The first complete Bible in English, Coverdale's Bible, was published in 1535, but its arrival was not an unmixed blessing, and it is far from clear how the readings were integrated into worship. The Injunctions specified that there was to be 'no reading aloud with any high voices [presumably chanting], and especially during the time of divine service or of celebrating or saying of mass'. In 1546 Coverdale's Bible was actually prohibited. Even possession of the officially sanctioned Great Bible was restricted to noblemen and gentry, their ladies and men of the merchant class. The clergy feared that in the wrong hands the Bible could lead to trouble; even Erasmus was known to have felt that the Lutherans, with their emphasis on the centrality of scripture, 'would bring about a tyranny of the Bible that would be worse than the tyranny of the church'. The adoption of a common service book for the whole country was an advance, but there was a determined conservatism in the new Articles of 1539 which secured the continuity of Confession as a necessity.

To many, Henry's quarrel with the Pope seemed no different from other monarchs' disputes, and there was probably an expectation that it would all be patched up in a year or two. Many priests and congregations preferred to wait on events rather than rush to adopt what might be no more than a new fashion, even, perhaps, a traitorous one. As a result the sixteenth century was no great age of church-building. There was a general simplification in the liturgy, and a few items, such as candles before images, were removed, but for the most part the churches stayed as they had been before Henry VIII came to the throne. Under his successor, Edward VI, there was an attempt to control preaching by the issue of a book of prepared homilies. Full sermons were only to be preached four times a year and on prescribed topics. But at least it was now the parish priest who was to preach, and, with the completion of the Book of Common Prayer in 1549, England could be said to have acquired its own independent Church. The penalty for failing to use this unified form of service was six months' imprisonment or life for a third offence. The result was the wholesale destruction of books of service, missals, antiphoners, breviaries and the like in a riot of book-burning that has left survivals such as the Psalter at Ranworth in Norfolk very rare indeed.

By 1563 the Thirty-Nine Articles of religion, to which an Anglican clergyman had to subscribe until very recently, were established. Yet the end of the century saw not so much reform in the Church as enrichment of individuals from the confiscation of its assets. One change that must have been distressing in many churches was the confiscation of plate and linen. The buildings were becoming gradually barer, though it is clear that parishioners were not uniformly anxious for radical change. The persecution of Protestants under Mary and of Catholics under Elizabeth roused more sympathy for their fate than hatred of their principles. The reign of Mary Tudor instilled a bitter hatred of Popery that lasted well into the nineteenth century, and the term Roman Catholic began to be used from about 1570. There were increasingly sharp divisions between those committed to either reform or continuity. The Archdeacon of Lincoln, for instance, proclaimed in 1553 that the new Book of Common Prayer was 'stuffed with blasphemies, stored with errors, which, under the name of religion, took away religion, diminishing the sacraments, condemned the whole world'. A former parson of St Michael Paternoster Royal in London was even more intemperate in the opposing cause, claiming that 'your peevish, popish, private, pedlary, pelting mass agreeth with the Lord's blessed supper and communion nothing at all'.

Such attitudes and the accompanying uncertainty did little to foster any interest in church building or even the gift of new fittings. At best churches were kept weatherproof, but it was hardly a sound investment to spend much on beautifying a structure that might rouse the disapproval of the authorities. Yet the totalitarian approach of the mid-sixteenth century was as nothing compared to the revolution in fittings that was produced in the seventeenth century. For the most part changes were seen in clerical dress, which was not long-lasting and could easily be donned or altered to proclaim an allegiance. The

Elizabethan settlement brought some security and further uniformity. It was under its auspices that congregational worship was limited to Sundays, a practice that has effectively lasted to this day. It was also made a legal requirement with fines for non-attendance. Yet, even so, there was a degree of local variety. A manuscript of 1564 records that:

> Some say the service and prayers in the chancel; others in the body of the church. Some say the same in a seat made in the body of the church; some in the pulpit with their faces to the people. Some keep precisely to the order of the book; others intermeddle Psalms in metre. Some say with a surplice; others without a surplice. The table standeth in the body of the church in some places; in others it standeth in the chancel. . . . Some receive kneeling, others standing, others sitting.[1]

However, there were still numbers of clergy anxious to see the new uniform liturgy accepted. Bernard Gilpin of Houghton-le-Spring in County Durham is a case in point. He worked as a teacher as well as being the senior parish priest of a group of fourteen villages, and he ran a school in his large parsonage. Such men left a distinct mark on the practices of their district but their contribution to the church structure was generally restricted to further tidying and stripping of ornaments, to whitewashing over paintings and so on. Men like Father Gilpin, however, were conservative. By the end of the century the Puritans were increasingly heard attacking such 'superstitious practices' and 'idolatrous fittings' as survived. The Millenary petition of 1603 sought to outlaw the use of rings at weddings and the sign of the cross at baptism, and opposed Confirmation as superfluous. It complained at the use of surplices and the practice of bowing the head at the name of Jesus, and it was signed by almost one thousand clergymen.

By then, however, King James was on the throne, and he attempted to preserve the rights of parishioners to traditional uses in their churchyards, offensive to Puritans, but likely to be popular. Another conservative was William Laud, whose term as Archbishop of Canterbury from 1633 to 1641 saw a determined effort to re-establish a decent and uniform liturgy. This had a widespread impact on the layout of sanctuaries, and a number of churches, such as Terrington St Clement in Norfolk, installed elaborate font covers. Laud, as we have seen, was a strenuous advocate of uniformity, and his concern extended to all aspects of church ordering. On a visit to Puritan Cambridge he demanded the pulling down of houses that had encroached on the churchyard of Great St Mary's and were built against the south wall of the church. But he was an intolerant visitor, and paid with his life for his efforts to force his version of churchmanship on the entire country.

Contemporary records of episcopal visitations, some by Laud himself, give a clear picture of the pattern of worship in the 1630s and of the equipment used. Most people made their communion at Easter and the other great festivals, though the mass was widely celebrated every month or so. Laud recorded two thousand communicants at St Giles Cripplegate, Milton's parish church. At each communion a large chalice was used, for it was the habit to drink deeply rather than merely taste the wine. The Presbyterian practice of using communion tokens to allow proper planning was not unknown, and many churches were beginning to install pews. In some places, such as Great St Mary's Cambridge, the congregation used to stand for the sermon, though that might last an hour or more, and men regularly wore hats in church, especially for the sermon. The term priest was still in general use in the north of England, but elsewhere the incumbent was now generally known as the parson. It was all a marked change from the muttered mass beyond the screen of a hundred years before. Within seven years of Laud's appointment, however, the country was split by the civil war that had both a religious and a political context.

The success of the Puritans and Parliamentarians meant a much more radical re-examination of the fitting out of churches, and one a good deal more vigorous than Laud's. The Puritans are widely credited with destruction but, although they campaigned vigorously against many aspects of the liturgy, such as the festivities that accompanied the Christmas services, their efforts to reform buildings were restricted to specific aspects of the pre-Reformation structures. They were convinced of the evil of images and thus their representatives and even their soldiers busily decapitated statues and smashed stained-glass windows. The destruction was widespread, though, once again, there were remote villages scarcely worth bothering about. The survival of some of the richest screens, such as that at Plymtree in Devon (albeit without its rood), was partly due to their isolation.

The decorative plasterwork of 1639 in St Mary, East Knoyle, Wiltshire, incorporates biblical texts. The Rector at the time, Christopher Wren's father, was put on trial by Puritans for inserting this decoration. (Colin Cunningham)

Plymtree is about halfway between Exeter and Honiton, but set some half dozen miles north of the main road, and there were many other places as isolated at that time. Also it is clear that the urge to destroy was not universal. For many it was sufficient to cover wall paintings with whitewash, and images on screens could easily be coloured over.

None the less the legacy of the Commonwealth was bare walls, clear glass and empty niches. William Dowsing was the official commissioner responsible for inspecting churches in Cambridgeshire and Suffolk in 1643 and 1644, and his *Journal* reports in detail the energetic removals and destruction he perpetrated. He records:

> At St Bene't's: 'ther was 11: superstitious Pictures, 14: Cherubims & 2: Superstitious Ingraveing. One was to pray for the Soule of John Canterbury & his wife.'
> At Little S. Mary's: 'We brake down 60: superstitious Pictures, some Popes & Crucyfixes, & God the father siting on a Chayer, & holding a Globe in his hand.'
> At Holy Trinity: 'We brake down 80: Popish Pictures, & one of Xt: & God the Father above.'[2]

Considering that Cambridge was one of the centres of the Puritan reform movement, the total number of images is surprising. However, Dowsing's visitation in Suffolk provided even more offensive material for him to destroy.

> At Benacre: 'There was 6 superstitious Pictures, one Crucifix, and the Virgin Mary twice, with Christ in her arms, and Christ lying in the Manger, and the 3 Kings coming to Christ with their presents, and St Catherine twice pictured; . . . And 3 Bishops with their Mitres; and the Steps to be levelled within 6 weeks. And 18 Jesus's, written in Capital Letters, on the Roof, which we gave order to do out; and the story of Nebuchadnezzar; and *orate pro animabus* [pray for the souls], in a Glass window.'[3]

Sometimes a second visit was required. He visited Ufford on 27 January, and noted:

> We brake down 30 superstitious Pictures; and gave direction to take down 37 more; and 40 Cherubims to be taken down of Wood; and the chancel levelled. There was a Picture of Christ on the Cross, and God the Father above it; . . . and took up 6 superstitious Inscriptions in Brass.

He was back in August, and recorded:

Where is set down what we did, Jan the 27th. '30 superstitious
Pictures; and left 37 more to brake down'; and some of them we brake
down now. In the Chancel, we brake down an Angel; 3 *orate pro anima*,
in the Glass; and the Trinity in a Triangle; and 12 Cherubims on the
Roof of the Chancel; . . . and the Steps to be levelled. And we brake
down the Organ Cases, and gave them to the Poor. – In the Church
there was on the Roof, above a 100 JESUS and MARY, in great Capital
Letters; and a Crosier Staff to be broke down, in Glass; and above 20
Stars on the Roof. There is a glorious Cover over the Font, like a Pope's
Tripple Crown, with a Pelican on the Top, picking its Breast, all gilt
over with Gold. And we were kept out of the Church above 2 hours,
and neither Churchwardens . . . that were enjoined these things above
three months afore, had not done them in May, and I sent one of them
to see it done, and they would not let him have the key.[4]

Only very occasionally was he able to report, as he did of Chattisham
'nothing to be done'.

The Puritan quarrel was with images and the worship of images,
rather than with ornament or the beautification of the House of God for
its own sake. Thus, while statues and windows were defaced, the
majority of churches were left rich with stone tracery in their windows,
with pinnacles and crockets, decorated parapets and crosses on the
exterior. Many of these have since been lost to the ravages of the weather,
but in the seventeenth century our late medieval churches still had their
carving sharp and fresh. Inside, the Puritans were prepared to ignore
carved bench ends, such as those at Isleham, and decorative carving on
screens that were retained. Where stalls survived, mostly in former
collegiate churches, there were often misericords with a range of scenes
of animals, daily life or rich foliage, spared because they were invisible
beneath the lowered seat. Thus, while the Puritans are regularly and
rightly attacked for the vandalism of their attack on images, it has to be
recognised that they did leave a great deal untouched.

The Reinvention of Ritual

Church-building had been rare throughout the seventeenth century.
The unsettled state of the Church was a strong disincentive to
building and Protestant forms of worship required little more than a
convenient space for congregation and minister. Ralph Josselin, the
vicar of Earl's Colne in Essex in the 1640s, kept a diary that shows
how a typical Protestant parson managed in church. He recorded
that 'wee took down all images and pictures and such like in glass'.
He wrote of a November day that he 'went not to Church untill
eleven, and I continued preaching untill sun was set', and elsewhere

Holy Trinity, Berwick-upon-Tweed, is a rare example of a church built in the mid-seventeenth century. (Colin Cunningham)

that he 'preacht in my litle coat as I goe every day'. At communion 'wee all sat round and near ye table', however, he was disturbed by 'ye unreverent carriage of divers in sitting with yr hats on when the psalme is singing'. That was probably standard under the Commonwealth, but is a far cry from what is commonly thought of as traditional Church of England ceremony. The theological Reformation had taken place, and the resulting changes to churches were well under way, but the pattern of mattins and evensong, the reduced version of the medieval Offices, developed only slowly.

The few churches that were built, such as Holy Trinity in Berwick, have a spare dignity that accords with the times. The church at Berwick lacks the usual pinnacles of a medieval church, and is without tower or spire. In general, there was no real opportunity to develop a new architectural language. Even the restoration of the monarchy in 1660 did not really give any impetus. However, there were other factors that had a considerable architectural impact. The seventeenth century effectively saw the emergence of architects as specialist designers. The course of natural decay and occasional disaster brought opportunities for rebuilding, especially in towns. The Fire of London in 1666 afforded Christopher Wren some of his finest opportunities, and his eventual collaboration with Grinling Gibbons enriched the City churches enormously. Similarly, as we have seen, the destruction by fire of All Saints, Northampton, in 1675 quickly led the city fathers to provide that prosperous borough with a brand new church of considerable splendour. A few new churches were built in rural parishes, carefully designed as works of art, and advertising the generosity and taste of their patrons. The little brick church of St Mary Magdalene at Willen in Buckinghamshire, for instance, was the gift of the headmaster of Westminster School, and he employed Robert Hooke, a former pupil, as his architect.

These new churches were designed for what was now the accepted pattern of worship. An altar surrounded by rails was adequate for the very occasional communion services and there was no need for a spacious chancel. On the other hand preaching required a substantial pulpit, and growing urban populations needed seats, so the common form for churches was like a large hall, often fitted with galleries. In the early years of the eighteenth century growing middle-class wealth meant that many town churches were sumptuously equipped although there was still little development in the functional requirements. Indeed the Church of England was settling into a regular pattern of morning and evening prayer each Sunday, with communion seldom more than three times a year.

The later eighteenth century is often thought of as a period of relative barrenness in Anglicanism. Country churches were usually provided as ornaments in a park. For the most part the most significant additions to a parish church were likely to be sumptuous monuments for deceased members of the local nobility. The connection between Church and State secured the position of the clergy as respectable and usually very comfortable, responsible for a degree of decency and for conventional observance in their churches. Parson Woodforde, the vicar of Weston, not far from Norwich, is often cited as the typical eighteenth-century parson, for he kept a diary from 1758 detailing his daily activities. But his reputation is as a *bon viveur*, and the diary is full of notes about what he ate, the fruit from his garden and the meat he consumed. Time and again he describes ill-attended services:

> I read Prayers, churched a woman [and] read the Act of Parliament against profane swearing as directed by Law . . .
>
> I read Prayers and Preached and christened a child by name Joseph this afternoon at Weston Church. None from Weston House today at Church.
>
> I read Prayers and Preached this Morning at Weston Church. None from Weston House at Church – It being a very cold, windy, and wet Day.
>
> I read Prayers and Preached this Afternoon at Weston Church, and also christened a Child. None from Weston House at Church, had but a small Congregation being very wet.[5]

The impression is, however, as much that the congregation and the folk from the big house did not attend regularly, though this was not always the case, as other entries show:

This being a Day appointed to be observed as a publick Fast in these seditious times and France . . . having declared War against us unprovoked, I walked to Church about 11. o'clock and read Prayers provided on the occasion at Weston Church this Morning, a large Congregation attended Divine Service which I was very glad to meet on the Occasion.

and:

I read Prayers & Preached this Afternoon at Weston Church which was very full of People. Mattishall Singers were at Church and sung exceedingly well, attended with a bass-Viol and an Hautboy . . .[6]

And Woodforde did more than merely take services and draw his stipend:

I read Prayers, Preached, Churched a Woman, and christened two children by name Christopher and John, this afternoon at Weston Church. A large congregation at Church, Mr and Mrs Carr there. All People well pleased with the Alteration at the Church. This afternoon was the first time of my using the reading Desk and Pulpit, since its being removed, and also of a new Common Prayer Book in my Desk. I can be heard much better than where it was . . .[7]

The alterations to his church appear to have been minimal. The medieval screen survives there to this day, and though the stained glass windows had evidently been broken by Puritans, the fine painted Tree of Jesse on the north wall of the nave had at worst been painted over with whitewash. Today it is revealed again. Almost the only other addition from the eighteenth century appears to have been a domed tankard made in London in 1773 to augment the Communion service that Woodforde used occasionally. But there is also evidence in his diaries of genuine care for his parishioners. He regularly fed the poor and helped the sick, and this was linked to his religious observance. His entry for Christmas Day in 1791 is typical:

This being Christmas I walked to Church this Morning and read Prayers and administered the Holy Sacrament to 22 Communicants. Gave for an Offering at the Altar 0. 2. 6. None from Weston House at Church this Morn' the Weather being very cold, wet and windy and extreme bad Walking, being all Ice under [foot]. My Foot extremely painful, hard Matter to get to and from Church, but thank God I went thro' it all better than I expected. The following old Men dined at my House being Christmas Day and each had a shilling apiece to carry home to their Wives, 0. 6. 0.[8]

The impression that the eighteenth-century parson was an ignorant glutton is not borne out. Hogarth's caricatures show clerics in an unfavourable light, wigs awry and faces contorted as they harangue bored congregations from overblown pulpits. Some eighteenth-century pulpits certainly were overblown, and this was a period when parsons eagerly seized a social status that cut them off from their congregations. It was enough to make them a target for satire, yet there was one element in this change that was generally positive: a parallel increase in their educational level. Churches, however, were increasingly designed as artworks by professional architects to express the taste and demonstrate the influence of powerful patrons. It was not yet an age of specialist architects, committed to nothing but church work, but the traditional work of the local craftsmen was less valued and only in remote rural areas was it still the norm. Mostly such work was confined to remaking or extending pews, and to small repairs. Yet in most remote rural areas there was not the wealth to improve churches, nor even sometimes, to maintain them properly, and outside the main centres of population or beyond the reach of wealthy patrons, the eighteenth century was a period in which many smaller churches were left to decay slowly.

None the less the eighteenth century – the Age of Enlightenment – produced a number of intellectual clerics, from Bishop Berkeley down, and it is clear that the standard of preaching was frequently high. It was also the time when Methodism grew out of the Church of England, and it is worth remembering that John Wesley first preached in the tiny Oxfordshire parish church of St Mary North Leigh. A plaque on the pulpit records his visit, but the church itself dates back to Saxon times at least. Most conventional Anglicans were suspicious of the 'enthusiasm' of the Methodists, but their devotional piety had its impact on the church. Yet there was a continued devotion in many places, and in the first decades of the nineteenth century the rise of scholarly antiquarianism provided an impetus for repair of decaying churches. Under an energetic archdeacon this could have a significant effect, and the visitation records of Henry Kaye Bonney, who was Archdeacon of Bedford from 1821 to 1844, show how he urged improvements in churches under his supervision. When he visited the church of The Virgin Mary at Keysoe in 1823, he ordered:

> that the open [i.e. unrented] seats be neatly repaired according to the Ancient Pattern, set strait, cleansed and oiled; the Porch be cleansed, the Doors be oak grained; Casements be placed in the North and South windows of the Church and Chancel; a new dark blue covering for the Communion Table and Pulpit Cushion be purchased; the stairs up the Tower and the floor thereof be repaired; a new plated Flagon and proper Font Bason be purchased.[9]

Bonney's concern was with basic repair and orderliness, but his taste was different from the ritualist revivers who were to take the lead in the 1840s. He regularly pressed for blue cushions (a colour that is fashionable in church furnishings today), and frequently ordered the use of casement windows, painting of woodwork or stone repair with proprietary cement of the kind that was abhorred by later architects. In fact Bonney's efforts, and those of others like him, were all too soon swept aside. In 1823 Bonney also visited St Mary Clophill and ordered:

> that a new plated Paten and Flagon be purchased; the Belfry and floor of the Middle Chamber of the Tower be repaired; the first and second Bell-wheels be repaired, and boards placed inside the Bellchamber Windows . . . ; the brickwork of the Windows be coloured so as to harmonise with the rest of the Fabrick; the Font be thoroughly cleansed from wash and repaired with Parker's Cement and washed a stone colour; a new Font Bason be purchased; the Minister's and Clerk's Prayer Books be repaired; the brick floor at the West end of the Church be relaid; there be a new Cloth for the Reading Desk, Pulpit Cushion and Communion Table; a mullion of stone instead of wood inserted in the West Window.[10]

It was a thorough and detailed set of instructions, but three years later the archdeacon was admitting that the church was inconveniently placed for the villagers. The vicar had offered £50 and promised to double that sum if the parishioners would build a new church in the centre of the village. By 1849 this had been done to the designs of Benjamin Ferrey, an architect committed to the proper revival of Gothic architecture.

Poor attendance at churches such as Weston Longville had long been a cause for concern, and that coupled with the increasingly rapid growth of towns had brought a realisation that the current provision of churches was inadequate. In 1818 the country was divided into a mere 9,500 parishes but the new industrial towns of the Midlands and the north were growing rapidly, and London was already scandalously overcrowded. Without radical development the conventional, established Church of England would be unable to cope, unable to find space for burials, and unable to accommodate those who came to hear the preaching. As late as 1834 it was calculated that in east London a population of 353,460 souls was served by ten parishes with eighteen churches and chapels between them (that is, about one church for every 19,000 people). Even had they wanted to attend, there was no longer room enough in churches for more than about 10 per cent of the urban population. Yet at the same time it was thought advisable to encourage attendance as one means of inculcating loyalty and obedience to the established order.

St George, Everton, Liverpool,
by Thomas Rickman, with a
roof of cast and wrought iron,
the latest materials in 1812.
(Colin Cunningham)

In 1818 the government allocated one million pounds for building new churches. Popularly known as 'Waterloo' churches, these were a celebration of the British triumph in the long French wars as well as a necessary provision for the growing multitude. Initially they were in the conventional classical style with columns and porticoes, but the costs proved too high. The new church at St Pancras, with vestries copied from the caryatid porch of the Erechtheion, cost over £76,000, and the feeling developed that this was an extravagant waste of public money. The original intention had been to build each church for about £10,000 and this could be done more economically in the Gothic style – Commissioners' Gothic – and such churches are often of brick only with stone dressings and tall pointed windows. Some architects made use of the latest materials, with cast-iron columns and tracery. In Liverpool, T.M. Rickman had already shown the way, with his lacy iron roof for a new church in Everton.

One unforeseen outcome was the respectability these new churches brought. A new church in a new neighbourhood marked out the

The new church of Holy Trinity, Cloudesley Square, Islington, in its smart new suburb. This Commissioners' church was designed by Charles Barry in 1826. A lithograph by C.J. Greenwood, 1850. (Guildhall Library, Corporation of London)

streets around as especially respectable, even to the extent of justifying landlords in charging higher rents. In Dalston in Hackney, St Mark's was built in 1864–5 with the houses facing it being noticeably grander than those in the back streets (and bringing in significantly higher rents for the developer who had generously given the site for the church). But this was in no way seen as a disadvantage, and Commissioners' churches spread rapidly across the land, some 214 of them in all. The pattern consisted of a large hall with galleries on three sides, and an organ in the west gallery, with the font beneath, and usually a shallow recess at the east end for the altar. Such structures provided welcome employment for young architects, among them Charles Barry, later to win fame with the rebuilding of the Houses of Parliament. And the pattern, and the profit, continued till the mid century. Often the completion of a new church was an excuse for issuing a handsome engraving to demonstrate the respectability of the area. But it was still not enough. In Bethnal Green the parish church was supplemented by a Commissioners' church, St John's, but this was followed by the building of no fewer than ten further churches with parishes carved out of the existing one. The work was a combined effort by the

'Reformed' and 'unreformed' churchyards contrasted, from Mowbray's *The Reformation and the Deformation*, 1868. (Courtesy of Pusey House, Oxford)

Bishop of London James Blomfield, himself a traditionalist cleric, and William Cotton, a rich banker and East London manufacturer. The pattern continued well into the nineteenth century.

However, the provision of seats merely for the continuation of the conventional services seemed unsatisfactory to many young clergy, and the middle years of the nineteenth century saw developments that had every bit as much impact on the average parish church as the Puritan onslaught of the seventeenth century. There was a reaction among a group of clergy who became known as the Oxford Movement.[11] In the early 1830s this group, concerned at the liberalism of recent theology and worried that the Catholic Emancipation Act (1829) might lead many people away from the Church of England, began to re-examine the values of the medieval church. Above all they hoped to restore what they believed were the spiritual values of the pre-Reformation Church. Their interests coincided with a move, begun in Cambridge,[12] to encourage churchwardens and vicars to ensure their churches were

Old St Giles, Cambridge,
dating back at least to the
twelfth century, had been so
much altered that the
congregation decided to
replace it altogether rather
than attempt further
restoration. The two churches
stood side by side for only a
few weeks before the old
building was demolished.
(Cambridgeshire Collection)

decently ordered and fitted out. The Ecclesiologists, as they were
known, claimed theirs was the only correct way to order a church, and
even published a journal with regular, and often scathing, criticisms of
new churches. They were much influenced by A.W.N. Pugin
(1812–52),[13] whose passionate writings declared that all architecture
since the Reformation was degraded, and that the only true
architecture was Christian architecture. He sought to ensure that new
buildings followed Gothic principles with construction honestly
shown in traditional materials, and ornament used to emphasise
construction rather than just to cover a surface.

Together the Oxford Movement and the Ecclesiologists wrought a
revolution in worship over the next two generations, and started a wave
of church 'restoration' and improvement as great as in any previous age.
There was a great deal of building, but it is important to remember
that the new movement did not automatically represent a major
revolution in liturgy. Liturgical change was slow, much slower than the
spread of the new architectural style, but there was a resurgence of
interest in the sacramental elements of worship, and much greater
emphasis on the Communion as a weekly, if not daily, feast. The priests

of this movement, known as ritualists, set about making their services as beautiful as they could. Their reinvention of a supposedly historical liturgy and the passion for archaeologically accurate recreations of Gothic architecture went hand in hand. There was good reason for this in that so many churches had been left with little beyond the barest maintenance for generations. A substantial number of parish churches were actually in need of repair and many needed to reopen or rebuild blocked-off chancels. The best precedents were used, and the details are often convincingly Gothic. Sometimes only the freshness of the tooling indicates nineteenth-century, as opposed to medieval, work.

Rebuilding was often begun at the very moment when congregations were shrinking, in an effort to halt the decline. None the less, at its best a campaign of refurbishment could produce a structure in which every element had a role to play in the activity of worship. Stalls for the choir, a new pulpit and lectern for the Word, and an organ to enrich the praise were often topped off by a new roof that ensured the continued life of the structure, and which might also be decorated yet further to express the glory of God. The extent of repair and rebuilding (often described as 'restoration') were considerable. It is possible to find examples of Victorian imitation of almost all the decorative elements of the medieval church and, though there are relatively few cases where the whole vocabulary was recreated in a single building, some churches were left richer than they had ever been. More often remains of the fine decoration in carved roof members, fonts or other fragments might be left undisturbed out of economy, and there was increasing respect for them as original pieces. Yet there were many places where the priority was not recreation of medieval features, and damaged pinnacles, crockets and carvings were often removed, tracery replaced and sometimes 'corrected' to fit with an architect's idea of the best pattern for a particular period. Where fine stone was at a premium, many churches had once been plastered and limewashed, but the surfaces were decaying, and Victorian architects eagerly scraped off the remains to allow repointing of the stone beneath. The result is that many churches now, particularly the flint churches of East Anglia, display a dull grey outside where once was white or creamy colour. So great was the enthusiasm for this degree of refurbishment that by 1877 the wholesale destruction of genuine medieval workmanship had become a scandal and a Society was founded for the Protection of Ancient Buildings. There was not, however, any immediate change in attitudes to the ecclesiastical heritage. The last years of the nineteenth century and the first decade of the twentieth saw continuing rebuilding, and few churches were left without some degree of refurbishment. It was a testament to a widespread commitment to worship and a concern for the proper state of the Established Church and its buildings.

The same concern had led the Victorians to supply brand new churches in expanding towns and cities, and the structures they raised in the industrial towns of the Midlands and the North are among the finest buildings of their age. Built in the wake of the Oxford Movement and under the watchful eye of the Ecclesiologists these churches dominated their surroundings in much the same way as had their medieval counterparts, and they were equipped with towers and spires, pinnacles and crockets, stained glass and sculpture that proclaimed the faith and biblical knowledge of those who paid for them. Leading architects found church-building both lucrative and creative. William Butterfield did almost nothing else, and his church of St Augustine at Penarth near Cardiff (1864–6) is a particularly fine example, while All Saints Margaret Street (1850–9) in London is probably his masterpiece as well as the flagship of the Ecclesiological movement. The tradition continued into the twentieth century with examples such as Sir Ninian Comper's St Mary Wellingborough begun in 1908 but not completed until 1930.

Naturally the revolution was not confined to exteriors, and the interiors of churches were fitted out as richly as at any time since before the Vikings. Fine patterned floor tiles, carved roof timbers, patterned walls and carved pews, organs and altar rails, candles, vases and altar cloths proliferated up and down the land. A whole industry grew up on the back of church refurbishment, with a series of specialist manufacturers for glass, ironwork and vestments. William Morris's company made fine stained-glass windows, though Morris's connection with the Society for the Protection of Ancient Buildings led him to decline orders for new windows in old churches. A.R. Mowbray of Oxford is typical of those who made a living out of church furnishing. A deeply devout man, he was fully committed to the tenets of the Oxford Movement, and determined to ensure that the range of fittings the ritualists wanted, but which had been unobtainable before, should be as widely available as possible.

The development was not without problems. Increasing ritualism was feared, misunderstood and fiercely contested, even in cases before the Privy Council. Traditionalists considered the new approach a dangerously Popish fashion, and some priests were even committed to prison for their determination to restore a richer liturgy. Much that is now conventional, even old-fashioned, in the Church of England, was new and radical in the mid-nineteenth century. When the vicar of Stow-on-the-Wold first used a surplice his parishioners called him 'the Pope's washerwoman', and thought the letters IHS he had stencilled on the walls of his chancel were his initials. Initially even the use of a pair of candles on the altar was considered unacceptable. Stone altars were actually ruled illegal on three occasions between 1845 and 1857, as was the use of a cross on the holy table. The ceremonial use of a

The hierarchy of symbols in
the new tiled floor of St Mary-
le-Tower, Ipswich (1860–70),
includes a crowned M for Mary
in the porch, angels in the
chancel and round the altar
symbols of the bread and wine.
(Colin Cunningham)

crucifix and even of banners was declared unlawful in 1870 as were
processions, making the sign of the cross (in 1874), and the
distribution of candles on Christmas Day. None the less scholars,
architects and priests all continued to devise ways of adapting medieval
English ceremonial to the usage of the 1662 Prayer Book. Sir Ninian
Comper recreated the English altar, with parclose screens topped with
carved angels and rich hangings, while Percy Dearmer wrote *The
Parson's Handbook* (1899) as a manual of good practice.

By the end of the century, however, the Church of England had
absorbed this revolution, while maintaining many longer established
practices. The pattern of Sunday worship centred on mattins and
evensong still predominated. The sermon was still a central element,
but, while the evangelical wing of the church still abhorred ritualism
and concentrated on prayer and preaching, high churchmen were
able to erect baldachins over altars, to reserve the sacrament and to
decorate their churches with stations of the cross and sets of six
candlesticks on the high altar. The variety was considerable.

Towards a Liturgy for Today

The experience of the First World War brought enormous social
changes, and with them came new attitudes to religion and to the
establishment as people turned against what they perceived as the
excesses of the Victorians. It is an attitude that has prevailed until
quite recently, but in church architecture it has run parallel to further

revolutions in the approach to liturgy. Not that the latest architecture had any immediate impact on Anglican church building – the Church, after all, was a body concerned with traditions, and moved slowly in matters of taste. There were still churches to be built in the ever-expanding suburbs, but the preference was for traditional forms in brick or stone rather than for the new white cubic concrete of the Modern Movement, while the Arts and Crafts traditions of fine workmanship were the driving force behind most designs.

The social revolution of the postwar years, and particularly the huge programme of rehousing, occupied the efforts of many clergy, and attention turned away from ceremonies in church as the prime focus. There was less emphasis on worship as the centre of the whole life of a congregation, and the business of caring for the community took a greater prominence. This was, in fact, little more than a concentration on activities that had been a part of much nineteenth-century Christian activity, but the concept of relevance, and of Christian ministry to all, gained in importance as social barriers began to be lowered. None the less traditional mattins and evensong remained the principal services in most churches throughout the first half of the twentieth century.

The three new factors – relevance, a concern for social welfare, and a rejection of past taste – operated to bring about yet further changes, in particular a move to greater simplicity. In church after church the Victorian patterned walls were whitewashed over, and there was a conscious desire to abandon the 'dim religious light' of the typical nineteenth-century church. Many Victorian fittings were moved, though often no further than to a corner of the vestry. The spread of electric light meant that oil lamps and candles were increasingly consigned to the rubbish bin. For the most part, however, rural churches were not rebuilt or altered beyond this simplification in the first half of the twentieth century.

It was in the suburbs that the new architecture of Anglicanism was most obvious. Some 250 churches were built in the inter-war years. By and large it was the High Church wing that paid most attention to buildings as works of art, and churches such as St Saviour in Eltham, by Cachemaille Day & Lander (1931), were equipped with sanctuaries in a modernised version of traditional forms. The new material, concrete, was used in parabolic arches, in simple churches such as St Philip Osmondthorpe, Leeds, which enclose a unified space with passages instead of deep aisles separated by arcades, and there was more emphasis on the openness of the interior space. More exciting spaces were occasionally created, such as the leaf-shaped Holy Family Church at Blackbird Leys in Oxford (Colin Shewring, 1964–5).

Such changes were the subject of much debate. Architects simply enjoyed the opportunity to create new and interesting shapes, but leaders of the Liturgical Movement, such as Peter Hammond, Rector of Bagendon in Gloucestershire, argued that liturgical function should be the prime consideration.[14] Hammond was interested in the centralised church – a form that had first been developed as early as 1915 by the Catholic architect Dominikus Bohm. On the continent the need for new or rebuilt churches, both Lutheran and Catholic, after the Second World War led architects such as Rudolf Schwarz to spend time reconsidering the whole nature of a church space. His conclusion was that there were effectively two types – the traditional form of the church as a journey, in which the faithful progressed from baptism at the entrance to communion at the east end, and the church as crucible, in which the congregation surrounded the altar that was the focus for their worship. This idea found a ready audience in Britain among clergy who wanted to see greater congregational involvement in worship. They put the same stress on the communion as had the ritualists of the nineteenth century, but were unhappy about the isolation of the celebrant in the sanctuary, often beyond a near empty chancel. Where new churches were to be built the problem could be overcome by buildings in which the nave, chancel and sanctuary were united in a single space. Many new Anglican churches featured a unitary space, and the old division of the chancel arch was abandoned.

Yet even so the liturgy had been remarkably slow to develop. The Book of Common Prayer, published in 1662, was still the authorised

Sunday service in Bolton, photographed by Humphrey Spender in 1937. Note the Gothic revival interior, complete with painted images of saints and symbols, organ and choir. (Courtesy of Bolton Museum & Art Gallery)

form of usage in all Anglican churches. There was an attempt to bring this up to date in 1928, and the arguments at this point between the traditionalist and Anglo-Catholic wings of the church can be seen as giving a new impetus to what was known as the Liturgical Movement. Yet it was not until 1936 that the General Assembly of the Church gave the formal order for a revision, and that was not issued until 1940. The traditional services of prayer and preaching remained widespread well after 1945.

Sir Basil Spence's church of St Oswald, Tile Hill, Coventry, of 1957–8, complete with its original fittings, organ and hangings. (University of Warwick, History of Art Photographic Department)

Once again the aftermath of destruction gave a new impetus to church-building and to worship. The devastation of bombing led to two types of church-building. In the first place there was rebuilding or repairing war-damaged structures. A number of churches had been completely gutted, and were rebuilt as replicas, though the details usually reveal that they are twentieth-century versions rather than precise recreations of what was destroyed. In a few cases, as at Hawksmoor's St George in the East, London, only the walls were left, and an entirely new church was created inside them. The new building included an open courtyard inside the former west end and housing for the clergy in the former turrets, as well as space for a church office and a community centre in the former crypt.

The main postwar effort was, of course, to provide housing. Thus in Coventry in the 1950s, for instance, new churches went along with new suburbs. Sir Basil Spence, architect of the new cathedral, was commissioned to design several simple churches for them, in which a key decision was the choice of an identical brick to the housing on the estate. They were even erected by Messrs Wates, the contractors for the new estates. Yet none of this predicated any dramatic change in the liturgy. Robert Maguire's All Saints Church in Crewe (1964–5), on the other hand, is a fine example of the new type of unifying of space that none the less accommodates all the liturgical requirements of the sacraments.

In older churches it was less easy to adopt the new approach to liturgy and to adapt to increasingly informal worship. A common solution was the provision of a nave altar, set below the chancel step, to bring the priest closer to the congregation. The inevitable result was that chancels were left empty, as in the seventeenth century. They have

The church as crucible:
All Saints, Crewe, by Maguire
and Murray (1963–5), is a
single square space. The
congregation surrounds the
altar and the font is actually
behind it. Note the careful
control of lighting. (Photo by
John Whybrow. Reproduced
by courtesy of Robert Maguire
and Keith Murray)

not, however, been abandoned, but are used for the occasional great
festival such as Christmas or Easter. In the last generation there has
been a steady, if slow, increase in congregational involvement. This has
brought some pressures on space in sanctuaries as more people are
involved in the distribution of the bread and wine. But whether the
readings are by priest or lay, whether the offerings are brought up by
churchwardens or by groups of parishioners, there is little impact on
the architecture of churches that were devised in the Middle Ages to
give prominence to just such activities whoever performed them.

One modern influence has been that of radio and television. This
mass medium has allowed congregations unparalleled access not only
to the new technology itself, but also to the practices of other
Anglican churches, and, as ecumenism has progressed, to patterns of
worship in other denominations and even other faiths. The first
broadcast services were simply traditional services made available over
the air waves. However, the reception of these in living-rooms and
parlours, perhaps with a cup of tea to hand, only served to increase the
pressure for a more relaxed pattern of worship that was felt to be more
meaningful to the general public. This attitude has been further

developed in the house church movement, where worship takes place in ordinary homes rather than in specially designed buildings.

Along with this variety of practices came a greater reliance on images from television as aids to worship. A parallel concern was that the liturgy was unintelligible to outsiders and might militate against conversion. Organ music, with its special skills and traditional musical forms, became less popular among those who wanted modern worship to be accompanied by modern music. This led to the practice of using groups of musicians, guitarists and so on, from the congregation, which in turn created problems of accommodation, the need for a platform to raise the performers into view, and a requirement for yet more sophisticated electric circuitry. A few churches have even been built with screens on which the words of hymns can be projected, or which can be used for images. All too often such things are simply strung across a chancel arch, and appear merely temporary. Many churches nowadays have quite sophisticated sound systems, but few have fittings specially designed to fit the church, as does St Nicholas in Yarmouth. Along with the rejection of Victorian paraphernalia went the disappearance of specialist manufacturers with a commitment to design specifically for churches. Today it is often a matter of assembling everyday fittings to create the atmosphere required by the particular liturgy.

One final problem is a pressure for flexibility. There is a frequent call for reordering of churches and one common target has been the church pew. Designed long before the concept of the ergonomic chair was understood, many are uncomfortable. They are certainly restrictive, and congregations often want to remove them altogether. St Peter's at Oundle in Northamptonshire is one of many churches that has replaced pews with movable chairs. They sit rather uncomfortably with the arcades when the chairs are set out in an arc; but the gain in flexibility is undeniable. Perhaps the lesson is that, as our world shrinks and we come into increasingly frequent contact with other denominations and other faiths, we will inevitably be faced with difficulties in using buildings designed for the liturgy of an earlier generation. Yet it is those very buildings that retain the priceless link with the communion of saints that stretches back to the earliest years of Christendom.

Managing Change

The inevitable tensions between contact with the past and anticipation of future developments lies at the heart of Anglican church use. Different congregations are served by different churches, the very latest in liturgical fashion and architecture as well as the most ancient fabric. Yet contact within deaneries and dioceses, and increasing mobility among clergy, has meant that the pressure for change in older churches has grown steadily. With congregations often widely scattered the desire for space to socialise after the service brings pressure for kitchen facilities, often within the church. Public legislation, such as the requirement for access for the disabled, has another impact, bringing ramps or new doorways.

These pressures on ancient churches have become increasingly frequent, yet the value of the historic fabric is also recognised as important in the continuity of witness. As early as 1921 the Council for Care of Churches was established to advise parishes and to coordinate the work of the Diocesan Advisory Committees, which consider applications to reorder churches and oversee their repair and maintenance. This system has allowed the Church to remain outside general planning legislation and, at its best, provides a range of expert advice on such things as electric fittings, bell hanging and clock repair, as well as on techniques of repair and the history of individual structures. The disadvantage is that the process is time-consuming, which makes change slow – but the alternative of working through the Local Planning Authority might be just as slow, and the argument in favour of this external control rests on an assumption that changes should be carefully considered and that there is a value in the historic fabric.

Now that church attendance is less than 10 per cent of the population, it is easier to see that value as simply one of heritage. Each parish church encapsulates much of the history, aspirations and endeavours of the inhabitants of the area. Some would see this as the only value in these old buildings, though, as I have argued, the Church also values their evidence of continuity of worship. But churches have a wider audience than merely their committed members, so national bodies such as English Heritage and its equivalents in Scotland, Wales and Northern Ireland do a great deal to support the repair and restoration of many fine churches. The heritage value of churches is reflected in the official list of buildings of architectural and historical merit. Only about 1 per cent of the nation's stock of buildings are listed, but a vastly higher proportion of churches are among them. The lists are graded I, II* and II, and grade I churches are outstanding. In many cases listed churches can be given financial support to help preserve them for future generations of both Christians and non-Christians. The lists have now been extended to include twentieth-century and even postwar churches where they are of real distinction. The problem for their users is that they were designed as complete entities and survive in a more complete form, with original lighting and hangings for instance, than their medieval counterparts. If, once again, there is a tension between a new fashion for church usage and the retention of 1950s fittings, it should not be assumed that things have no value unless they are at least a hundred years old. Once destroyed they cannot be recreated, and who of us has not regretted that nice old utensil of grandma's we threw out and now cannot afford from the antique shop!

The need for comparative evaluation has resulted in two types of organisation, the official and the voluntary, who keep a watch on buildings of value. The Royal Commissions on Historical Monuments (RCHM England is now amalgamated with English Heritage) have been publishing inventories of listed buildings since 1910. They hold an invaluable archive of photographs and other material relating to listed churches, and regularly record threatened structures. The various County Record Offices now also hold most church archives, leaving the old parish chests redundant, and there are a number of other special public collections, such as the Church of England Record Centre, recently established in Bermondsey, and Lambeth Palace Library. The sort of accumulation of historical knowledge of these organisations is essential to the full understanding of churches, and in ensuring that unnecessary or damaging restoration is avoided.

The Church of England requires parishes to have the structure of their church examined every five years, and the necessary repairs are graded according to their urgency. It should be no surprise that structures as complex as parish churches, given the age of most of them, require extensive maintenance and often careful restoration. Because each building is unique it requires great sensitivity either to alter or to ensure that major restoration is effectively carried out. However, the rescue of a fine church has an impact far beyond the group of worshippers who use it regularly. Fortunately there is a considerable body of expertise among the many architects who specialise in church work, and

The decaying spire of St Peter and St Mary, Stowmarket, Suffolk, was dismantled in 1975. Its restoration in 1994 by Andrew Anderson was both a fine technical feat and an important symbolic statement. (Courtesy of Andrew Anderson)

many have built up a lifetime of experience of the materials and structures of their area.

The work of professionals and official bodies is supplemented by voluntary organisations. Local Civic Societies are often powerful lobbies in support of the proper repair of churches. There are also six national amenity societies – The Society for the Protection of Ancient Buildings, The Ancient Monuments Society, The Georgian Group, The Victorian Society, The Twentieth Century Society and the Council for British Archaeology – which have a measure of government support and are represented in the diocesan advisory system. The Society for the Protection of Ancient Buildings is the oldest, and campaigns on the principles for which it was established – that conservation is preferable to repair or restoration which so often constitutes replacement. They also lay on courses in specialist techniques of repair, and on the use of traditional materials, which not infrequently turn out to be a long-term saving as well as being better for the building. The other societies are groupings with particular enthusiasms and set out to develop interest and expertise in their own area. The Victorian Society was a creation of the 1950s and the Twentieth Century Society is even more recent, but they all share the aim of campaigning for buildings of their period.

Enthusiastic campaigners and the cumulative knowledge of archivists, government agencies and other scholars may seem to shift the focus of care for churches away from the parishioners who actually use them. Certainly we are a long way from the days when they actually undertook the repairs and maintained the nave. There are occasional conflicts, and when those have to be the subject of judicial decisions by Chancellors, the chief legal executive of each diocese, one side or other is almost inevitably disappointed. However, there are probably more unrecorded cases in which disagreements are argued out before that stage, and where some contribution from experts outside the parish (even outside the Church) can help a congregation to work with its building and get the best out of it. Unfortunately it is less fashionable these days to build just for the Glory of God. Difficulties of financing major repairs or rebuilding too often drive congregations to choose the simplest and cheapest option, and it has to be admitted that the merely modest and functional is seldom a great contribution to the heritage. Many people, it is true, are keen to commission art works, especially new stained-glass windows, and there are certainly some fine new churches, but the extravagance of late medieval buildings of faith is most nearly matched nowadays in structures such as the Hindu temple at Neasden. Our surviving stock of historic churches is the more valuable.

Even so it is not always possible to maintain a particular church. Great structures were built in thriving communities that later dwindled. The tiny Northamptonshire village of Fotheringhay once boasted a huge collegiate church associated with Fotheringhay Castle. In 1573 the choir was pulled down by Dudley, Duke of Northumberland, leaving the villagers with a vast nave and tower. Queen Elizabeth I paid for two fine monuments in the church, but even she could not be persuaded to provide financial help for the building. The structure withstood the elements for centuries, and is, understandably, listed grade I. But it is vastly too large for the local population and for many years winter worshippers were welcomed with a blanket as well as prayer and hymn book in an effort to make the service bearable.

Sometimes even a faithful remnant does not survive. Some villages are entirely depopulated, and their churches abandoned. The church may then be formally declared redundant, deconsecrated and demolished, or perhaps converted to another use. In some areas the fabric is just left to decay, and the ruin and its churchyard may become a nature sanctuary. Norfolk has a number of such churches. This is proving worrying for some Christians because ruined churches can easily be misused. Accordingly the Church established a Redundant Churches Fund (now the Churches Conservation Trust), which exists to preserve outstanding churches for which there is no realistic use. It is not the only organisation dedicated to helping or conserving remote or abandoned churches, but its work exemplifies their heritage value. Funds are set aside by the Church towards their conservation, and they remain open to the public as precious reminders of the faith that built them. They are used for occasional services and for suitable events organised by the local community. A very few redundant churches are in towns, but for the most part they are, like St George's Shimpling in Norfolk or St Mary Stocklynch Ottersey in Somerset, remote but entrancing reminders of the way in which Christians have worshipped their God in generations past.

Ancient churches in towns advertise the rich history of their community, but the survival of imposing town churches from more recent periods as well is a reflection of our urbanised culture.

The storage problem is solved at St Mary, Bures, Suffolk, by making rooms in the base of the tower. This was part of a careful and attractive scheme of 1990 by the Whitworth Co-Partnership. (Photo by David Brittain; architects the Whitworth Co-Partnership)

However, the old parish church seems to be an essential element of the rural scene, as permanent almost as the landscape itself. As such they are a part of our common heritage, witnesses in stone to a faith that shaped so much of the built environment of these islands. But a church is above all a house of prayer and a focus for worship, so the sound of church bells on a Sunday or candlelit carol singing at Christmas are equally elements of the Christian heritage. The activity justifies the building, and the buildings create what has been described as 'a bridge of holiness' between today and our collective past. An old, or even redundant, church may conjure up images of medieval congregations worshipping in a timeless Merrie England – but the bustle of a busy church, with coloured frontals, a priest to celebrate the Eucharist and a congregation singing their hearts out in a favourite hymn gives meaning to the whole structure and is an actual contact with those past generations who built and beautified so many churches of all periods.

Further Reading

Church architecture and church history have both fathered a whole army of publications dealing with various aspects or periods and it is not possible to provide anything like an exhaustive list of titles. What follows is a selection of the books I have used in preparing this one, and which I have found useful and approachable.

For detailed description of individual churches the most readily available sources are the county volumes of *The Buildings of England, The Buildings of Wales, The Buildings of Scotland* and *The Buildings of Northern Ireland* by Sir Nikolaus Pevsner *et al*., published by Penguin Books.

Adleshaw, G.W.O. and Etchells, F. *The Architectural Setting of Anglican Worship*, 1948

Anson, Peter F. *Fashions in Church Furnishings 1840–1940* London, Faith Press, 1960

Bertram, Jerome *Monumental Brasses as Art and History*, Stroud, Sutton Publishing, 1998

Betjeman, John (ed.) *Collins Guide to Parish Churches of England & Wales*, London, William Collins 1958, reissued 1980

Bottomley, Frank *The church explorer's guide to symbols and their meaning*, 2nd edn, Otley, Smith Settle, 1995

Brooks, Chris and Saint, Andrew (eds) *The Victorian Church*, Manchester, Manchester University Press, 1995

Carpenter, S.C. *The Church of England 597–1688*, London, John Murray, 1954

Chadwick, Owen *The Victorian Church Part 1 1829–1859*, 3rd edn, 1971; *Part 2 1860–1901*, 2nd edn, 1972

Clark, B.F.N.L. *Church Builders of the Nineteenth Century*

Cocke, Thomas H. *Recording a church: an illustrated glossary*, 3rd edn, York, Council for British Archaeology, 1996

Cox, J.C. and Ford, C.B. *Parish Churches*, Batsford, 1934, rev. edn, 1961

Dix, Dom. Gregory *The Shape of the Liturgy*, Dacre Press, 1945

Duffy, Eamon *The Stripping of the Altars: Traditional Religion in England 1400–1580* Yale and London, Yale University Press, 1992

Fletcher, Ronald (ed.) *The Biography of a Victorian Village: Richard Cobbold's Account of Wortham, Suffolk 1860*, London, Batsford, 1977

Friar, Stephen *A Companion to the English Parish Church*, Stroud, Alan Sutton, 1996

Goodenough, Simon *The Country Parson*, Newton Abbot, David & Charles, 1983

Hammond, Peter C. *Liturgy and Architecture*, 1960

Hammond, Peter C. *The Parson and the Victorian Parish*, London, Hodder & Stoughton, 1977

Howell, Peter and Sutton, Ian (eds) *The Faber Guide to Victorian Churches*, London, The Victorian Society, 1989

Leatherbarrow, J. Stanley *Victorian Period Piece: Studies occasioned by a Lancashire Church*, London, SPCK, 1954

Lloyd, Roger *The Church of England 1900–1965*, London, SCM Press, 1966

Moule, A.C. (ed.) *William Dowsing's Cambridge Journal*, Cambridge, 1926

Osborne, June *Stained Glass in England*, Stroud, Sutton Publishing, 1997

Neale, J.M. *Church enlargement and church arrangement*, Cambridge, Camden Society, 1843

Painter, Kenneth (ed.) *Churches built in Ancient Times: Recent Studies in Early Christian Archaeology*, London, Society of Antiquaries, 1994

Parsons, Gerald (ed.) *The Growth of Religious Diversity: Britain from 1945* (vol. I), London, Routledge/Open University, 1993

Salmon, Frank *Gothic and the Gothic Revival*, Papers from the 26th Annual Symposium of the Society of Architectural Historians of Great Britain, Manchester, 1998

Stamp, Gavin *et al. The Twentieth Century Church*, London, Twentieth Century Society, 1998

Welsby, Paul A. *A History of the Church of England 1945–1980*, London, Oxford University Press, 1984

Yates, Nigel *Buildings Faith & Worship: the liturgical arrangement of Anglican churches 1600–1900*, London, Oxford University Press, 1991

Sources and Notes

Chapter One

1 *The Collins Guide to Parish Churches of England & Wales*, ed. John Betjeman (London, 1980), p. 13
2 The Church in Wales was formally disestablished only in 1920, so its buildings share most of the characteristics of English parish churches, for all the bulk of the population had been estranged from the Anglican church for several generations before then.
3 William of Malmesbury, *De Antiquitate Glastoniensis Ecclesiae*, ed. T. Hearne (Oxford, 1729)

Chapter Two

1 Matthew, chapter 28, verse 19, and chapter 26, verses 26–9
2 *The Didache*, trans. C. Bigg (1898; rev. A.J. Maclean, 1922)
3 J.D.C. Fisher, *Christian Initiation: Baptism in the Medieval West*, Alcuin Club Collection, vol. XVII (London, SPCK, 1965), p. 174
4 Book of Common Prayer, 1662, Rubrick for the Ministration of the Publick Baptism of Infants
5 F.A. Paley, *Baptismal Fonts* (London, 1844), pp. 7–8
6 Matthew, chapter 26, verses 25–8
7 The letters stand for the Greek words *Iesos Huios Soter*, meaning Jesus Son [of God] Saviour
8 See Anna Jameson, *Sacred & Legendary Art* (London, Longmans, 1891), 2 vols
9 Book of Common Prayer, 1662, Institution for the Solemnization of Matrimony, opening prayer
10 Ibid., Rubric for the Solemnization of Matrimony
11 Acts of the Apostles, chapter 6, and chapter 13, verses 1–3

Chapter Three

1 Book of Common Prayer, 1662, Concerning the Service of the Church
2 *James Woodforde: The Diary of a Country Parson, 1758–1802*, ed. John Beresford (Oxford, Oxford University Press, 1935, pbk 1987)
3 *The Yattendon Hymnal*, edited by the poet laureate, Robert Bridges
4 See, for instance, *A Hundred Hymns for Today* (1969) and *More Hymns for Today* (1980)
5 Thomas Hardy, *Under the Greenwood Tree, or The Mellstock Quire* (1872)
6 *The Biography of a Victorian Village: Richard Cobbold's account of Wortham Suffolk 1860*, ed. Ronald Fletcher (Batsford, 1977)
7 T.S. Eliot, *Four Quartets* (Little Gidding)

Chapter Four

1 *Kilvert's Diary: Selections from the Diary of the Revd Francis Kilvert*, ed. William Plomer (London, Jonathan Cape, 1938, 2nd edn, 1960, repr. 1977, pp. 93–4, 98–9, entries for Easter 1870
2 Ibid, pp. 90–5, entries for Easter 1870
3 Acts of the Apostles, chapter 2, verse 3
4 See, for instance, *Hall's Dictionary of Subjects & Symbols in Art* (London, Longmans, rev. edn, 1979)
5 Apollonia was an early martyr from Alexandria who had her teeth drawn before being killed for refusing to sacrifice to the pagan gods

Chapter Five

1 Estimates vary between 277 and 294 people executed under Mary
2 The college buildings are now a part of the King's School, Canterbury
3 The school has now been rebuilt again, yet further from the parish church, but the link is retained. There is also a separate service of commemoration in one of the Leeds synagogues for the school's Jewish population

Chapter Six

1 Preface to the Acts of 1777, known as Gilbert's Acts, quoted in Hammond, *The Parson and the Victorian Parish*, p. 46

Chapter Seven

1 Quoted in S.C. Carpenter, *The Church in England 597–1688* (London, 1954), p. 330
2 'William Dowsing's Cambridge Journal', ed. A.C. Moule, in *The History Teacher's Manual* (1926). Dowsing visited St Benet's on 28 December, Little St Mary's on 29th–30th, and Holy Trinity on Christmas Day 1643
3 'William Dowsing's Suffolk Journal', ed. C.H.E. White (Ipswich, 1885), p. 26. Dowsing visited Benacre on 6 April 1644
4 Ibid., pp. 18, 29. Dowsing visited Ufford on 27 January and 31 August 1644. Happily, he was unable to destroy the great font cover, which is now one of the wonders of that part of Suffolk
5 *James Woodforde: Diary*, ed. Beresford: p. 60: 1 October 1769; p. 350: Sunday 3 May 1789; p. 394: Sunday 27 February 1791; p. 398: Sunday 1 May 1791
6 Ibid.: p. 433: Friday 9 April 1793; p. 455: Sunday 23 February 1794
7 Ibid.: pp. 126–7: 10 November 1776
8 Ibid.: p. 409: 25 December 1791. Woodforde lists six old men; and the dinner consisted of roast beef, plum pudding and mince pies
9 Bedfordshire County Record Office: 'Visitation Notebook of Archdeacon Bonney, 1823–39', quoted in *Bedfordshire Churches in the Nineteenth Century*, Bedfordshire Historical Record Society, vol. 77, Part II, Parishes H–R, ed. Chris Pickford (Bedford, 1998), pp. 405–6
10 Ibid., Part I, Parishes A–G, ed. Chris Pickford (Bedford, 1994), pp. 201–2
11 So-called because its founders were all members of Oriel College, Oxford. The followers of the Oxford Movement were also known as the Tractarians after the series of tracts they published
12 The Cambridge Camden Society was founded in 1839. It later changed its name to the Ecclesiological Society and its members were known as the Ecclesiologists
13 Pugin was the son of a French Huguenot immigrant. He converted to Roman Catholicism in 1835. One of his best known books was called *The True Principles of Pointed or Christian Architecture* (1842)
14 His message was eventually spelled out in his book *Liturgy and Architecture* (1960)

Index

This index includes only the principal topics, places and persons. Page numbers in italics indicate an illustration.